County boundaries afte

D0854353

Llangefni
Bangor

Mold

C L W Y D

G W Y N E D D

Dolgellau

Newtown

Aberystwyth

P O W Y S

Llandrindod
Wells

D Y F E D

Brecon

Haverfordwest
Carmarthen

WEST
GLAMORGAN

MID

G W E N T

GLAMORGAN

Newport

SOUTH
GLAMORGAN

Cardiff

A Guide to
the birds of Wales

Red Kite

David Saunders

A Guide to
the birds of Wales

Constable London

First published in Great Britain 1974
by Constable and Company Ltd
10 Orange Street, London WC2H 7EG
Copyright © 1974 David Saunders

ISBN 0 09 459360 4

Set in 'Monophoto' Baskerville
Filmset and printed in Great Britain by
BAS Printers Limited, Wallop, Hampshire

This book is dedicated to all those who
seek enjoyment watching birds in Wales

Contents

Illustrations

Introduction

On coming to live in Pembrokeshire some fourteen years ago two things soon became apparent to me. First, the exciting variety of bird habitats to be found in Wales; secondly, the fact that information concerning them and the species they supported was hard to come by. There was no reference work for the birds of Wales like the *Birds of Scotland* by Baxter and Rintoul or the *Birds of Ireland* by Kennedy, Ruttledge and Scroope. At that time there was no Welsh Bird Report, indeed, some counties were even without annual reports. Despite this, there were many enthusiastic bird-watchers, though these tended to be very scattered in the areas of low population. One was struck by the fact that many, like myself, were immigrants from other parts of Britain. Although the situation is improving, it is a fact that, with only a few notable exceptions, the Welsh take little interest in their bird life, or indeed in their wildlife generally.

In the years that have elapsed since my arrival important developments in the ornithological sphere have taken place, chief among them the now annual publication of a Welsh Bird Report, and a slowly growing liaison between the various clubs and societies that exist. The continued absence of up-to-date avifaunas for much of Wales is to be regretted. This means that those who require background information before visiting an area outside the well-known localities are sometimes at a loss to obtain it. My purpose in this book is to introduce bird-watchers, both resident and visiting, to some of the lesser-known haunts, besides describing the 'musts' in anyone's itinerary. By doing so I hope to stimulate even more interest in bird-watching and bird-recording in this most interesting part of Britain. Whenever possible the reader should try to keep notes of his observations and send them to the appropriate county recorder—their addresses are listed later in the book. As more information is collated, revised county avifaunas will appear and these in turn will lead to a greater degree of ornithological activity. Properly channelled, such interest can only be for the benefit of the birds which provide so many of us with so much interest and enjoyment.

As this book was completed, elections were about to take place for the new county councils resulting from the reorganisation of local government which will take effect from April 1974. This has led, despite fierce opposition, to the merging of some counties, so that Wales, for administrative purposes, is now divided into the following counties:

Gwent	originally Monmouthshire
South Glamorgan	originally Cardiff and the Vale of Glamorgan
Mid Glamorgan	originally the industrial valleys of north Glamorgan and an area extending from these, through Bridgend to the sea at Porthcawl
West Glamorgan	originally Port Talbot, Neath, Swansea including Gower, and the region immediately to the north
Dyfed	originally Cardiganshire, Carmarthenshire and Pembrokeshire

Powys	originally Breconshire and Radnorshire
Montgomeryshire	originally Montgomeryshire
Gwynedd	originally Anglesey, Caernarvonshire and Merioneth
Clwyd	originally Denbighshire and Flintshire

Although these changes will be in force shortly after the publication of this book, I have retained the old, much loved, and familiar county system. Ornithology in Wales is based on this at present, but because of the above changes I draw the reader's attention to the possibility of alterations in name—and perhaps area—covered by some of the ornithological organisations and naturalists' trusts mentioned in later chapters.

The check lists of birds which follow each of the county sections exclude both the vagrant species, many of which have only occurred on single occasions during the present century and those which may formerly have occurred, and in some cases nested, but no longer do so, having changed their range. I have included only those birds which I consider an enthusiastic observer willing to travel about his or her county may reasonably expect to see during a year or two's fieldwork.

It would not have been possible to write this book without the help of many good friends, and I would especially like to thank the following who so willingly gave their time to answer my questions: E. Bartlett, R. P. Cockbain, W. M. Condry, P. J. Dare, P. E. Davis, J. W.

Donovan, R. A. Eades, D. M. Hanford, J. Harrop, Mrs
A. Heathcote, P. Hope-Jones, J. Humphreys, W. G.
Lewis, R. Lovegrove, J. J. Morgan, Col H. Morrey
Salmon, A. J. Prater, M. Preece, D. H. V. Roberts and
A. Smith. E. V. Breeze-Jones, Harold Grenfell, J.
Lawton-Roberts, J. Taylor and Keri Williams all kindly
loaned me photographs, and I only wish it had been
possible to include more examples of their excellent work.
J. A. Bateman (Keeper of Zoology) of the National
Museum of Wales provided a small selection of photographs and the water-colour of the red kite from the
national collection. My wife Shirley, besides checking the
typescript, shouldered the entire problems of house-
moving and home extensions while I went a-birding and
a-writing. I am forever in her debt. My thanks are also
due my publishers—particularly Benjamin Glazebrook—
for their patience during my slow production of the
manuscript.

Chapter 1

Wales—a brief introduction

Wales is an upland country, about 60 per cent of its total area (8,018 square miles) exceeding 500 feet in altitude. It is bounded on three sides by the sea—Bristol Channel, St George's Channel and the Irish Sea. On the fourth, along the eastern border extending between the Dee and Severn estuaries, the land drops abruptly to the English plain. Though small and basically upland in character Wales has a great variety of habitats, and scenically is one of the most beautiful parts of Western Europe, whether it be the mountains or coastline.

Geologically the history of Wales is one of instability and change, making it a rich area for those interested in the study of rocks and land formations. The oldest rocks are found in Anglesey and in parts of the Lleyn and St David's peninsulas. Cambrian and Ordovician rocks comprise most of the northern mountain zone, the thickest succession in Britain of the former occurring on the Harlech Dome, south Snowdonia. Softer Silurian rocks extend in a great arc from the Denbighshire coast to Pembrokeshire and Carmarthenshire. Here, except where glacial action has been severe or harder igneous rocks intrude, the terrain is gentler and more rounded than in the higher mountains. Bordering on the South Wales coalfield is an outcrop of Old Red Sandstone which runs in a narrowing band east to west, finally reaching the coast at St Brides Bay and on the Castlemartin and Dale peninsulas. Where resistant material is present, high ground—with some particularly impressive escarpments—occurs at sites like the Carmarthen Vans and Black Mountains.

During the Pleistocene era Wales was heavily glaci-
ated; at times the whole land was covered, at others the
lower levels were tundra with local ice sheets on high
ground. Ice also moved south from Scotland, Ireland and
northern England to encroach upon Wales. Good evidence for this is apparent at places as widely separated as
the Lleyn Peninsula, Cardigan Bay south of Aber-arth
and in Pembrokeshire where glacial erratics from Arran,
Ailsa Craig, Galloway and the Isle of Man have been
discovered. Throughout the country there are numerous
examples of glacial action—U-shaped valleys, cirques,
screes, perched blocks, diversions of drainage and over-
flow channels.

The majority of Welsh rivers are short, like those
flowing into Cardigan Bay or the somewhat longer ones
which rush through the South Wales coalfield and into
the Bristol Channel. The three longest rivers having
their source in Wales, but not their complete course, are
the Dee, Severn and Wye. Where each enters the sea,
forming as they do part of the boundary with England,
important estuary areas are formed, the latter two combining in a single unit. Elsewhere, except for the Burry
Inlet and associated channels, estuaries in Wales tend to
be of a rather restricted size.

A striking feature of the upland regions are the numerous lakes and pools. Those merely in the boggy hollows
of plateau regions usually attract only the ornithologist
and botanist. The larger lakes—Llyn Tegid at Bala being
the largest natural freshwater—especially when situated
in deep valleys or mountain corries, provide a great
scenic attraction. Many, impounded by glacial moraines,
are deep, even though they occur at quite high altitudes.
Llyn Dulyn (the Black Lake) situated at 1,747 feet in

Snowdonia is 189 feet deep; more spectacular still are its
precipitous sides, dropping at one spot 55 feet within
three feet of the shore. Llyn Cau in Merioneth is one of
the finest corrie lakes in Britain. With its high rainfall and
abundance of natural waters it is not surprising that both
the hydro-electric and water engineer have turned their
attentions repeatedly to Wales—not without protracted
disputes, one must hasten to add. Where natural lakes
have proved unsuitable for their requirements large
reservoirs have been constructed by throwing dams across
narrow valleys. Water impounded by such schemes not
only supplies the needs of Welsh industry and population,
but also large English conurbations like the West Mid-
lands and Merseyside.

  The coast of Wales, including estuaries, extends for
nearly a thousand miles, exhibiting as it does virtually all
shoreline physiographical features. It is an irregular coast
with fine cliff headlands alternating with lower shores and
beaches. Monmouthshire has an estuarine coast while in
east Glamorgan there are low sea-excavated cliffs. The
Gower and Castlemartin peninsulas have possibly the
finest coastal scenery in Wales, their cliff lines intersected
by bays where the sea has cut into softer strata or along
fault lines. Both have numerous sea caves, stacks, natural
arches and blow-holes to delight the visitor. Pembrokeshire is rich in islands, ranging from Skomer the largest,
down to many a sea-washed rock and gull-sentinelled
stack. North Wales also has its islands—famed Bardsey
off the tip of Lleyn, Puffin Island and the lesser-known
gems of Anglesey. Some of the largest dune systems in
Wales occur in the north—Newborough Warren, Morfa's
Dyffryn and Harlech, the latter two originating behind
shingle embankments. These sandy regions are in great

demand by holidaymakers as recreation areas, by the services as airfields and ranges and by the Forestry Commission who now have extensive plantations on some.

The coastline of Wales has been described as being in the youth of its development, and so far in these early formative years there is plenty of evidence of sea-level changes. In Cardigan Bay there are five Sarns—narrow ridges of loose boulders and stones extending seawards. The largest, Sarn Badrig, runs from the Merioneth coast for 21 miles, of which 9 are exposed at extremely low tides. These interesting features may well be the peaks of a much larger low area, now long submerged—the Cantref y Gwaelod of Welsh folk-lore? Drowned valleys like that of Milford Haven and its lesser creeks, the discovery of peat deep below marine deposits, and the submerged forests located at several points provide further evidence for sea-level change.

Wales has a changeable climate, while the height and configuration of the land may cause marked weather differences over quite short distances. There is an ample rainfall, and high amounts may fall within very short periods causing sudden flooding. Fortunately such records as 2.90 inches in half an hour near Cowbridge in July 1880 are rarely emulated. As expected the north-western mountains have the highest annual rainfall with totals of over 100 inches, the highest peaks in Snowdonia having about 200 inches. The driest parts are the coastal regions and those valleys immediately in the eastern lee of the mountains. The south and south-west coasts are the sunniest spots, places like Tenby and Dale competing to claim the title of the resort with the most hours of sunshine. Wales is a windy country, inland the mountains and narrow valleys accentuate speeds by their funnelling

effect. The exposed western headlands of Caernarvonshire and Pembrokeshire are among the windiest in
Britain and may expect at least thirty gales in a year.

With a difficult terrain it is hardly surprising that
Wales in prehistoric times was extremely thinly populated. A lack of suitable implement materials, flint only
occurring as a storm beach erratic of glacial origin,
would also have restricted man's development of the
region. Colonisation and contact were probably easier by
sea and river than by overgrown routes through marshy
valleys. Iron Age settlers arrived about 250 B.C., a couple
of centuries later than their first colonisation of Britain.
The Romans completed their conquest in A.D. 75, but were
only in control of the lowland zones, though even so there
were areas—notably the extreme south-west—barely
under their jurisdiction. About A.D. 400 important movements of people took place into Wales when Brythonic
speaking Celts came from the north, gradually consolidat-
ing their position by conquest over the next 300 years.

Between A.D. 778 and 796 Offa's Dyke was constructed,
not, it seems, so much as a purely military barrier but as
one denoting a frontier between Celt and Saxon agreed
after peaceful negotiation. It follows remarkably closely
the line of the present day Welsh–English border. About
1070 the first Normans arrived, their settlements growing
around castles, wooden structures later replaced with fine
mason-crafted keeps. Further encroachment by the
English took place in the thirteenth century, culminating
in the Treaty of Rhuddlan signed in 1284. The present
political map of Wales stems from this era, though it was
not until 1536 and 1542 that the Tudors joined the two
countries by an Act of Union, and revolt and insurrection
finally ceased.

The population of Wales has always been small by
comparison with the rest of southern Britain. It was estimated to number 278,000 in 1536 and over the next 300
years rose to 1,046,073. By 1961 it was 2,640,632 and in
1971 2,723,592. Although the population has continued
to rise the majority of this increase has occurred in comparatively few areas, generally at the expense of the rest
of the country. People have tended to vacate rural areas
—in particular those in central Wales—to seek alternative
opportunities in urban zones, not only those in the
Principality but also further afield. In 1961 about 70 per
cent of the population was classed as urban, yet these
only occupied 13 per cent of the available land; the
main concentrations being in the mining, industrial and
port areas of the south and south-east, and along Deeside
and the Wrexham region in the north. It is in these
northern industrial areas that the most spectacular increases are taking place at present.

Man, since his first appearance in Wales, has been
continually altering and adapting the countryside to his
own needs and requirements, usually with scant regard
for its original state and inhabitants. In prehistoric times
about 70 per cent of Wales was woodland—on the
highest ground conifers, at lower altitudes oak while
alder carpeted the valley floors. Climatic change caused
the initial retreat of trees from high ground, at one time
even oak occurred up to about the 2,000-foot contour.
Coincident with the growth in human population, was
an increase in the amount of tree felling and of grazing
by domestic animals, most particularly sheep. By 1871
woodland acreage had been reduced to only 127,000
acres compared with an estimated 3,570,000 acres at its
zenith. Now only fragments of the older woods remain—

the hanging oakwoods of valley sides, and a few areas of
steep sea slopes which even man has failed to harness to
an agricultural system. Intensive grazing and the spread
of bracken are both inhibiting factors to the natural re-
generation of native woodland.

Since its establishment in 1919 the Forestry Commission has been most active in its planting programme.
One cannot drive far anywhere in Wales without encountering its coniferous woodlands, some of which rise
to the summit rims. Unfortunately in general this vast
habitat, in varying stages of development, does not assist
the bird life of these regions. Elsewhere in upland Wales
man's influence has altered little for centuries, sheep still
being the dominant factor. From an ornithological view-
point the increase in human leisure activities, taking as
it does more visitors over a greater part of the year to
high ground, could well prove detrimental to certain
species with a local distribution in Wales, like merlin,
golden plover and dunlin. Such pressures may prevent
the establishment of species which might otherwise come
to breed in Wales, given undisturbed (and this includes
by ornithologists) areas.

Lowland Wales has for the most part lost its great bogs
and marshlands; of the remaining small fragments some,
fortunately, are nature reserves, so giving us an insight
into these most fascinating of habitats. Drainage has produced rich farming areas, while industry has long cast
covetous eyes on these level regions. Now the respiratory
functions of vast steel works billow smoke across land
where curlew nested and wild geese sought winter sanctuary. Until recently the remoter coastal areas have es-
caped serious depredation by man. However, at an
accelerating rate during the past thirty years this situa-

tion has changed, with oil pollution incidents involving seabirds an all too regular occurrence, while the exploitation of possible oil from marine wells in St George's Channel and the Irish Sea adds yet a further dimension to this problem. Industrial waste dumped in these same areas or accumulated there via our river systems poses another threat; the disaster that affected many thousand guillemots and other seabirds during the autumn of 1969 in the Irish Sea seems likely to have been due to such contamination sources. The major Welsh estuaries have all had schemes mooted for their development, none more so than the Dee, one of the most important coastal bird areas in Britain.

There are, however, bright sides to the story. Even in industrial areas interesting habitats for birds remain or have indeed been created, the construction of reservoirs and park lakes being especially noteworthy. The growth of the County Naturalists' Trusts in Wales since the early 1960s and the increasing emphasis on local conservation together with the wider efforts of national organisations like the Nature Conservancy and Royal Society for the Protection of Birds bodes well for the future, though one may hardly need to add much still remains to be done. Ornithologists can play their part. The more people watch and enjoy birds in Wales the greater the notice of conservation that will be taken by those who, in the interests of the general population, have the task of improving communications, expanding industry and residential areas and implementing the other changes which the latter years of the twentieth century dictate.

Chapter 2

A brief history of Welsh ornithology

For the earliest references to birds in Wales one must go back over a thousand years to the time of Hywel Dda (Hywel the Good). It is for excellent reasons that Hywel is the only Welsh prince to be termed 'Good'. He maintained peace with the English, and although doing homage to both Edward, son of Alfred, and to Athelstan, remained independent of their rule. Possibly these close contacts with the Saxon court inspired him in his greatest work, the codification of the Welsh laws and customs. This he accomplished about the year 945, aided by 'archbishops, bishops, abbots and good teachers from all parts of Wales'. References to birds in the laws of Hywel Dda are all related to falconry, the falconer occupying a high position in the King's household. The nest of a sparrowhawk was valued at twenty-four pence compared to that of a hawk (goshawk?) at one pound. If the falconer, by means of his birds, managed to kill either a heron, bittern or crane the king was obliged to perform several services for him, among them holding his horse while the birds were secured, and while the falconer mounted and dismounted.

Early Welsh poetry followed rigid Bardic lines—odes to God, odes in praise of Princes, and later, love poems and eulogies of lesser personages. In the mid-fourteenth century Dafydd ap Gwilym, a native of south-west Wales where he had no doubt been influenced by the Norman occupiers, commenced a new style. One of his favourite themes was nature and in his works some twenty species of bird are referred to, including the swan, eagle, woodcock, swallow, magpie and linnet.

The first to leave actual written records of birds,
though one must hasten to add that these were generally
quite incidental to their main tasks, were the various
chroniclers who travelled through Medieval Wales.
Giraldus Cambrensis (Gerald the Welshman), born at
Manorbier Castle, Pembrokeshire in 1147 was one of the
greatest scholars of his day. In 1188 he accompanied
Archbishop Baldwin through Wales preaching the Third
Crusade, during which the prelate was to die in Palestine.
Giraldus wrote down his impressions in his 'Itinerary
and Description of Wales'. This includes a few ornithological passages—he mentions the high esteem placed
on the falcons which bred in Pembrokeshire, and quotes
the Archbishop, perhaps tiring of his journey, as saying
that 'the nightingale followed wise counsel, and never
came into Wales; but we, unwise counsel, who have
penetrated and gone through it'. There are few breeding
records for the nightingale in Wales and at the present
time it remains a very scarce visitor to this part of
Britain. Perhaps the most intriguing of all Giraldus' com-
ments is that concerning a golden oriole heard in
Caernarvonshire, or was it a green woodpecker as some
of the party considered?

John Leland who catalogued the antiquities of Wales
between 1536 and 1539 was one of many early travellers
to mention eagles nesting. However, not one of them
actually encountered a breeding site themselves despite
some most graphic accounts. There would seem to be no
doubt that the golden eagle once bred in Wales, dis-
appearing some time in the seventeenth or eighteenth
century from its last strongholds in Snowdonia. George
Owen in his *Description of Pembrokeshire* (1603) devotes
four pages to 'Of abundance of foule that the County

yeeldeth, and of the feverall fortes thereof'. Nearly forty species are mentioned, including bittern, teal, oyster-catcher, woodcock, curlew, guillemot, fieldfare, black-bird and hedge sparrow.

John Ray and Francis Willughby visited Wales in 1658 and 1662 and are described by W. M. Condry in his book *Snowdonia* (1966) as 'the two most celebrated English naturalists of their time'. Towards the end of the same century Edward Lloyd, possibly the greatest of all naturalists to have worked in Wales, made repeated visits to the northern uplands. He is best remembered for his botanical discoveries, one of which—the Snowdon lily *Lloydia serotina*—is named after him. We are the poorer for the loss by fire in 1810 of his unpublished manuscript notes including those on birds.

One of the most prolific correspondents of Gilbert White, the curate of Selborne, was Thomas Pennant, a Welshman born in 1726 at Downing Hall near Mostyn, Flintshire. Although one of the most eminent of the great eighteenth-century naturalists, being author of master-pieces like *A Tour in Scotland* (1771), *British Zoology* (1776), and *A History of British Quadrupeds* (1793), Pennant's con-tribution to the natural history of Wales is, to say the least, disappointing. Zoological information in his *Tour of Wales* (1784) is scarce, barely half a dozen species being mentioned with regard to Snowdonia.

As the nineteenth century progressed so interest in birds grew, involving a much wider spectrum of society than the few learned observers of the previous 150 years. There was a rapid improvement in communications. Roads, particularly in the mountainous north and central regions, were opened up and made suitable for less hardy travellers. The railway was thrusting into even the remotest parts of Wales, so that visitors could move about with a previously unheard-of ease, no longer suffering the problems of Archbishop Baldwin and his retinue. More books were being published, even the authors of the numerous 'guide-books' often found it of interest to include for their readers a chapter or two on the flora and fauna. Birds were usually pre-eminent, and no ornithological historian can fail to neglect such unlikely sounding titles as *A History of Aberconwy* (1835) by Reverend Robert Williams, or the *Llandudno Visitors Guide Book* (1855) by Richard Parry.

In 1853, when the collecting of field sport trophies was at its height, the breech-loader was invented; this more efficient weapon enabled an even greater degree of destruction to be meted out by sportsmen and gamekeepers. No town worthy of its name failed to boast of a taxidermist's shop, and hardly a country house was without its collection of mounted birds in glass cases. Game birds and wildfowl usually formed the basis of most collections but the possession of rarer species was a prize for which high fees were paid. Virtually all information concerning rarer avian visitors during the nineteenth century came from such sources. In their introduction to *The Birds of Brecknock* (1957) Geoffrey C. S. Ingram and Col H. Morrey Salmon so aptly sum up the situation—'What a picture of the nineteenth-century ornithologists; they must have kept their guns always at full-cock and one has a feeling that, if there happens to be only a sight-record, the observer must have missed with both barrels.' A glance at the early avifaunas quickly confirms this view, with numerous statements like 'one shot', 'a good specimen obtained', 'sent to the taxidermist', 'examined in the flesh' etc.

However there were those observers, indeed a growing number, who were keeping records, beginning the compilation of local lists and contributing notes to journals like the *Field* and *Zoologist*. With field observation still in its infancy and collecting at its peak it seems hardly surprising that such workers drew heavily for their information on specimens obtained. Our information would be that much poorer without their efforts, for taxidermists and the majority of collectors seemed lethargic where the keeping of records was concerned. One of the most important early works was a series of papers by Thomas Campbell Egerton modestly entitled, 'An attempt to ascertain the Fauna of Shropshire and North Wales' which appeared in the *Annals of Natural History* between 1835 and 1838.

In South Wales one of the first local lists was compiled by Lewis Weston Dillwyn of Swansea, Member of Parliament between 1832 and 1841. In 1840 his 'Contributions towards a History of Swansea' was published, followed in 1848 by 'Materials for a Fauna and Flora of Swansea and Neighbourhood'. Although omitting waders and seabirds the *Zoologist* published in 1850 and 1851 'A Catologue of Birds taken in Pembrokeshire; with Observations on their Habits, Manners etc' communicated by James Tracy, the Pembroke taxidermist. Through his hands passed several of the specimens used to illustrate Yarrell's *A History of British Birds* (1839). These included the first yellow-billed cuckoo to be recorded in Britain, shot on the nearby Cawdor estate at Stackpole where Tracy's father was a gamekeeper. In Carmarthenshire a curious list was published in 1858 by William Davies in his 'Llandeilo-Vawr and its Neighbourhood: Past and Present'. Some eighty-two species are mentioned though the names given for some seem rather odd—small willow wren, bare-faced crow, water quail and jaypie. A particularly important local list, and the first to be published for Cardiganshire, was the work of J. H. Salter, head of the Botany Department of University College, Aberystwyth 1891–1908, an indefatigable ornithologist who kept notes on his observations until his death in 1942. His 'Observations on Birds in mid-Wales' appeared in the *Zoologist* in 1895.

Such local lists and the many separate notes in natural history journals formed the basis for the larger county avifaunas. North Wales, i.e. the counties of Anglesey, Caernarvonshire, Denbighshire, Flintshire, Merioneth and Montgomeryshire, were covered by H. E. Forrest in his massive work *The Vertebrate Fauna of North Wales* published in 1907, to be followed by a supplement in 1919. Although half a century has elapsed, and a massive amount of new information has been collected concerning the avifauna of these counties, the only up-to-date work to have followed Forrest is the *Birds of Flintshire*. Compiled by the Flintshire Ornithological Society this was published in 1968. Although avifaunas are planned for most of the other North Wales counties, a perhaps understandable tendency for field- rather than desk-work continues to delay the appearance of these much needed volumes.

South Wales has been better served. In 1882 *The Birds of Breconshire* by E. Cambridge Phillips, for sixty years a Justices Clerk in the county, was published. Twelve years later *The Birds of Pembrokeshire and its Islands* by the Reverend Murray A. Mathew appeared. Mathew had come from West Somerset to Pembrokeshire for health reasons, and he wrote of his result that, 'although meagre,

it may serve as the foundation upon which an ampler
account of the birds of the county may some day be
based.' In 1900 the first of several Glamorgan avifaunas
was produced, one of the compilers being Robert Drane,
an East Anglian domiciled in Cardiff where he was a
chemist, and best remembered as the discoverer of the
Skomer Island bank vole. *A Handbook of the Natural History
of Carmarthenshire* by T. W. Barker (1905) includes a list
of that county's birds.

   In the 1930s, inspired by Forrest's work on the fauna
of North Wales, Col H. Morrey Salmon and the late
Geoffrey C. S. Ingram commenced the task of compiling
avifaunas for the seven counties of South Wales. In 1936
their *Birds of Glamorgan* was published, followed in 1937
by *The Birds of Monmouthshire*. In collaboration with
R. M. Lockley *The Birds of Pembrokeshire* was published in
1949. Although Breconshire (1954) and Radnorshire
(1955) followed in quick succession a further eleven
years elapsed before the final county—Cardiganshire—
was completed, this time in collaboration with W. M.
Condry. Revised editions of *The Birds of Monmouthshire*
appeared in 1963 and Glamorgan in 1967. A noteworthy
aspect of most of these avifaunas is the relatively cheap
format adopted, so that the price is well within the budget
of even the youngest enthusiast. It is hoped that re-
visions of the other earlier works of these two fathers of
modern ornithology in Wales are not too far away.

   The first half of the present century saw the publication of a number of general works on or including items
concerning birds in Wales. *Bird Life in Wild Wales* (1903)
by John A. Walpole-Bond; *Wild Life in Wales* (1913) by
George Bolam; *Bird Haunts and Nature Memories* (1922)
by T. A. Coward; *Watchings and Wanderings among Birds*

(1931) by H. A. Gilbert and A. Brook; *Birds in Britain Today* (1933) by Geoffrey C. S. Ingram and H. Morrey Salmon. One must not overlook the slim volume *Changes in the Fauna of Wales within Historic Times* by Colin Matheson, published at two shillings in 1932 by the National Museum of Wales. This contains a chapter on birds which have become extinct as breeding species in Wales, including honey buzzard, bittern (returned to breed in late 1960s), spoonbill, and crane. There is also a chapter on introduced species including red-legged partridge, blackgrouse and little owl.

As the interest in birds grew so clubs and societies began to form, some had only a brief life, others have flourished and play their important role in the ornithology of Wales today. The oldest of these organisations is the Cardiff Naturalists' Society, founded in 1867, though a separate ornithological section did not commence until 1946. Although a Pembrokeshire Field Naturalists' Club existed during the late nineteenth century it was not until 1938 that the Pembrokeshire Bird Protection Society was established. It enlarged both its scope and geographical area in 1946 by becoming the West Wales Field Society embracing the counties of Cardigan, Carmarthen, Merioneth and Pembroke. A further change took place in 1961 when the Field Society became the first Naturalists' Trust in Wales, and in 1972 handed over responsibility for voluntary conservation work in Merioneth to the North Wales Naturalists' Trust. There is now no ornithological society, as such, in West Wales, matters including the production of an annual Dyfed Bird Report being in the hands of the County Bird Recorders. The Cambrian Ornithological Society covers North Wales except for Flintshire which has its own Society, and Montgomeryshire with its Field Club. Radnorshire is linked with Herefordshire, the Brecknock County Naturalists' Trust has an ornithological section while Monmouthshire has its own Society. The newest member of these organisations is the Gower Ornithological Club, founded in 1956 and covering the Gower Peninsula and Swansea.

Ornithologists in Wales seem in some respects rather parochial, there has in the past been comparatively little contact and liaison between the clubs and societies. A significant step forward was made in Aberystwyth in 1967 when a gathering of representatives from the various ornithological organisations launched the Welsh Bird Report. This has appeared annually in the journal *Nature in Wales* since 1967, though its inclusion there does, through lack of space, tend to stifle its natural growth and expansion. At the time of writing late in 1972 there is talk of an annual or biennial Welsh ornithologists' conference, this could become an important focal point for future activities, particularly the co-operative enquiries which are planned.

Bird migration is without question one of the most fascinating aspects of ornithology and Wales has led the way in one aspect of its study. In 1933 R. M. Lockley founded Britain's first Bird Observatory on Skokholm Island off the Pembrokeshire coast. Except for the war years bird migration has been watched and studied here continuously ever since, undoubtedly inspiring other workers in this field so that now there is a chain of Observatories situated on remote islands and headlands in Britain. One of these is Bardsey Island, Caernarvonshire where an Observatory opened in 1953 though was temporarily closed from 1971 until 1974.

Turning now to the field of ornithological conservation
the Royal Society for the Protection of Birds paid hono-
raria to voluntary watchers in Pembrokeshire as long ago
as 1925. They acquired their first reserve in Wales—
Grassholm, Pembrokeshire—in 1948, and since then another Pembrokeshire island—Ramsey—and the mainland reserves of the Gwenffrwd, Carmarthenshire and
Ynyshir, Cardiganshire. A major new development took
place in 1971 when the first Wales Representative of the
R.S.P.B. took up his post with an office in Newtown. The
Nature Conservancy opened their Welsh activities in
earnest in 1954 when Cwm Idwal was declared a
National Nature Reserve, other declarations have followed, while besides the reserves there are regional
offices in both Bangor and Aberystwyth. Although covering all branches of natural history, the County Naturalists'
Trusts which formed in Wales during the early 1960s
often have strong ornithological leanings. Besides managing their own reserves they work in close co-operation
with others like the R.S.P.B., Nature Conservancy,
Forestry Commission, County Planning Authorities and
Water Boards.

In Wales there is a longer history of conservation for
an individual species of bird—the red kite—than in any
other part of Britain. Over the past eighty years a small
number of dedicated ornithologists have been involved in
efforts to ensure that this rare raptor remains a breeding
species. A full account has been given by one of their
number—Col H. Morrey Salmon on pages 67 to 79 of
Welsh Wildlife in Trust, published in 1970 by the North
Wales Naturalists' Trust. The following summary has
been prepared from the information presented in this
valuable paper. By the 1870s Wales was the sole remain-

ing locality in Britain for the kite, and even here it was
confined to a few oak-fringed valleys in the south central
region. Several people, among them Cambridge Phillips
of Breconshire and J. M. Salter of Aberystwyth, were
appalled by a situation in which the few remaining pairs
were continually harried and their nests if found, de-
stroyed. A letter in 1903 from the latter to the British
Ornithologists Club resulted in the first of several kite
committees which through the ensuing years have largely
been responsible for the continued survival of this bird as
a breeding species in Britain. Although there have been
setbacks like a food shortage following the myxomatosis
epidemic in the mid-1950s and contamination by toxic
chemicals in the early 1960s, the population now seems
to be in as healthy a state as at any time during the past
one hundred years. In 1972 22 pairs bred rearing 16
young from 12 successful nests, the spring population
being between 55 and 60 individuals.

No branch of natural history has so many devotees as
ornithology; birds it is often said, are the most observable
and most observed of all animals. Based on its rich ornithological history their study in Wales is now a fine art
backed by a group of vigorous societies. Ornithologists
are rapidly realising that their hobby cannot be pursued
in these rapidly changing times without reference to conservation and many take part in co-operative enquiries.
In some areas ornithological societies and naturalists'
trusts have tended to go their separate ways, but in Wales
they generally work in close liaison and in West Wales
and in Breconshire ornithological matters come completely under the aegis of the naturalists' trusts. Such
close co-operation surely marks the next phase in the
ornithological history of Wales.

Chapter 3

General information

Although much information of a local nature is given in the relevant county chapters, there are wider aspects which the ornithologist in Wales may find of value and these are given here.

Avifaunas
At present Wales lacks an avifauna along the lines of *The Birds of Scotland* by Baxter and Rintoul, *The Birds of Ireland* by Kennedy, Ruttledge and Scroope, or even the shorter *Ireland's Birds* by Ruttledge. Such works not only provide an invaluable source of information, but also, through the gaps which they indicate, inspire and encourage ornithologists in their observations and search for knowledge. The absence of a Welsh avifauna is much regretted, and one hopes that not too many years will elapse before such a work is published.

When one considers county avifaunas, South Wales has been particularly well endowed, mainly through the energies of Col H. Morrey Salmon and the late Geoffrey C. S. Ingram. All the southern counties have been covered since the late 1940s, a revised edition of *The Birds of Glamorgan* (1967) being the most up to date. The economical format adopted in most of these works, means that the price is low, well within the range which the majority of ornithologists can afford. This should mean that revised editions can appear fairly frequently, say about every twenty years or so, as our knowledge increases. Unfortunately this has not proved to be the case, and the accounts of birds in Carmarthenshire, Pembrokeshire and Radnorshire are now somewhat out of date.

Except for the notable exception of Flintshire, the North Wales counties constitute a large region without any recent county avifaunas, indeed none has been written since *The Vertebrate Fauna of North Wales* (1907) and its supplement (1919). However, Welsh ornithologists are deeply conscious of this gap and strenuous efforts are being made in several counties in order to bring the situation up to date.

British Trust for Ornithology
Founded in 1933 the Trust with a headquarters staff at Beech Grove, Tring, Herts. collects information from its members and interested non-members concerning birds in Britain. Some of its enquiries are long standing like the Nest Records Scheme and the Annual Index of the Heron Population. More recently, species studied in detail have included the peregrine, and the information collected during this enquiry provided the first circumstantial evidence of the accumulation of chlorinated hydro-carbons in the bodies of animals at the upper end of food chains. Two of the largest enquiries conducted by the B.T.O. are the Birds of Estuaries Enquiry and the Atlas of Breeding Birds. The latter, a five-year project completed in 1972, is the first detailed inventory of our breeding birds, and will be invaluable in assessing changes in our bird populations. Regional Representatives of the B.T.O. are appointed mainly on a county basis and act as focal points for the exchange of information between ornithologists, and are always willing to advise on the birds of their own areas.

Countryside Commission
When the Countryside Act became law in August 1968,

the Countryside Commission replaced the National
Parks Commission, assuming its functions but at the same
time extending its sphere of action to the whole of England and Wales instead of being restricted to specially
designated areas. One of the most important parts of the
Commission's work, however, is concerned with the
National Parks, of which there are at present three in
Wales—Brecon Beacons, Pembrokeshire Coast and
Snowdonia. If a new National Park is to be designated,
no change in land ownership takes place and no special
rights of public access are available to private land which
they have not previously enjoyed. The Commission draws
up proposals for establishing long-distance footpaths, like
the Pembrokeshire Coast Path (167 miles) and the Offa's
Dyke Path (168 miles). Information services are an important part of the Commission's work, each of the National
Parks having several offices where guide books and
pamphlets concerning the National Parks are easily
available. Addresses of information centres are given in the
appropriate county sections, while the offices of the
Countryside Commission are at:

   1 Cambridge Gate,
   Regent's Park, London NW1 4JY.

Field Studies Council
There are three Field Studies Centres in Wales and another just over the border in Shropshire. These arrange
a wide variety of courses between March and September
mainly for senior pupils and university students, though
others are arranged for the interested amateur. All
natural history subjects are covered as well as geology,
geography and art. Full details are available from:

Field Studies Council, 9 Devereux Court, Strand, WC2; or from the Centre wardens at:

Dale Fort Field Centre, Dale, Haverfordwest, Pembrokeshire;

Orielton Field Centre, Pembroke;

Preston Montford Field Centre, Nr Shrewsbury;

Rhyd-y-Crenau (Drapers Field Centre), Betws-y-Coed, Caerns.

Forestry Commission

The Forestry Commission in Wales is divided into the Wales (North) Conservancy administering the counties of Anglesey, Caernarvon, Cardigan, Denbigh, Merioneth, Flint, Montgomery and Radnor with its headquarters at:

Victoria House, Victoria Terrace, Aberystwyth, Cards. SY23 2DA; and the Wales (South) Conservancy administering the counties of Brecon, Carmarthen, Glamorgan, Monmouth and Pembroke with its headquarters at:

Churchill House, Churchill Way, Cardiff CF1 4TU.

From a purely ornithological view the vast areas of mainly conifer woodland—in 1972 there were some 126,000 hectares (312,000 acres)—may not be as rich in bird life as mixed or purely deciduous woodland; nevertheless there are exceptions. Both black grouse and siskin, increasing species in Wales, resort to developing conifer plantations. More important to the community at large has been the increasing efforts, though of course secondary to the task of producing timber economically, made by the Forestry Commission to open up its holdings for recreational purposes. Besides camp and picnic sites there are now over thirty Forest Trails and Walks in

Wales, each with descriptive leaflet, while other publications include a Guide to the Snowdonia Forest Park and
another to the Glamorgan Forest. Where applicable such
publications are mentioned in the county chapters, but
full details of all those available may be obtained from
either of the Welsh headquarters or from:

H.M. Stationery Office, 109 St Mary Street, Cardiff.

Nature Conservancy Council
Established in 1949 the Nature Conservancy advises on
nature conservation, establishes and manages nature reserves and carries out research. The Conservancy works
in close liaison with voluntary bodies like the Naturalists'
Trusts. In Wales there are now twenty-nine National
Nature Reserves covering just over 8,900 hectares
(22,000 acres) and three Forest Nature Reserves. Although some of the reserves are of no particular ornithological interest, others like Newborough Warren
(Anglesey), Dyfi Estuary (Cards.) and Skomer (Pembs.)
are of the highest importance. Descriptive leaflets are
available for some reserves and several Nature Trails
have been established. Access to reserves varies greatly,
permits are required for some of the smaller ones and also
for sections of the larger reserves away from rights of way.
Full information concerning National and Forest Nature
Reserves in Wales and the work of the Nature Conservancy may be obtained from the two regional offices:

North Wales—covering the counties of Anglesey,
Caernarvon, Denbigh, Flint, Merioneth and Mont-
gomery: The Nature Conservancy, Headquarters and
Research Station, Penrhos Road, Bangor, Caerns;

South Wales—covering the counties of Brecon, Cardigan, Carmarthen, Glamorgan, Monmouth, Pembroke

and Radnor: The Nature Conservancy, Plas Gogerddan, Aberystwyth, Cards.

Naturalists' Trust

All the Welsh counties are covered by Naturalists' Trusts, in two cases—West Wales and North Wales, several counties are included in the same organisation. Details are given in the county sections concerning the relevant Trusts, together with a brief summary of their activities. General information concerning the Naturalists' Trust movement is available from:

Association of Nature Conservation Trusts, Nettleham, Lincoln

Nature in Wales

Founded in 1955 as the journal of the West Wales Field Society (now West Wales Naturalists' Trust) *Nature in Wales* is published twice a year and now shared with the North Wales Naturalists' Trust and the Radnorshire section of the Hereford and Radnor Nature Trust. Edited by T. A. Warren Davis and L. S. V. Venables, the Managing Editor is Dillwyn Miles, 4 Victoria Place, Haverfordwest, Pembs. from whom copies may be purchased by non-members of the above Trusts at 55p (Trust members receive the journal free).

Although covering all aspects of natural history in Wales, there are frequent ornithological papers, recent titles including 'The Chough in North Wales', 'Ornithological Beachcombing in Merioneth' and 'Our Vanishing Swans'. The 'Welsh Bird Report' (see page 41) is published annually in *Nature in Wales*.

Ornithological Societies

There is at present no single society covering the whole of
Wales and the reader is referred to the county sections.
Although not included in these, the Merseyside Naturalists' Association covers much of North Wales besides the
Liverpool area and north-west England. Field meetings
are held from time to time in North Wales, but indoor
meetings are confined to the Liverpool area. The 'North-
western Bird Report' for 1966–71 is available price 40p
(post extra) from the Hon. Sec. Eric Hardy, 47 Wood-
sorrel Road, Liverpool, L15 6UB. Annual subscription
to the Association is 25p.

Royal Society for the Protection of Birds

Founded in 1889 the Society is probably the best known
and certainly the largest (140,000 members by October
1973) natural history organisation in Britain. It owns or
leases five reserves in Wales—Ynyshir (Cards.), Dinas
and Gwenffrwd (Carms.) and Grassholm and Ramsey
(Pembs.). An important development in Wales was the
appointment of a representative and the opening of a
regional office in April 1971:

    R.S.P.B. (Wales Office), 18 High Street, Newtown,
    Montgomeryshire.

    Honorary local representatives whose main task is the
publicising of the work of the R.S.P.B. through such activities as film shows, lectures and exhibitions have been
appointed for some areas. It is anticipated that this
scheme will expand, so that the names and addresses
given in the county sections will be amended from time
to time and anyone wishing to receive up-to-date information is advised to contact the Welsh Office direct.

    For those below the age of 17, the Young Ornithologists' Club is a must, field meetings are held in many areas and numerous holiday bird-watching courses are arranged including several in Wales. Further information is available from:

Young Ornithologists' Club (R.S.P.B.) The Lodge, Sandy, Beds.

'*Welsh Bird Report*'
Following a meeting in 1967 of representatives of all regional organisations concerned with birds in Wales, a 'Welsh Bird Report' (for 1967) was published in the September 1968 issue of *Nature in Wales* (see page 40). Subsequent annual reports have appeared in the same journal. Inclusion in such a wide-ranging journal means that space is limited, so that, unfortunately, the report is greatly condensed. Publications elsewhere of reports have always stimulated and encouraged bird-watchers, and here in Wales the same would undoubtedly occur if a report was allowed to develop separately, and so be allowed to include the fullest information possible. Much of value would result. Reprints of the reports are available, price 10p from the Editors:

P. Hope Hones, Bedwen, Bro Enddwyn, Dyffryn Ardudwy, Merionethshire;

P. E. Davis, Ty Coed, Tregaron, Cardiganshire.

ANGLESEY

IRISH SEA

13

1

Amlwch

10

Holyhead

12

9

3

11

8

Llangefni

4 Beaumaris

5

6

2

7

14

CAERNARVON
BAY

0   5   10

miles

Chapter 4

Anglesey

The most northerly point in Wales is probably one of its least known localities, a small sea rock known as Ynys Badrig (Patrick's Island), its English name is Middle Mouse. Small numbers of cormorants, gulls, razorbills and guillemots nest, and probably the only visitors are those few stalwart ornithologists who make regular surveys of the bird populations. There is also an East and a West Mouse, each having small numbers of nesting gulls. All three are widely separated but lie within a mile of the north coast of Anglesey, surely one of the best known of the Welsh counties. A mere three hundred yards at its narrowest point, and four miles at its widest from the mainland of north-west Wales, Anglesey is the largest island in England and Wales and one of the largest in Britain. It was divided from the rest of Wales—despite some assertions that roads existed across what is now the Menai Straits in the fifth century—by land subsidence in early Neolithic times.

Unlike the rest of Wales, Anglesey is a lowland county, its highest point being 720 feet above sea level on Holyhead Mountain. Much of the land is below the 500-foot contour, being a series of parallel ridges divided by short river valleys, most of which run north-east to south-west. Marine erosion during late Tertiary times is responsible for the low altitude of the island which besides Holyhead Mountain has only eight other small areas above 500 feet. Roughly rectangular in shape, the island lies on a north-west to south-east axis being approximately 20 miles long and 14 miles wide. An interesting feature is Holy Island some seven miles long and up to three miles wide, separated from the west coast by an estuarine area across which two embankments carry transport links.

Anglesey is steeped in history, there are numerous burial mounds and megalithic monuments, the oldest dating back at least 4,500 years. Druidism flourished here, no doubt new influences were slow, or even failed to reach, this far corner of Wales. However, about A.D. 61 the Romans crossed the Menai Straits, conquered the tribes and prevented further druid festivals. Holy men found Anglesey much to their liking. Seiriol established cells on the Penmon peninsula and on Puffin Island off its eastern extremity, Cybi who gave us the Welsh name for Holyhead—Caer Cybi (Cybi's fortress), while one

Black Guillemot

story relates how Patrick set sail for Ireland from
Llanbadrif. Viking pirates from their Irish lairs often
pillaged along the Welsh coast and Anglesey was no exception. The English came under Edward I, who from
his huge retinue produced master craftsmen in stone who
built Beaumaris Castle at the western end of the Menai
Straits. Unlike most castles Beaumaris has never heard
the clashing of steel weapons or the roar of cannon in
anger and remains in quite good condition today. Because of difficulties of access Anglesey has retained its
very Welsh character, it was not until 1826 that the first
of the two bridges crossing the Menai Straits was constructed. This was the suspension bridge which still
carries the road traffic, the engineer being the indomit-
able Thomas Telford. In 1850 the railway bridge, recently severely damaged by fire, was constructed by
Robert Stephenson, son of the famous George.

Anglesey is mainly an agricultural county, devoted at
the present time to dairy farming, though in the past it
produced large quantities of grain, so gaining its name
'Mon Mam Cymru' the 'Mother of Wales'. Industry unfortunately has not passed the island by, the Romans
mined copper on Parrys Mountain near the north-west
corner, and it was here that in 1768 a rich ore vein was
discovered by more modern miners and soon the largest
copper mine in Europe was in operation. The ore was
mainly exported by sea from the nearby harbour at
Amlwch, however the boom was short lived and by the
time of Waterloo the workings were closing down. As
copper becomes harder to obtain in the last years of this
century, will we see yet another phase of Anglesey's
mining history when man finds it necessary to dig out
even low grade ores? Some coal mining was carried on in

south-west Anglesey as early as 1450 and was carried on
sporadically until about 1875 when the workings were
flooded. Limestone quarrying has been, and indeed still
is, an important industry, with the workings on the
Penmon peninsula coast providing nesting sites for seabirds—mainly herring gulls and lesser black-backed gulls,
while kittiwakes have also established colonies. Some of
these may only be of a temporary nature as the sites alter
when further blasting takes place. More recent industrial
developments have been the construction on the north
coast of a nuclear power station and near Holyhead an
aluminium smelter.

Of the many lakes on Anglesey twenty-five are considered to result from glacial activity and these, together

Arctic Tern

with their associated marshlands, provide bird habitats almost unique in Wales. It is a pity that so far none of the Anglesey lakes and marshland have been included in a nature reserve, their rich bird life, both resident and wintering meriting this. As their importance is more widely accepted, and this can only be done by more concerted observation to provide background information, perhaps it will be possible for a representative area to be designated a reserve. On the coast naturalists have been more fortunate, with important reserves at Newborough Warren and the Cemlyn Lagoon. There are, however, still disappointing aspects. Cliff climbing at the seabird colonies on Holy Island and the virtual disappearance of the Little Tern as a breeding bird from the Anglesey beaches are problems very much in ornithologists' minds at the present time. The proposed, and much fought-over, plan to offload giant tankers lying off the north coast of Anglesey, the oil to be pumped through pipes to Liverpool, may well have detrimental effects on the island's bird life in the event of pollution occurring. The ornithologist visiting Anglesey should keep careful records of any observations, for several species—e.g. kingfisher, great spotted and lesser spotted woodpeckers, marsh and long-tailed tits, nuthatch, redstart, garden warbler and chiffchaff—have a rather local breeding distribution on the island. This fact might be overlooked by the visitor encountering some of these species during his stay. Anglesey has much to offer the ornithologist at all seasons. In summer there are the seabird cliffs, in winter the lakes and marshlands with their wildfowl, and on both spring and autumn passages the chance of observing large movements of birds and, with luck, the discovery of rare bird visitors to Wales.

Information

County Avifaunas
Forrest, H. E., *The Vertebrate Fauna of North Wales*
(London, 1907) together with the supplement to this
work published in 1919, is the only avifauna available at
the present though, needless to say, it is long out of date.
Walker, T. G., 'The Birds of Anglesey', pp. 165–203 in
Natural History of Anglesey ed by W. Eifion Jones (1968).
This gives a brief introduction to the county's bird life
together with a Check List.

Bird Report
Records of birds on Anglesey are published annually in
the *Cambrian Bird Report* published by the Cambrian Ornithological Society. Price 30p plus postage from the Hon.
Sec.

County Bird Recorder
Dr P. J. Dare, Tan-yr-allt, Trefriw, Caerns.

Ornithological Society
The Cambrian Ornithological Society covers the counties
of Anglesey, Caernarvonshire, Denbighshire and Merioneth. Indoor meetings are held during the winter months
at Colwyn Bay, Llandudno and Bangor. Field meetings
are arranged throughout the year, mainly in the society's
area, but occasionally further afield. Special help is available for beginners attending meetings. Besides the
Cambrian Bird Report a cycostyled newsletter is circulated
to members five times a year. Subscription £1.00 per

annum for adults, 50p for juniors. Hon. Sec. E. Griffiths, Longleat House, Longleat Avenue, Craigside, Llandudno.

Naturalists' Trust
The North Wales Naturalists' Trust covers the counties of Anglesey, Caernarvonshire, Denbighshire, Flintshire, Merioneth and Montgomeryshire. Founded in 1963 the Trust owns or leases a number of reserves, of which three are in Anglesey. Hon. Gen. Sec. Mrs M. J. Morgan, 154 High Street, Bangor. Subscription £1.00 per annum, students 50p, juniors 25p.

R.S.P.B. Representative
D. Nicholas, 17 Ffordd Mwfa, Llangefni, Anglesey; K. Williams, Police Station, Trearddur Bay, Anglesey.

B.T.O. Representative
A. J. Mercer, Llywenan, Nerddyn Gwyn, Brynsiencyn, Llanfairpwll, Anglesey.

Tourist Information
Anglesey Tourist Association, 27 High Street, Llangefni. Official County Guide price 13p (incl. postage).

1. CEMLYN LAGOON SH3393: From the early 1930s this lagoon in north-west Anglesey was managed as a private nature reserve on part of the Hewitt Estate. After the death of Captain V. Hewitt the estate was purchased by the National Trust, in co-operation with Anglesey County Council, as part of the Enterprise Neptune appeal. In 1971 the North Wales Naturalists' Trust entered into a reserve agreement with the National Trust

and now manages the pool with its shingle ridge. Follow the unclassified road west from Tregele SH3592 for about a mile and a half, when it passes close to the south edge of the pool. A track leads along the western shore and good views may be obtained from this; there are car parks at SH329936 and SH336932. A footpath from close to the latter car park takes visitors out along the shingle bank.

Both common and Arctic terns nest at the lagoon, being joined in some years by Sandwich terns. Other species breeding in the area include mallard, red-breasted merganser, shelduck, oystercatcher and ringed plover. Numbers of both mallard and wigeon reach about 400 in most winters and the majority of our other wintering duck can be observed here including golden-eye, the lagoon being the main stronghold for this species in the county. Whooper and Bewick's swans occasionally arrive, though rarely stay long. Red-throated divers are seen in most winters at the lagoon or in Cemlyn Bay and are joined by sea duck such as eider and common scoter or auks like razorbills and guillemots.

2. CEFNI ESTUARY SH3967: Forming a natural western boundary to Newborough Warren is the Cefni Estuary with its adjacent sand flats and salt marshes. A footpath leaves the A4080 at SH411671 west of Newborough and after passing through coniferous plantations skirts the perimeter of the Cefni salt marsh to continue towards the estuary mouth. This section is part of the Newborough Warren National Nature Reserve where access on the east bank away from this marked path is by permit only. The western shore may be viewed from the vicinity of Bodorgan village.

Mallard breed in Newborough Warren and then gather in July and August on the estuary when up to 1,000 may be seen; wintering numbers are considerably smaller, normally not exceeding about 100. Shelduck also breed in the area and in mid-winter up to 400 can be seen on the sand flats. Wigeon are the most numerous wintering duck, up to 2,750 having been recorded.

An increasing feral population of greylag geese is now resident on Anglesey, where the first recorded nest was located at Llyn Dinam sh310775 in April 1970. The geese visit the Cefni estuary from time to time, about 130 being present in late September 1970.

The area is good for waders both in winter and during the spring and autumn passage movements, while oyster-catchers and redshank breed on the salt marsh. Curlew can build up to about 1,000 during migration while other regular visitors, though in considerably smaller numbers, include whimbrel, bar-tailed godwit, spotted redshank, little stint and sanderling.

Hope Jones, P., 'Birds Recorded at Newborough Warren, Anglesey, June 1960–May 1965', *Nat. in Wales* 9 (1965): 196–215.

3. INLAND SEA SH2779: A tidal lagoon, in the shelter of Holy Island, formed by the Stanley Embankment carrying the A5 and at its southern extremity the causeway carrying the B4545 from Holyhead to Valley. Access to the shore is most convenient on the eastern bank where a footpath runs between the two causeways, a distance of little over a mile.

Common and Arctic terns, together with a few pairs of roseate terns, nest at several points in the area and may be observed here well into September, the first having arrived from their West African wintering grounds during mid-April.

4. LLYN BODGYLCHED OR BULKELEY LAKE SH5877: This, the largest area of open water on the eastern peninsula of Anglesey, may be observed from either the B5109 Beaumaris to Pentraeth road or the unclassified road running north from Beaumaris Llanddona. A footpath from the latter road commences near the Bulkeley Memorial and passes close to the lake.

Normally between fifty and sixty whitefronted geese winter at the lake, feeding in the surrounding fields, this is their only regular site in Anglesey. Wigeon are the commonest winter duck with up to 150 occurring together with smaller numbers of mallard, teal, tufted duck and pochard.

5. LLYN CORON SH3770: Although not the largest, Llyn Coron is one of the most important Anglesey lakes. Situated about a mile and a half east of Aberffraw, the lake may be reached by a minor road following the Afon Ffraw. A footpath from Bodorgan Station SH387702 runs close to the northern shore, while others leaving the A4080 at SH379693 and SH374693 give access to the southern side of the lake.

Breeding species include great crested grebe, little grebe, tufted duck and coot. In winter the flock of wigeon at some times exceeds 2,000, while teal, mallard, pintail, shoveler, tufted duck, pochard and goldeneye occur in flocks of less than 100. Unusual visitors have included black-throated divers and gadwall.

6. MALLTRAETH POOL SH4068: At the head of the Cefni

Estuary an embankment known as Malltraeth Cob was
built during the last century to prevent flooding further
up the valley. Behind this a shallow brackish pool has
formed with the A4080 marking the opposite boundary.
Birds on the pool may be observed with ease from the
road; access to the surrounding land, which forms part of
the Newborough Warren National Nature Reserve, is by
permit only.

The pool is an excellent place, indeed probably the
best in Wales, to watch waders at close quarters, particularly during the spring and autumn passage, though
some species like dunlin may be seen throughout the
winter. Regular visitors include ringed plover, whimbrel,
black-tailed godwit, green sandpiper, spotted redshank,
little stint, curlew sandpiper and ruff. Rarer visitors in
recent years have been spoonbill, glossy ibis, Temminck's
stint, avocet and red-necked phalarope.

7. NEWBOROUGH WARREN SH4263: Six hundred years ago
a series of great storms swept Anglesey and on its most
southerly peninsula a once prosperous farming community was driven away as vast quantities of sand,
hurled ashore by the sea, crept inland. So, what is now
known as Newborough Warren, with its sand hills, salt
marshes and pools was formed. The only major change
to have taken place in this, one of Wales richest biological
areas, has been the extensive planting of conifers by the
Forestry Commission since 1947. However, about a
thousand acres of dune, together with areas of foreshore,
salt marsh and the rocky island of Ynys Llanddwyn, (see
page 59) were declared a National Nature Reserve
in 1955.

The reserve is easily reached from the A4080 which

passes through Newborough village sH4265. There are
six access routes into the reserve, movement away from
these requires a permit, which may be obtained from the
Nature Conservancy, North Wales Office. Cars may be
taken down the rough track from Newborough through
the plantations to a car park close to the shore; access by
the other routes is entirely on foot. Intending visitors are
advised to obtain a copy of the Reserve leaflet from the
Nature Conservancy, North Wales Office, which includes
a map with details of the routes into the reserve.

Some fifty-five species of bird regularly breed on Newborough Warren, the most noticeable being the herring
and lesser black-backed gulls which together number
about 7,000 pairs, mostly in the western dunes with
smaller groups elsewhere. Common, Arctic and roseate
terns have all nested in small numbers, but now only the
little tern does so regularly. In 1946 there were forty
pairs at one site where now only about two pairs attempt,
usually unsuccessfully, to nest. Increased public pressure
seems to have been the most likely cause of this decline,
as it has at the few other sites in Anglesey of this,
Britain's rarest breeding seabird.

Montagu's harriers have nested in the past, but now this
fine raptor is only an occasional visitor on passage, while
hen harriers, however, occur in most winters. Merlins
breed on the reserve as do short-eared owls. Other breeding species include Canada geese, lapwing, curlew, grey
partridge, stonechat, whinchat and redpoll.

Hope Jones, P., 'Birds Recorded at Newborough Warren,
Anglesey, June 1960–May 1965', *Nat. in Wales* 9 (1965):
196–215.

8. PENMON PENINSULA sH6381 : This, the most easterly

peninsula of Anglesey, contains several seabird colonies and may be reached by following the unclassified road from Penmon village to the point. The main colonies are in the Trwyn Dinmor quarries on the northern shore, but a scattering of sites may be encountered west to Tandinas Quarry SH5882.

Herring gulls are the most numerous species with the occasional pair of great black-backed gulls, while in the Penmon south quarry there is a colony of lesser black-backed gulls. Look out for common gulls, several pairs having nested here since about 1965; their nearest other regular breeding haunt is in Co. Down. There are several kittiwake colonies, though blasting operations have caused some birds from the main site to move across to Puffin Island. Razorbills and guillemots nest at several points, while a pair or two of black guillemots, another arrival in Anglesey during the past decade, occupy nest sites amongst the boulder scree.

9. PENRHOS NATURE RESERVE SH2781: In 1969 Anglesey Aluminium Metal Limited built their smelter in the north-east of Holy Island, the land having once been part of the former Stanley Estate. Although a large area of land has been taken over by the industrial complex much more, basically unspoiled ground remains, though this too is owned by the Aluminium Company. Following a suggestion made by Ken Williams, currently village police constable for Trearddur Bay, the woodland and uncultivated headlands have been designated a Nature Reserve managed by an Association of honorary wardens. A Nature Trail with thirteen points runs around the headland and a Nature Room is also available for the use of visitors. Trail leaflets (price 3p) and further informa-

tion are available from the Reserve Secretary, Montcalm, Trearddur Bay, Anglesey. The Reserve entrance is on the right of the A5 immediately one has crossed the Stanley Embankment from the mainland of Anglesey to Holy Island.

A rich variety of woodland and open-country birds should be encountered along the trail and its associated footpaths which also provide a good vantage point for bird-watching on the northern section of the Inland Sea (see page 51).

10. POINT LYNAS SH4893: A narrow promontory in north-east Anglesey seems to offer opportunities for watching seabirds, both on passage and during feeding movements, particularly during the late summer and autumn. Kitti-wakes from the colonies on Puffin Island and the Penmon Peninsula make regular movements spanning several hours after dawn and before dusk. During July, August and September all five British breeding terns can be ob-served in the vicinity of the Point. Both great and Arctic skuas regularly pass, as do common scoter and auks, the latter in considerable numbers at times. On the cliffs south from the Point into Freshwater Bay, there are gull colonies together with small numbers of shags, and the occasional fulmar and pair of razorbills.

11. PUFFIN ISLAND SH6582: Half a mile off the Penmon Peninsula lies the 70-acre Puffin Island also known as Priestholm or Ynys Seiriol, the latter after Saint Seiriol who lived there in the sixth century. The remains of more recent habitation include a medieval monastery, a telegraph station and a marine biological station. Most of the island's bird life can be adequately observed from

the sea, and boats ply from Beaumaris, where enquiries should be made.

Although originally not the largest puffin colony in North Wales, that on Puffin Island has attracted the attention of many writers since at least 1662 when Ray noted them breeding there. Like many others in Britain, the colony has declined during the present century and now numbers less than 100 pairs compared with about 2,000 pairs in 1907. Some suggest that the presence of brown rats has been responsible for the decrease, but this can hardly be the whole answer for other colonies have likewise been affected in the absence of this mammalian predator. The island's main claim to ornithological fame at the present time is its vast herring gull colony, estimated in 1970 to contain about 15,000 pairs making it one of the largest in Britain. Accurate census work on the island is made difficult by the dense undergrowth which has become established since the rabbit population was decimated by myxomatosis. There is a cormorant colony of about 200 pairs, while on the north-west cliffs small numbers of razorbills and guillemots nest and there is an expanding kittiwake colony.

12. SOUTH STACK SH2082: The Stack is the most westerly point in Anglesey and may be reached by road either from Holyhead or from Trearddur Bay SH2579. A flight of 350 steps descends 150 feet to a footbridge by which one crosses to the Stack where a lighthouse was constructed in 1809. Small colonies of razorbills, guillemots and puffins nest on the mainland cliffs and may be observed from a point three-quarters the way down the steps or from the footbridge. Other seabirds resident here include fulmars, shags and the three large gulls. These,

together with further auks, occupy the cliffs north into
Gogarth Bay where there is also a small cormorant
colony, and along the cliffs south of the Stack. In this
latter area the largest concentration of razorbills and
guillemots in Anglesey is located and these may be seen
from Ellins Tower, the fortified building below the café
about a quarter of a mile back along the road from the
South Stack steps. The possibilities, which judging from
its position seem many, of the Stack being an ideal position for observing seabird passage have hardly been explored. As a contribution to European Conservation
Year 1970, the North Wales Naturalists' Trust published
a short illustrated leaflet, *Birds and Flowers of the South
Stack*, an imaginative venture justly rewarded by a
Prince of Wales Award. The leaflet is available from the
North Wales Naturalists' Trust (price 2½p plus postage).

13. THE SKERRIES SH2694: Nearly two miles off Carmel
Head, the north-westerly tip of Anglesey lie a group of
low rocks known as The Skerries, their total area not exceeding 42 acres. A lighthouse erected in 1717 stands on
Ynys Toucan. Although out of reach to all but the more
enterprising observers—permission to land is required
from Trinity House—the rocks have much to offer at
migration time, an aspect of Anglesey's ornithology yet
to be studied in detail. The only recent visit of any length
was made in September 1961 when in three weeks ninety
species were recorded, including vagrants like bittern,
black redstart, bluethroat, ortolan bunting and little
bunting. Further work, no doubt, would be as equally re-
warding, as would detailed watches for seabird movement.
    Breeding birds are few, though once there was an im-

portant Arctic tern colony with a few pairs of common and roseate terns. Puffins have also nested in the past and a few pairs probably still remain. Other breeding species include shag, oystercatcher, great black-backed and herring gulls and rock pipit.

Mercer, A. J., 'Migration Studies on The Skerries, Anglesey, September 1961', *Nat. in Wales* 8 (1963): 109–15.

14. YNYS LLANDDWYN SH3862 : Although part of the Newborough Warren National Nature Reserve, this peninsular islet, connected to the mainland by a sandy isthmus, is so different in character that it deserves a section of its own. Saint Dwynwen sought solace here in the fifth century and twelve hundred years later a church, now ruined, was built and dedicated to his memory. More modern buildings include an automatic lighthouse and cottages. Ynys Llanddwyn may be reached by driving from Newborough village to the car park at SH405634 and then walking west along the shore. Alternatively one can walk some two and a half miles through the conifer plantations directly from the village to the islet.

Both cormorants and shags breed on the rocks close to Ynys Llanddwyn, the latter being of special interest in that they may be observed incubating in November, with chicks visible in January and February. Elsewhere the breeding season commences in late March or April. Other breeding birds include oystercatcher, ringed plover, great black-backed gull, stonechat and rock pipit. Rather unusual in a maritime habitat were the mistle thrush breeding records of 1962 and 1963, the nest site being on a rock outcrop.

Llanddwyn Bay, to the east of the island, is frequented

by a variety of wintering divers, grebes and duck. Great northern and red-throated divers are regular in winter occasionally black-throated divers, the rarest of the three in Welsh waters may be seen. Great crested and slavonian grebes are also regular winter visitors as are common scoter, while long-tailed duck, velvet scoter, eider and red-breasted mergansers are occasionally reported in most winters.

Check list

RB Resident breeder   MB Migrant breeder
WV Winter visitor   PV Passage visitor
                v Vagrant

Black-throated Diver	v	Grey Heron	RB
Great Northern Diver	WV	Bittern	RB
Red-throated Diver	WV	Mallard	RB
Great Crested Grebe	RB	Teal	RB
Red-necked Grebe	v	Garganey	PV
Slavonian Grebe	WV	Gadwall	WV
Black-necked Grebe	WV	Wigeon	WV
Little Grebe	RB	Pintail	WV
Fulmar	RB	Shoveler	RB
Manx Shearwater	PV	Scaup	WV
British Storm Petrel	PV	Tufted Duck	RB
Leach's Petrel	v	Pochard	RB
Gannet	PV	Goldeneye	WV
Cormorant	RB	Long-tailed Duck	WV
Shag	RB	Velvet Scoter	v

Common Scoter	WV	Grey Plover	WV
Eider	V	Golden Plover	WV
Red-breasted Merganser			Has bred
	RB	Turnstone	WV
Goosander	V	Snipe	RB
Shelduck	RB	Jack Snipe	WV
Greylag Goose	RB	Woodcock	WV
Feral population		Curlew	RB
White-fronted Goose	WV	Whimbrel	PV
Brent Goose	V	Black-tailed Godwit	PV
Barnacle Goose	V	Bar-tailed Godwit	WV
Canada Goose	RB	Green Sandpiper	PV
Mute Swan	RB	Wood Sandpiper	PV
Whooper Swan	WV	Common Sandpiper	PV
Bewick's Swan	WV		Has bred
Buzzard	RB	Redshank	RB
Sparrowhawk	RB	Spotted Redshank	PV
Marsh Harrier	PV	Greenshank	PV
Hen Harrier	WV	Knot	WV
Peregrine	PV	Purple Sandpiper	WV
Merlin	RB	Little Stint	PV
Kestrel	RB	Dunlin	WV
Partridge	RB	Curlew Sandpiper	PV
Quail	V	Sanderling	PV
Pheasant	RB	Ruff	PV
Water Rail	WV	Grey Phalarope	V
Corncrake	PV	Great Skua	V
	Has bred	Arctic Skua	PV
Moorhen	RB	Great Black-backed Gull	
Coot	RB		RB
Oystercatcher	RB	Lesser Black-backed Gull	
Lapwing	RB		MB
Ringed Plover	RB	Herring Gull	RB

Common Gull	RB	Skylark	RB
Little Gull	V	Shore Lark	V
Black-headed Gull	RB	Swallow	MB
Kittiwake	RB	House Martin	MB
Black Tern	V	Sand Martin	MB
Common Tern	MB	Raven	RB
Arctic Tern	MB	Carrion Crow	RB
Roseate Tern	MB	Rook	RB
Little Tern	MB	Jackdaw	RB
Sandwich Tern	PV	Magpie	RB
Has bred		Jay	RB
Razorbill	RB	Chough	RB
Guillemot	RB	Great Tit	RB
Black Guillemot	RB	Blue Tit	RB
Puffin	MB	Coal Tit	RB
Stock Dove	RB	Marsh Tit	V
Woodpigeon	RB	Willow Tit	RB
Turtle Dove	PV	Long-tailed Tit	RB
Has bred		Nuthatch	RB
Collared Dove	RB	Treecreeper	RB
Cuckoo	MB	Wren	RB
Barn Owl	RB	Dipper	RB
Little Owl	RB	Mistle Thrush	RB
Tawny Owl	RB	Fieldfare	WV
Short-eared Owl	RB	Song Thrush	RB
Nightjar	MB	Redwing	WV
Swift	MB	Ring Ouzel	PV
Kingfisher	RB	Blackbird	RB
Green Woodpecker	RB	Wheatear	MB
Great Spotted Wood-		Stonechat	RB
pecker	RB	Whinchat	MB
Lesser Spotted Wood-		Redstart	MB
pecker	RB	Black Redstart	V

Robin	RB	Pied Wagtail	RB
Grasshopper Warbler	MB	White Wagtail	PV
Sedge Warbler	MB	Grey Wagtail	RB
Blackcap	MB	Yellow Wagtail	PV
Garden Warbler	MB	Starling	RB
Whitethroat	MB	Greenfinch	RB
Lesser Whitethroat	MB	Goldfinch	RB
Willow Warbler	MB	Siskin	WV
Chiffchaff	MB	Linnet	RB
Wood Warbler	MB	Redpoll	RB
Goldcrest	RB	Bullfinch	RB
Spotted Flycatcher	MB	Chaffinch	RB
Pied Flycatcher	PV	Brambling	WV
Dunnock	RB	Yellowhammer	RB
Meadow Pipit	RB	Reed Bunting	RB
Tree Pipit	PV	House Sparrow	RB
Rock Pipit	RB	Tree Sparrow	RB

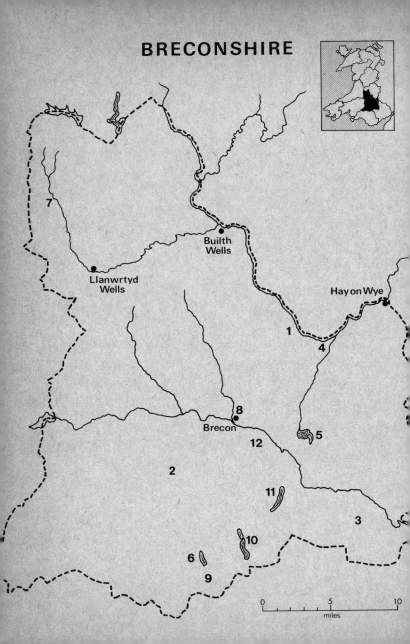

BRECONSHIRE

Builth
Wells

Llanwrtyd
Wells

Hay on Wye

1

4

8
Brecon

12

5

2

11

3

10

6

9

7

0   5   10
miles

Chapter 5

Breconshire

Breconshire, 733 square miles, is by far the larger of the two inland counties of Wales, the other being Radnorshire which abuts it in the north and north-east. In the north the boundary runs along the Elan and Claerwen valleys with their great reservoirs of Caban Coch and Claerwen. The eastern boundary runs south-east, following the tumbling Wye past Builth Wells until it reaches the outskirts of Hay-on-Wye, a distance of nearly thirty miles. Herefordshire, then Monmouthshire are now on its eastern flank as it forsakes the lowlands to climb across Hay Bluff (2,219 feet), northernmost of the high Black Mountain ridges, before eventually descending to reach the Usk valley just west of Abergavenny. From here more high ground is traversed as the boundary, now with Glamorgan, brushes the South Wales coalfield, finally reaching the upper Swansea valley near Ystradgynlais. The Afon Twrch leads onto the Carmarthen Van thence on north through the Crychan and Tywi Forests, the latter shared with Cardiganshire until the Claerwen is reached once more.

Although occupying much of the high ground in this the southern heartland of Wales, Breconshire is skirted, or intersected by a number of important valley systems including the Usk and Wye. These have in the past, as indeed they do today, provided man with access routes into the area and beyond towards the maritime regions of the south-west. Neolithic man grazed his herds here but has left few remains save for impressive megalithic tombs whose lichen-encrusted slabs have stood 5,000 years or more. Bronze Age man lived here, there is a

circle of his standing stones at Saith Maen near Aber-
crave. Iron Age hill forts are numerous and include one
of the most dramatic in Wales, that at Pen-y-Crug, just
north of Brecon, with five ramparts and ditches to defy
the most vigorous of foes. Their time-mellowed contours
are ideal for those who wish to savour the view south to
the Brecon Beacons and Fforest Fawr or north-west to
Mynydd Eppynt.

When the Romans thrust their legions beyond the
Severn and into south-east Wales they encountered a
resilient people—the Silures—who, through incessant
skirmishing, ensured the invaders' occupation was primarily a military one. Their fort known as Cicutio at Y
Gaer west of Brecon was an important staging post, and
from it routes penetrated farther into Wales. The
Normans came this way, using the Wye valley as a route
within a few years of their arrival in England. This became part of the land of the Marcher lords who ruled,
almost independent of the king, from the security of
their many castles, now wind-whistling ruins. That at
Castel Dinas (1,471 feet) is probably at a higher altitude
than any other in Wales and this site was also used in the
Iron Age. Occupying part of the Marcher Lordship of
Brecon was the Great Forest (Fforest Fawr) a royal
hunting area which despite its name was primarily open
moorland above 1,500 feet, the only large areas of trees
being on the valley sides.

Fforest Fawr is at the centre of a mountain block, the
largest of the three natural sections into which the county
may be divided, extending from the Carmarthen Van,
across the Brecon Beacons, thence north-eastwards on to

Pied Flycatcher

the Black Mountains. This hill land, mainly of Old
Red Sandstone rises to 2,906 feet at Pen-y-Fan while
there are some forty other peaks exceeding 2,000 feet in
its 130-mile expanse. The rivers generally run south towards the Bristol Channel, the largest, the Usk, divides
the Black Mountains from this almost contiguous area
while to the north-west lies Mynydd Eppynt, another of
Breconshire's natural sections. The last of the Pleistocene
Ice Ages finally thawed in this part of Wales about
10,000 years ago. An Alpine/Arctic flora thrived in the
tundra climate at the ice edge. As the land warmed still
more such plants only survived on the higher, generally
north-facing, crags and screes, where some remain until
the present day. This then is a botanists' hunting ground
with a few plants at the southern edge of their range in
Britain.

North of the Usk, and with the River Wye on the east
and the Irfon, one of its tributaries, in the west as
boundaries, lies Myndd Eppynt a sandstone ridge rising
to nearly 1,600 feet. On the north side there are short
narrow valleys plunging to the Irfon while to the south
the streams that run to the Usk have carved more gentle
courses. Whether north or south these features are worth
exploring by the ornithologist. The actual uplands are
much used by the military as a training area so that
access away from the few roads is restricted. Enquire
locally before setting off across the moors.

Northwards still, before one reaches the county boundary along the Elan reservoirs, is an extension of the
Cambrian Mountains, their highest point in Breconshire
being Drygarn Fawr (2,104 feet) with a great deal of

Redstart

other ground about the 2,000-foot contour. Straddling
the upper reaches of the Irfon on the border with
Cardiganshire is the extensive Tywi Forest.

Forestry is an important occupation in Breconshire,
which is almost completely an agricultural county with
some 50 per cent of its area rough pasture. Much of this
is common land, indeed there are over 150,000 acres,
more than in any other Welsh county, consequently sheep
rearing is widely practised. The lower regions are used
mainly for beef rearing with some dairy herds in the
main valleys and a little arable farming. Only light industries have been established though some coal mining
is carried out in the Ystradgynlais area where the South
Wales coalfield intrudes upon the rural solitude of
Breconshire.

Tourism is important, a fact recognised in 1957 when
the Brecon Beacons National Park was designated, this
covers 381 square miles in Breconshire with smaller sections in neighbouring Carmarthenshire and Monmouthshire. Situated within the Park and providing water for
the thirsty industrial areas to the south, are a number of
important reservoirs including the Usk, Taf Fechan and
Talybont.

Although lacking the attractions of a sea coast, islands
and estuaries, Breconshire has been well served by ornithologists and there is an active ornithological section of
the Breconshire Naturalists' Trust. About 100 species of
bird breed in Breconshire, but the populations in some
areas are poorly known especially the northern area in
the Cambrian Mountains and the Black Mountains in
the east. An ornithologist visiting these regions, especially
if prepared to leave the vicinity of roads and work the
high tops, may add greatly to our knowledge of the

county. Observations at the many reservoirs have shown their value to migrating waders and terns, and in winter wildfowl; these sites are commended to all who watch birds in Breconshire.

Information

County Avifaunas
Phillips, E. Cambridge, *The Birds of Breconshire* (Brecon 1899).
Ingram, Geoffrey C. S. and Salmon, H. Morrey *The Birds of Brecknock* (1957) *Brycheiniog* III
Griffiths, J., 'Bird-Life in Breconshire' (Brecknock Museum, 1968). Although not an avifauna this short work provides a most readable general account of the county's birds.
'Breconshire Bird Report', 1969, *Breconshire Birds* 3 : 3–17. This report gives a complete list of all species recorded in Breconshire from 1957 to 1969 inclusive, together with their known and considered status over that period.

Bird Report
Published annually in *Breconshire Birds*, a journal of the Brecknock County Naturalists' Trust, which also contains short ornithological papers, available from the Hon. Secretary of the Trust price 24p (post free).

County Bird Recorder
M. V. Preece, Stepaside, Llangynidir, Crickhowell, Breconshire.

Ornithological Society
No Society as such, but the Brecknock County Naturalists' Trust arranges winter meetings in Brecon and other
centres with field meetings throughout the year; a number of these are angled towards ornithology.

Naturalists' Trust
The Brecknock County Naturalists' Trust was founded
in 1964 and now manages several reserves; besides
Breconshire Birds it publishes a quarterly journal *The
Breconshire Naturalists*. Hon. Sec. H. M. Budgen, Byddwn.
Llanhamlach, Brecon. Subscription £1.00 (adults) 50p
(juniors), £1.50 (family).

Royal Society for the Protection of Birds Representative
Not yet appointed.

British Trust for Ornithology Representative
M. E. Massey, Windyridge, Penorth, Brecon, LD3 7EX.

Tourist Information
Brecon Beacons National Park, Information Officer, 6
Glamorgan Street, Brecon.
    The Brecon Beacons Mountain Centre, Near Libanus,
Brecon.

1. BRECHFA POOL SO1137: In view of the scarcity of open
water in north Brecon this small pool on the southern
edge of Brechfa Common has an importance out of all
relation to its size. Its close proximity to the River Wye
also proves an advantage in attracting birds moving
through the valley. Although a Site of Special Scientific
Interest (mainly for its botanical importance), farm

rubbish has been dumped there, a practice which must not be repeated if this valuable area is to be maintained. In early 1974 the pool was declared a Trust Nature Reserve. It is close to an unclassified road leading south from the A479 Builth Wells to Llyswen road at so117400 to the A4073 at so120362.

Both mallard and coot breed regularly. Black-headed gulls now breed fairly regularly but not successfully in dry summers, though about thirty young were reared in 1972. Mallard, teal, wigeon and Bewick's swan have all been noted in winter, the first three species being regular visitors. Waders seen at, or close to, the pool have included golden plover, snipe, curlew, greenshank, spotted redshank and dunlin.

2. CRAIG CERRIG GLEISIAD SN9522: This National Nature Reserve of 283 hectares (698 acres) about six miles south-west of Brecon includes one of the richest sites for alpine plants in southern Britain. Formed by glacial action the armchair-shaped hollow is lined by crags and screes which rise to 2,000 feet at Craig Cerrig Gleisiad and 1,750 feet at Craig Cwm Du. This area is surrounded by the typical grazed moorland of this part of Wales. Good general views may be obtained from the A470 road at SN9720. A permit is available from the Nature Conservancy, South Wales Regional Office.

Birds occurring in this area include buzzard, red grouse, raven, ring ouzel, wheatear and whinchat.

3. CRAIG Y CILAU SO189158: Overlooking the Usk Valley about two miles south-west of Crickhowell is a spectacular limestone escarpment rising 400 feet to a point 1,500 feet above sea-level; an extremely rich botanical site, de-

scribed as the best place for plants on inland limestone;
157 acres were declared a National Nature Reserve in
1959 (leased by the Natural Environmental Research
Council from the Duke of Beaufort Estates). The Reserve is best approached by leaving the A40 or A4077 in
Crickhowell and taking the unclassified road to Llangattock. Pass through the village, bear right at the chapel
and continue for a further mile and a quarter to the
cattle grid at so186168 just beyond which there is limited
parking where a footpath climbs south into the Reserve.
A leaflet is available from the Nature Conservancy
South Wales Regional Office.

At least forty-nine species of bird breed on the Reserve, while sixty-seven bred on or close by in the five
years 1966–70. A number make good use of the cliff
crevices, ledges and gullies including buzzard, kestrel,
stock dove, raven, jackdaw, ring ouzel and wheatear. In
the valley woods marsh tit, willow tit, redstart, wood
warbler, pied flycatcher and tree pipit may be seen.
Casual visitors have included merlin, nightjar, lesser
spotted woodpecker and grasshopper warbler.

Black-headed gulls breed on Pwll Gwy Rhoc so1815, a
mountain pool on Mynydd Llangattock above the reserve. This also has an impressive list of waders noted on
passage, fourteen species having occurred since 1966, including ringed plover, whimbrel, green and wood sandpipers, redshank, spotted redshank, greenshank and
knot; the latter species only rarely seen at inland waters
in Wales.

4. DDERW POOL so1437: Two small pools situated close
to the River Wye near Llyswen, of which one is easily
viewed from the A4079 Llyswen to Three Cocks road.

In view of the scarcity of such open freshwater areas in Breconshire, the maintenance of these pools in their present state is highly desirable.

Canada Geese bred at the pool in 1970, 1971 and 1972 the first breeding records of this species in Breconshire, though unsuccessful attempts were made in 1966 and 1967, one of the pair being shot at the nest. Coot also nest—eight pairs in 1969. However, the main attraction to the ornithologist visiting the pools is the hope of encountering birds on passage, both in spring and autumn, or as winter visitors. Little grebe, goosander, whooper swan, Bewick's swan, golden plover, jack snipe, common sandpiper, green sandpiper and redshank have all been noted.

5. LLANGORSE LAKE SO1326: This, the largest natural freshwater lake in South Wales, was formed by glacial action depositing a gravel moraine across the valley through which the Afon Llynfi, a tributary of the Wye, flows on its northward journey. An attempt was made to schedule this area of major natural history importance as a proposed Local Nature Reserve by the Breconshire County Council in 1954, but unfortunately this has not been implemented despite considerable efforts during the ensuing years. Meanwhile, problems of pollution and disturbance due to water sports increase annually, and the lake's future importance as a botanical and ornithological site is debatable unless such factors can be controlled. Good general views of the lake may be obtained from the B4560 Bwlch to Talgarth road, while access to the shore is possible at SO128270 just south of Llangorse village and at Llangasty Tal-y-llyn SO133262 on its southern shore.

Llangorse Lake is the main site of the great crested

grebe in Breconshire, normally up to fifteen pairs nesting. The little grebe, however, is a rare breeding species
in the county and is generally only a winter visitor to the
lake. Tufted duck nested at Llangorse Lake in 1970, the
first breeding record for the county since 1930, many
more occur in winter when they are joined by good
numbers of pochard, over 400 being noted in January
1969. Mute swans breed, while the late summer flock,
which has decreased in recent years with maximum
counts of about twenty, showed signs of recovery in 1972
when forty-five were recorded. Both whooper and
Bewick's swans visit the lake in winter. Waders call
briefly, particularly during the late summer southward
passage; ringed plover, green sandpiper, wood sandpiper, greenshank, spotted redshank, sanderling and ruff
have all occurred in recent years. The lake proves
equally attractive to passing terns, all the British breeding species save for the roseate tern being noted almost
annually. The fringe of reed beds supports a small population of reed warblers, with sedge warblers and reed
buntings, and during migration time provides a roosting
place for hirundines and wagtails.

6. LLWYN-ON-RESERVOIR SO00011 : Surrounded by conifer
plantations, this reservoir, which provides water for
Cardiff, is situated in the Taf Fawr valley north of
Merthyr Tydfil, from which it is reached by the A470
Brecon to Merthyr Tydfil road. A minor road runs right
around the perimeter.
  Grey herons nest in the nearby woods—there were at
least ten nests in 1971—though this is likely to suffer as
the conifers are felled, and they can usually be seen at
the reservoir. That other efficient avian angler the cor-

morant not infrequently visits the reservoir even though it is 22 miles from the sea (Swansea Bay). Great crested grebes are often to be seen and may have bred in 1969. Mallard breed, but more are seen in winter when small numbers of teal and the occasional wigeon, pintail and shoveler arrive, together with diving duck such as tufted duck and pochard. Goosander, smew and whooper swan are among the more unusual wildfowl recorded in recent years. The autumn wader passage has included ringed plover, green sandpiper, common sandpiper and green-shank.

7. NANT IRFON SN8552: A typical Breconshire valley, this one in the extreme north-west is reached by an un-classified road from Llanwrtyd Wells SN878468, which passes through sections of the Tywi Forest before crossing the Cardiganshire border and continuing to Tregaron. There is a National Nature Reserve of 87 hectares (216 acres) in the valley, part of which is sessile oak woodland. A permit is required from the Nature Conservancy (South Wales Regional Office) in order to enter the reserve. The ornithologist can, however, see much of the valley's bird life from the road.

Pied flycatchers breed in the deciduous woods, as do redstarts and wood warblers. Buzzards and ravens are always to be seen and on the higher rocky ground, ring ouzels. The common sandpiper, dipper and grey wagtail may be seen beside the river.

8. PRIORY GROVES SO0429: On the north-west outskirts of Brecon following the River Honddu, a tributary of the Usk, is an area of deciduous woodland known as Priory Groves. Between 5 May and 1 October a Nature Trail

arranged by Shell in conjunction with the Brecknock County Naturalists' Trust operates along a one and a half mile route through the wood. However, the area is well worth a visit in search of birds at any time of the year. The best approach to the Trail is from the B4520 Brecon to Builth Wells road at the Cathedral from where one walks through the churchyard and then past a rookery where there are usually about forty nests. Trail leaflets are available from Shell garages in the Brecon area, the Brecknock County Naturalists' Trust or National Park Information Centres.

All our more common resident woodland species may be seen in the Groves including green woodpecker, nuthatch, treecreeper, great and blue tit, song thrush, goldcrest and chaffinch. Summer visitors include blackcap, chiffchaff, willow warbler and wood warbler. Kingfisher, dipper and grey wagtail occur along the river.

9. TAF FAWR VALLEY SOO109: The Taf Fawr River, north of Cefn Coed y Cymmer, has scoured a deep valley in the carboniferous limestone on this the northern edge of the South Wales coalfield. Extensive cliffs have been formed on both sides of the valley and have been exploited by man engaged upon quarrying at several locations. The A470 Brecon to Merthyr Tydfil road follows the eastern bank of the river and so provides easy access.

On the west bank about one mile north of Cefn Coed y Cymmer, from which it is reached by an unclassified road, is the Penmoelaelt Forest Nature Reserve. Although only 7 hectares (17 acres) in extent it is one of only two known sites (the other is also in the valley) for Leys white beam *Sorbus leyana* discovered here in 1958. A permit to visit and a reserve leaflet are obtainable from the Nature Conservancy, South Wales Regional Office.

Birds which frequent the valley include buzzard, sparrowhawk, kestrel, green woodpecker, redstart, wood warbler and pied flycatcher.

10. TAF FECHAN VALLEY S00513: Said to be one of the most beautiful valleys in South Wales, it is reached by leaving the A470 Brecon to Merthyr Tydfil road at S0030081 and following the unclassified road. This passes the twin reservoirs reaching a junction at their head. Now the choice of routes is difficult. For a motorist the eastern road climbs over the watershed before plunging through the Talybont Valley and past a further reservoir. For those on foot the western road, said to be of Roman origin leads across the open hills to Brecon passing close to Pen-y-Fan (2,906 feet), the highest mountain in South Wales and the highest Old Red Sandstone peak in Britain.

The Taf Fechan reservoirs fluctuate greatly in level so are not attractive to breeding water birds. In late summer the exposed mud provides a rich feeding ground for waders and, although not extensively watched, ringed plover, greenshank and dunlin have all occurred; while among winter wildfowl visitors long-tailed duck, smew and whooper swan are noteworthy. Kingfishers, dipper and grey wagtails may generally be seen along the streams, while buzzards and ravens can often be seen soaring over the valley sides. Just above the reservoir head is the Taf Fechan Forest Walk which extends for about a mile from the Owl Grove Car Park S0048163. A descriptive leaflet is available from the Forestry Commission South Wales office.

11. TALYBONT RESERVOIR SO0918: This reservoir in the Talybont valley supplies water to Newport and is one of the most important wildfowl areas in the county. Leave the B4558 road in Talybont SO113227 and follow the unclassified road southwards for two miles to the reservoir dam. The road continues, following the western shore, and as the reservoir is only about 500 yards wide, good views are usually possible of any birds which may be present.

All three species of diver have occurred at intervals, while great crested grebes are regular winter visitors with forty-five present in February 1968.

The reservoir holds the largest concentration of wintering goosanders on an inland water in Wales, the maximum number recorded being about thirty-five. Good numbers of both dabbling and diving duck occur throughout the winter, with mallard being particularly numerous with up to 300 in mid-winter, while teal numbers peak at about 100. Tufted duck, pochard and goldeneye are the most numerous diving ducks, being joined occasionally by scaup, red-breasted merganser and even common scoter. Late summer proves good for waders when most of the common species are recorded annually; less frequent visitors have included sanderling, pectoral sandpiper and semi-palmated sandpiper. Common and Arctic terns pass through regularly in the same period, with little and Sandwich terns being noted occasionally.

12. TY MAWR SO0726: This small pool in the Usk Valley, about two miles south-east of Brecon, has the distinction of being the first reserve to be acquired by the Brecknock County Naturalists' Trust. Conservation work has been

carried out in order to maintain optimum conditions for wildlife. Leave the A40 by the B4538 Talybont road at so077274 and after half a mile bear right on an un-classified road, the pool is on the left.

Great crested grebe nested in 1970, and in 1971 little grebes were seen in late summer, but are not thought to have nested. Other breeding species include moorhen and coot. Winter wildfowl numbers are small, but have included gadwall. The pool seems a good locality to watch feeding swifts, swallows and martins, an unusual visitor being an Alpine swift in 1956.

Check list

RB	Resident Breeder	MB	Migrant Breeder
WV	Winter Visitor	PV	Passage Visitor
	V	Vagrant	

Great Crested Grebe	RB	Goldeneye	WV
Little Grebe	RB	Common Scoter	V
Cormorant	WV	Goosander	WV
Grey Heron	RB	Shelduck	WV
Mallard	RB	White-fronted Goose	V
Teal	WV	Canada Goose	RB
Gadwall	V	Mute Swan	RB
Wigeon	WV	Whooper Swan	WV
Pintail	WV	Bewick's Swan	WV
Shoveler	WV	Buzzard	RB
Scaup	V	Sparrowhawk	RB
Tufted Duck	WV	Red Kite	RB
Pochard	WV	Hen Harrier	WV

Osprey	V	Black Tern	PV
Peregrine	V	Common Tern	PV
Merlin	RB	Arctic Tern	PV
Kestrel	RB	Sandwich Tern	V
Red Grouse	RB	Stock Dove	RB
Black Grouse	RB	Woodpigeon	RB
Partridge	RB	Turtle Dove	MB
Pheasant	RB	Collared Dove	RB
Water Rail	RB	Cuckoo	MB
Moorhen	RB	Barn Owl	RB
Coot	RB	Little Owl	RB
Oystercatcher	PV	Tawny Owl	RB
Lapwing	RB	Long-eared Owl	RB
Ringed Plover	PV	Short-eared Owl	RB
Golden Plover	WV	Nightjar	V
Snipe	RB	Swift	MB
Woodcock	RB	Kingfisher	RB
Curlew	RB	Green Woodpecker	RB
Whimbrel	PV	Great Spotted Wood-	
Black-tailed Godwit	V	pecker	RB
Green Sandpiper	PV	Lesser Spotted Wood-	
Common Sandpiper	RB	pecker	RB
Redshank	RB	Woodlark	RB
Spotted Redshank	V	Skylark	RB
Greenshank	PV	Swallow	MB
Dunlin	RB	House Martin	MB
Great Black-backed Gull		Sand Martin	MB
	PV	Raven	RB
Lesser Black-backed Gull		Carrion Crow	RB
	PV	Rook	RB
Herring Gull	WV	Jackdaw	RB
Common Gull	WV	Magpie	RB
Black-headed Gull	RB	Jay	RB

Great Tit	RB	Chiffchaff	MB
Blue Tit	RB	Wood Warbler	MB
Coal Tit	RB	Goldcrest	RB
Marsh Tit	RB	Spotted Flycatcher	MB
Willow Tit	RB	Pied Flycatcher	MB
Long-tailed Tit	RB	Dunnock	RB
Nuthatch	RB	Meadow Pipit	RB
Treecreeper	RB	Tree Pipit	MB
Wren	RB	Rock Pipit	V
Dipper	RB	Water Pipit	V
Mistle Thrush	RB	Pied Wagtail	RB
Fieldfare	WV	Grey Wagtail	RB
Song Thrush	RB	Yellow Wagtail	MB
Redwing	WV	Starling	RB
Ring Ouzel	MB	Hawfinch	RB
Blackbird	RB	Greenfinch	RB
Wheatear	MB	Goldfinch	RB
Stonechat	RB	Siskin	WV
Whinchat	MB	Linnet	RB
Redstart	MB	Redpoll	RB
Robin	RB	Bullfinch	RB
Grasshopper Warbler	MB	Crossbill	V
Reed Warbler	MB	Chaffinch	RB
Sedge Warbler	MB	Brambling	WV
Blackcap	MB	Yellowhammer	RB
Garden Warbler	MB	Corn Bunting	V
Whitethroat	MB	Reed Bunting	RB
Lesser Whitethroat	MB	House Sparrow	RB
Willow Warbler	MB	Tree Sparrow	RB

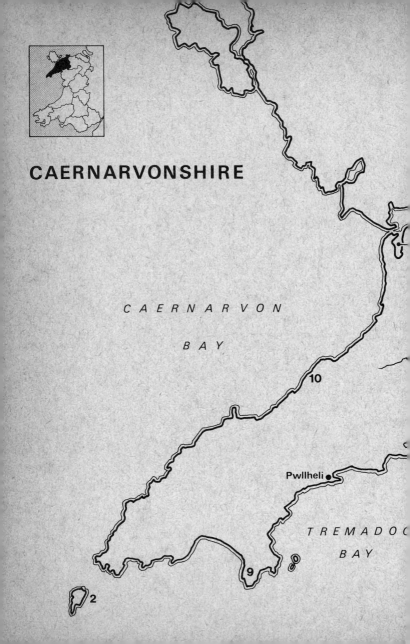

CAERNARVONSHIRE

C A E R N A R V O N

B A Y

10

Pwllheli ●

T R E M A D O C

B A Y

9

2

Chapter 6

Caernarvonshire

Despite the fact that Snowdon (3,560 feet) is situated in Caernarvonshire, this is not the most mountainous county in Wales. Indeed only about 12 per cent of the county's total land area (569 sq. miles) exceeds 1,500 feet while nearly 50 per cent is below 500 feet. With 127 miles of coastline, Caernarvonshire occupies a wedge-shaped section of north-west Wales, extending 56 miles north-east to south-west from the Llandudno Peninsula to the tip of the Lleyn Peninsula opposite the island of Bardsey. On the north–south axis the widest point is 22 miles between the Menai Straits at Bangor and the Glaslyn estuary at Portmadoc. In the east the Conway river valley forms most of the boundary with Denbighshire. Merioneth is its southern neighbour, the boundary here being initially the Afon Glaslyn but once this is left behind it follows a tortuous course across much high ground, passing just north of the slate-quarrying area around Blaenau Ffestiniog.

Although Snowdonia dominates the Caernarvonshire scene, let us take a brief look at that other prominent feature—the Lleyn Peninsula. Like those other Welsh peninsulas—maritime Pembrokeshire and the Gower—the Lleyn is rugged and windswept. A world of headlands and islands, of scattered villages and hamlets over which herring gulls continually patrol, a few wing-beats away from their cliff nesting grounds. The coastal fringe in spring is a blaze of spring flowers—thrift, sea campion and scurvy grass among them. There are interior hills forming a backbone of isolated summits which continue to the very south-western extremity.

Our ancestors greatly approved of the Lleyn. There are megalithic tombs on Cilan Head and at Penllech, but pride of place must surely go to the fortified village of Iron Age times (built on a Bronze Age site) at Tre'r Ceiri (Giants Town) on the Yr Eifl hill close to the north coast. Covering some five acres at a height of about 1,600 feet the village is the finest of its kind remaining in Britain. No visitor should fail to miss examining this encampment with its clusters of dry stone wall huts which look out over one of the finest views in North Wales.

In the early Middle Ages the Lleyn was a focal point for holy men and pilgrims who tended to follow a route along the north of the peninsula, a route marked with small churches like those which can still be seen in the villages of Clynnog, Pistyll, Nevin and Llangwnnadl. Their goal was Aberdaron, the embarkation point, as it is today, for those wishing to cross the tide-wracked passage to Bardsey. The island had achieved prominence as a holy place ever since Cadfan had arrived there in the sixth century to be followed by monks after the sacking of their monastery at Bangor Is-y-Coed, Flintshire, by a Saxon horde shortly after the battle of Chester in A.D. 600. Even this remote peninsula was involved in the castle-building encirclement of North Wales by Edward I; Nevin on the north and Criccieth on the south were brooded over by embattled towers. In the nineteenth century these small townships, together with others on or close to the coast, were important harbours with ship building being carried out at several points. Such activities have long ceased and the accent is now on the tourist. With long sandy beaches, superb cliff walks and

overleaf – *Chough*

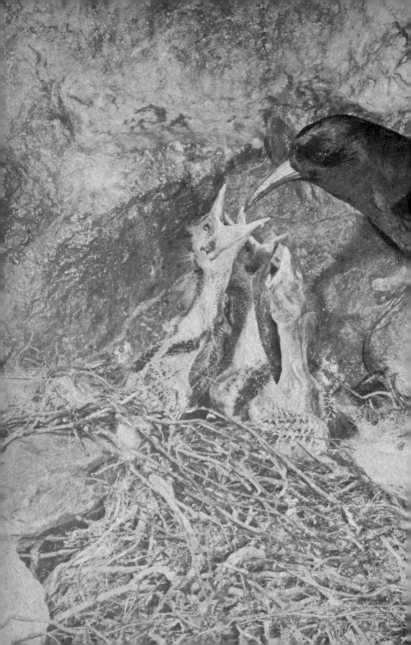

a rural hinterland, the whole area is much sought after by those seeking quiet solitude.

Caernarvonshire's Snowdonia region may be divided into five areas, each conveniently divided from the other by valleys which intersect the mountains. The largest of the five, the uplands of Carneddau in the north-east is bounded by the Conway Valley, Nant Ffrancon and the Llugwy. Carnedd Llywelyn (named after the last Llywelyn) rises to 3,485 feet, almost the height of Snowdon itself. For the most part these uplands are wide grassy ridges, intersected by rock peaks, screes and precipices, the latter often plunging to narrow lakes, some of which now serve as reservoirs. One has to move farther west to encounter more dramatic Snowdonia scenery. A narrow section of land climbs rapidly from the coastal plain about the Menai Straits bounded by Nant Ffrancon and the Llanberis valley. This is the Glyder range, much visited by the mountaineer. The numerous peaks and precipices reach their culmination on Glyder Fach where blocks and rubble of split and shattered volcanic rock—the result of extreme pressures and heat—give the impression, believed by some early visitors, of some huge, long-ruined megalithic structure.

Encompassed by the Llanberis Valley, Nant Gwynant and Nant-y-Betws is the mountain massif containing Snowdon itself. There are several paths for the hill walker which lead, with varying degrees of effort, to the summit—including the Watkin Path, Beddgelert Path, Snowdon Ranger Path and the Pig Track which passes over Bwlch Moch (the Pass of the Swine). For those who wish for a more relaxed route a mountain railway commences near Llanberis. Food discarded by climbers and walkers on the mountain together with garbage from the summit cafe provides a welcome food supply for scavenging herring gulls.

Westward beyond Nant-y-Betws is the Hebog; Moel Hebog rises to 2,566 feet and Moel Lefn 2,094 feet. The best way to explore here is by way of the Pennant valley above Dolbenmaen through which the Afon Dwyfor flows. The last section of Caernarvonshire Snowdonia lies south of the valley systems traversed by the road from Betws-y-Coed westwards to Beddgelert and on towards Portmadoc. The land here is not so high as farther north and except for Moel Siabod (2,860 feet) overlooking Capel Curig, most peaks do not exceed 2,000 feet. The area is bordered on the south by the slate region of

Woodcock

Blaenau Ffestiniog (Merionethshire) while to the east the
Gwyder Forest extends wide fingers of conifers along
valley sides and across ridges towards the peaks.

Caernarvonshire boasts of the presence within its
boundaries of what is possibly Britain's oldest industrial
site, that at Craig Llwyd near Penmaenmawr, where in
Neolithic times stone axes were produced for export to all
parts of the country. Although the slate-quarrying industry has not quite such ancient origins it can nevertheless be traced back at least until the thirteenth century
and now there are extensive workings in several locations,
the largest being the Dinorwic quarry at Llanberis.
There are a number of light industrial concerns in the
county and in the Conway valley a factory of the
Aluminium Corporation Ltd. Agriculture is however
dominant, with sheep, mostly Welsh Mountain, kept on
an extensive scale, while in the lower regions beef producing is carried on. Of the 10,125 hectares (25,000
acres) of woodland in Caernarvonshire, some 7,700
hectares (19,000 acres) are under Forestry Commission
control, the main forests being the Gwdyr, Beddgelert
and Machno while the Lleyn and Arfon forests are in the
process of development.

Of all Welsh counties Caernarvonshire has possibly the
widest range of habitats, from the highest mountains in
Wales down to estuaries, sea cliffs and islands. Consequently its avifauna is a rich one which has been much
studied in parts like the Conway estuary and in the extreme west Bardsey Island where migration has been re-
ceiving attention for many years—important work which
it is hoped can be allowed to continue. On account, perhaps, of the island-going urge of many bird watchers, the
section of land which they pass through to Aberdaron,

following the old pilgrim routes, is rapidly traversed, and consequently much of the Lleyn Peninsula is rather little known ornithologically, in particular away from the sea-bird cliffs. Sea-watching from Bardsey has proved re-warding and no doubt the Lleyn would prove so too, as would the Ormes near the eastern boundary; these are vantage points which are virtually unexplored. Although the number of common gulls nesting on Anglesey is small, further increases may take place, and the many small lakes in Snowdonia seem highly suitable for this species. In fact, inland-nesting of any gulls should be carefully recorded. Caernarvonshire is the headquarters of the chough in North Wales and observations on the require-ments of this, one of our rarer species, are urgently required; there are opportunities here for the careful watcher.

Information

County Avifaunas

Forrest, H. E., *The Vertebrate Fauna of North Wales* (London, 1907). This, together with a supplement pub-lished in 1919, is the only avifauna available though it is long out of date.

North, F. J., Campbell, B., and Scott, R., *Snowdonia* (London, 1949); Condry, W. M., *The Snowdonia National Park* (London, 1966). Both Snowdonia books contain lists of the birds of this region of North Wales, together with brief notes on their present status.

Bird Report
Records of birds in Caernarvonshire are published annually in the *Cambrian Bird Report*, published by the Cambrian Ornithological Society. Price 30p plus postage from the Hon. Sec.

County Bird Recorder
Dr P. J. Dare, Tan-yr-allt, Trefriw, Caerns.

Ornithological Society
The Cambrian Ornithological Society covers the counties of Anglesey, Caernarvonshire, Denbighshire and Merioneth. Indoor meetings are held during the winter months at Colwyn Bay, Llandudno and Bangor. Field meetings are arranged throughout the year, mainly in the Society's area, but occasionally further afield. Special help is available for beginners attending meetings. Besides the Cambrian Bird Report a cyclostyled newsletter is circulated to members five times a year. Subscription £1.00 per annum for adults, 50p for juniors. Hon. Sec. E. Griffiths, Longleat House, Longleat Avenue, Craigside, Llandudno.

Naturalists' Trust
The North Wales Naturalists' Trust covers the counties of Anglesey, Caernarvonshire, Denbighshire, Flintshire, Merioneth and Montgomeryshire. Founded in 1963 the Trust owns or leases a number of reserves, of which three are in Caernarvonshire. There is an active branch of the Trust in the Conway Valley which, besides active conservation work, has a full programme of lectures and field excursions.
Hon. Gen. Sec. Mrs M. J. Morgan, 154 High Street,

Bangor. Subscription £1.00 per annum, students 50p, juniors 25p.

Royal Society for the Protection of Birds Representatives
P. Mansell, 22 Tynrhos, Criccieth, Caerns; Dr P. and Dr J. Peregrine, Dept of Applied Zoology, U.C.N.W., Bangor.

British Trust for Ornithology Representative
A. W. Williams, Bro Hedd, Llanddeiniolen, Caerns.

Tourist Information
For information and a list of publications concerning the Snowdonia National Park write to the National Park Information Officer, Plas Tanybwlch, Maentwrog, Blaenau Ffestiniog, Merioneth. In Caernarvonshire there is a Countryside Centre at Llanberis.

The official guide to the county is available (price 20p) from the National Park Information officer (address above).

1. ABER OGWEN SH6172: The mouth of the Aber Ogwen, together with Bangor Flats, forms the muddy western extremity of the Lavan Sands. Access to the shore is best achieved near Capel Bangor, about a mile north along an unclassified road leaving the A55 at SH610710.

The numbers of wildfowl and waders occurring here make this a most attractive area for the ornithologist. For two species it is their main passage haunt in North Wales. Red-breasted mergansers gather here to moult during the late summer, the maximum number recorded being 236 in September 1971. Greenshank favour the area while on autumn passage and flocks of up to about thirty have been observed, a very good number for this bird in western Britain; spotted redshanks also occur at the same time. Redshank and oystercatcher flocks usually number at least 1,000 and in mid-winter up to fifty goldeneye are present. Casual visitors in recent years have included pintail, shoveler, scaup, velvet scoter, goosander, wood sandpiper, Arctic skua, black and roseate terns.

2. BARDSEY SH1221: Lying two miles off the south-western tip of the Lleyn Peninsula, Bardsey is easily the most important of the North Wales islands. It has an ecclesiastical history dating from at least A.D. 429, and legend has it that 20,000 saints are buried there. Pirates used the island as a base in the fifteenth and sixteenth centuries, while more recently there was a small farming community which for a time had its own 'King', the last one dying in 1926. Opened in 1953 a Bird Observatory has operated on Bardsey under a succession of wardens. The island boat departs from the mainland village of Aberdaron, and information concerning this and the Observatory is available from Mrs. Helen Bond, Bryn Eisteddfod, South Road, Caernarvon.

The most numerous seabird breeding on the island is the manx shearwater with an estimated population of 2,500 pairs. Other species include fulmar, shag, kittiwake, razorbill and guillemot. Land birds breeding on Bardsey include kestrel, cuckoo, raven, chough, stonechat and reed bunting. However, it is as a point for observing bird migration that Bardsey is particularly famed; though unfortunately its lighthouse is notorious as a death trap for migrants travelling at night during periods of heavy overcast. The birds become dazzled in the beams before striking the tower, usually with fatal results. On occasion, several hundred have been killed in a single night, ranging from our smallest species like wrens and gold-crests to birds like water rails and snipe.

The number of rare vagrants seen on the island in recent years is as impressive as in any other part of Britain and Ireland, save perhaps for those sites *par excellence* on Fair Isle and Cape Clear. Night heron, hobby, stone curlew, Sabine's gull, wryneck, shore lark, grey-cheeked thrush, black-eared wheatear, icterine warbler, Arctic warbler, firecrest, Richard's pipit, rose-coloured starling, yellow warbler, rock bunting, song sparrow and white-throated sparrow, to mention just a few. Clearly Bardsey, like Skokholm in Pembrokeshire, is an island not to be missed by the ornithologist in Wales.

3. CONWAY ESTUARY SH7878: The Conway estuary, which for part of its course forms the boundary between Caernarvonshire and Denbighshire, extends inland some ten miles, almost to Llanrwst. The upper section is ex-tremely narrow, but both above and below Conway town there are extensive mud flats with some salt marsh, while large mussel beds are located where the estuary opens to the sea. Access to the eastern bank is somewhat re-stricted by a railway line and is generally only possible at Glan Conway SH8076, Llandudno Junction SH7977, Deganwy SH7779 and to the north of Deganwy where Llandudno golf links are adjacent to Conway Sands. The western shore is accessible from several points be-tween Conway and the sea at Conway Morfa golf links. In the upper estuary Tal-y-carn bridge SH7871 is a good vantage point though numbers of birds here are generally small.

The estuary, together with Conway Sands is, according to the preliminary results of the Estuaries Enquiry organised by the British Trust for Ornithology, the third most important area for waders in Wales (excluding the Dee which is partly in England), following the Burry Inlet and the Monmouthshire coast.

In winter up to about 6,000 waders are usually present on the Conway estuary—oystercatchers number about 2,000, dunlin about 3,000 together with smaller numbers of curlew, redshank and knot. Jack snipe regularly winter on the saltings at Llandudno Junction. In the autumn Sandwich terns on passage gather in the estuary area or just offshore, usually roosting on the Morfa salt marsh, with 190 in late July 1971. Except for shelduck which reach 400 in the early spring, numbers of other ducks— mallard, teal and wigeon—are small, though the winter gathering of up to thirty pintail at Glan Conway should not be missed. Casual visitors include Bewick's swan, ruff, grey phalarope and snow bunting, the latter at Morfa.

4. CWM IDWAL SH6459: Situated above the Nant Ffrancon Valley, the 398 hectares (984-acre) National Nature Reserve, the first in Wales, was declared in 1954. Renowned as a geological and botanical site of extreme importance, naturalists have been visiting the area since Ray and Willoughby first travelled in these parts in 1658. Cars may be parked (limited space) near the Ogwen Mountain School on the A5 at SH650604, from where a track leads up the mountain to the reserve gate. From here one can walk round Llyn Idwal, a shallow glacial lake which regularly attracts cormorants to feed, though their nearest colony is on Puffin Island, fourteen miles to the north. Herons also visit the lake to fish, while herring

gulls come to splash and bathe. Around the margins grey wagtails are usually to be seen, and in summer common sandpipers. Whooper swans occasionally call in the winter and, except during severe weather, there are small parties of tufted duck, pochard and goldeneye present. Land birds which inhabit the cliffs and screes include buzzard, raven, ring ouzel and wheatear. A reserve leaflet is available from the Nature Conservancy (North Wales Regional Office) price 4p.

5. FORYD BAY SH4459: This shallow bay—it almost dries out at low water—is situated at the western extremity of the Menai Straits and sheltered from Caernarvon Bay by a sandy peninsula. An unclassified road follows the shore west from Caernarvon and good views of Foryd Bay are possible after driving some two miles along this. Access to the Morfa Dinlle peninsula and the western side of the bay is more difficult. Follow the A499 south-west from Caernarvon for nearly five miles, taking the turning for Llandwrog at SH457562, continue through the village until the coast is reached and then north past the disused airfield to the bay shore.

Generally this is a disappointing area with only small numbers of regular duck, mallard, teal, wigeon and shelduck, and waders such as oystercatcher, curlew, redshank and dunlin. Encroaching *spartina* limits the areas of open flats and can make observation difficult.

6. GREAT ORMES HEAD SH7683: Sheltering Llandudno, the Great Ormes Head, a Carboniferous Limestone massif, rises to 679 feet with sea cliffs reaching 250 feet. The Marine Drive, a perimeter road, provides easy access to all parts, while footpaths cross the interior at several

points. A Nature Trail has been established by Llan-dudno Urban District Council and the booklet (price 3p) is available from North Wales Tourism Council, Civic Centre, Colwyn Bay, Denbighshire.

The main ornithological interest on the Head is with-out question the seabird colonies, which together with those on the nearby Little Orme are the furthest east into Liverpool Bay that several species penetrate. Fulmars— they first nested here in 1945—and herring gulls nest at many points including the cliffs above the road near Pen-trwyn SH781838. Cormorants, kittiwakes, razor-bills, guillemots and house martins nest on the cliffs in the vicinity of the lighthouse SH756845 and may be viewed from above. Great caution (fatalities occur almost annually) should be exercised by the observer once he or she has descended from the road. Better views are possible from a boat and enquiries concerning these should be made at Llandudno harbour. Puffins once nested on the Great Orme and, although it is some years since they were proved to do so, occasional birds are seen offshore in most years. Could the odd pair still nest? It is some-thing an observant ornithologist might prove during June and July when the adults carry fish ashore in con-spicuous beakfuls.

7. GWYDYR FOREST SH7857: To the north and north-west of the village of Betwys-y-Coed and the A5 which passes through it, lies the Gwydyr Forest. At one time oak was the predominant tree with smaller numbers of other de-ciduous species like sweet chestnut and birch. Alas only a small section of the original forest still remains and should be sought on the slopes to the south of the village. Since 1921 the Forestry Commission has been active here, the

main species planted being sitka spruce, Douglas fir, Norway spruce and Japanese larch and the forest now covers some 6,000 hectares (15,000 acres). Some of the older plantations are being felled and extensive replanting is taking place. The Commission has established a number of facilities for visitors to the Forest—picnic sites, exhibitions, an arboretum and forest walks. The Gwydyr Forest Trail (leaflet price 5p, from the Forestry Commission, North Wales) commences at Ty Hyll Bridge at SH757575 on the A5 about two miles west of Betws-y-Coed. A booklet containing details of ten walks through the Forest, ranging in length from three-quarters of a mile to five and a quarter miles, is also available from the Forestry Commission (price 5p), also an invaluable guide the Snowdonia Forest Park (price $32\frac{1}{2}$p) which contains a chapter on woodland birds.

Both species of grouse—red and black—occur in the Gwydyr Forest area, the latter having moved into the developing plantations within the last twenty years. Interesting species of local breeding distribution in Wales also occur, including the woodcock (said to be more numerous here than elsewhere in the Principality) nightjar and siskin, the latter being a relative newcomer. Long-eared owls may possibly breed; careful listening after dark for its low sighing 'oo-oo-oo' calls could prove profitable. Crossbills have remained to breed following their invasion years and should be looked for at such times. Regularly occurring species include buzzard, raven, redstart, wood warbler and redpoll.

8. LAVAN SANDS SH6375: A huge area of sand flats which at low tide extends three miles out from the shore and, except for a channel close to the Anglesey side, almost

blocks access to the eastern end of the Menai Straits. Several unclassified and minor roads run north from the A55 towards the shore, the most convenient for the ornithologist are those at Aber SH653727, west of Llanfairfechan SH669738 and Llanfairfechan promenade.

Great crested grebes occur in large numbers, up to 420 have been recorded during the autumn, with a few remaining throughout the winter when occasional black-necked grebes may also be seen. The mouth of the Afon Aber SH6473 seems the most attractive point for wintering duck, with several hundred each of mallard, wigeon and shelduck, together with smaller parties of pintail and shoveler. Up to about 150 common scoter winter farther out into the bay. Oystercatchers and dunlin are the most numerous winter waders, with up to 5,000 of each, while knot number a few hundred. During the autumn passage both curlew and redshank numbers reach up to 2,000. Sandwich terns and common terns occur in good numbers during August and September, the former choosing to roost in ploughed fields near Aber along with gulls. Both peregrine and merlin hunt the shoreline regularly in winter. More casual visitors have included great northern diver, scaup, green sandpiper, little stint, curlew sandpiper, grey phalarope, Arctic skua and black tern.

9. PENCILAN HEAD SH2923: This, the most southerly headland on the Lleyn Peninsula, has the same breeding seabirds, though in generally smaller numbers, as at Penrhyn Glas. An unclassified road runs south from Abersoch SH3128 and this gives access to several points including the National Trust property of Tynewydd on the western side.

Most of the kittiwakes, razorbills and guillemots nest on the south-west cliffs between Trwyn y Fulfran SH287238 and the southern tip Trwyn Cilan SH294230. Although the whole colony is not visible from the land, good numbers may nevertheless be seen. Other breeding seabirds on the headland are fulmar, cormorant, shag and herring gull. Land birds include buzzard, raven, chough and stonechat. The St Tudwal's Islands off the eastern side also have a small seabird colony, but alas only one or two pairs of puffins remain where in the 1930s there were several thousand.

10. PENRHYN GLAS SH3343: Also known as Carreg y Llam, the cliffs at this point on the north side of the Lleyn Peninsula hold the largest auk colony in North Wales. Unfortunately, it is faced with two possible threats—further quarrying activity might remove the breeding ledges, while cliff climbing is a serious disturbance factor during the breeding season. Leave the A499 Caernarvon to Pwllheli road at Llanaelhaearn and follow the B4417 west for three miles, then a minor north from SH344429.

Although the complete colony is only visible from the sea, good views of some sections are possible from the cliff top. About 2,500 pairs of guillemots nest here, together with about 600 pairs of kittiwakes, 100 pairs of razorbills and smaller numbers of fulmars, cormorants, shags, herring gulls and occasionally a pair of great black-backed gulls.

11. SNOWDON SH6054: Although rich in geological, botanical and scenic interest comparable to upland regions anywhere in Europe, the higher slopes of the Snowdon

range support only a limited avifauna. The visitor is
well advised to follow one or other of the two Nature
Trails. These are on established routes, and the information contained in their accompanying leaflets (available
from the Nature Conservancy, North Wales Regional
Office) allows the maximum appreciation of the land-
scape, the geological forces which moulded it so magnifi-
cently and the plants, animals and birds which live there.

The Trail (price 2½p) that follows the Miners Track
(copper was mined high on the mountain during the last
century) leaves the A4086 Caernarvon to Capel Curig
road at Pen-y-Pass SH647557 at the head of the Pass of
Llanberis. In two miles the visitor climbs 236 feet to
reach Llyn Llydaw, a lake of glacial origin with a maximum depth of 190 feet. Here one is 1,416 feet above sea
level and for those more energetic and properly equipped,
the path continues to Llyn Glaslyn (1,975 feet) and on to
the summit of Snowdon (3,561 feet).

On the south-east slopes of Snowdon the Cwm y Llan
Nature Trail (price 3p) follows the lower section of the
Watkin Path, which also eventually leads to the summit.
Commencing at Bethania Bridge SH627507 on the A498
in Nant Gwynant, the visitor climbs to the now ruined
Snowdon Slate Works below Craig ddu at SH613524.

While following either Trail the visitor can expect to
see raven, carrion crow, and the occasional buzzard or
wandering party of choughs, while in the summer both
ring ouzels and wheatears breed in the area. In winter,
waters like Llyn Dinas SH6149, Llyn Gwynant SH6451
and Llynnau Mymbyr SH7057 hold small numbers of
tufted duck, pochard, goldeneye and occasional herds of
whooper swans.

Check list

RB	Resident Breeder	MB	Migrant Breeder
WV	Winter Visitor	PV	Passage Visitor
	v	Vagrant	

Black-throated Diver	v	Goldeneye	WV
Great Northern Diver	WV	Long-tailed Duck	WV
Red-throated Diver	WV	Velvet Scoter	v
Great Crested Grebe	WV	Common Scoter	WV
Red-necked Grebe	v	Eider	v
Slavonian Grebe	v	Red-breasted Merganser	
Black-necked Grebe	v		RB
Little Grebe	RB	Goosander	v
Fulmar	RB	Smew	v
Manx Shearwater	MB	Shelduck	RB
British Storm Petrel	MB	Greylag Goose	v
Leach's Petrel	PV	White-fronted Goose	WV
Gannet	PV	Brent Goose	v
Cormorant	RB	Barnacle Goose	v
Shag	RB	Canada Goose	RB
Grey Heron	RB	Mute Swan	RB
Mallard	RB	Whooper Swan	WV
Teal	RB	Bewick's Swan	WV
Gadwall	WV	Buzzard	RB
Wigeon	WV	Sparrowhawk	RB
Pintail	WV	Marsh Harrier	v
Shoveler	RB	Hen Harrier	PV
Scaup	WV	Peregrine	RB
Tufted Duck	WV	Merlin	RB
Pochard	WV	Kestrel	RB

Red Grouse	RB	Curlew Sandpiper	PV
Black Grouse	RB	Sanderling	PV
Partridge	RB	Ruff	PV
Quail	V	Grey Phalarope	V
Pheasant	RB	Great Skua	PV
Water Rail	WV	Pomarine Skua	V
Corncrake	MB	Arctic Skua	PV
Moorhen	RB	Great Black-backed Gull	
Coot	RB		RB
Oystercatcher	RB	Lesser Black-backed Gull	
Lapwing	RB		MB
Ringed Plover	RB	Herring Gull	RB
Grey Plover	WV	Common Gull	WV
Golden Plover	WV	Little Gull	WV
	Has bred	Black-headed Gull	RB
Turnstone	WV	Sabine's Gull	V
Snipe	RB	Kittiwake	RB
Jack Snipe	WV	Black Tern	PV
Woodcock	RB	Common Tern	PV
Curlew	RB	Arctic Tern	PV
Whimbrel	PV	Roseate Tern	V
Black-tailed Godwit	PV	Little Tern	MB
Bar-tailed Godwit	WV	Sandwich Tern	PV
Green Sandpiper	PV	Razorbill	RB
Wood Sandpiper	V	Guillemot	RB
Common Sandpiper	MB	Black Guillemot	V
Redshank	RB	Puffin	MB
Spotted Redshank	WV	Stock Dove	RB
Greenshank	WV	Woodpigeon	RB
Knot	WV	Turtle Dove	PV
Purple Sandpiper	WV	Collared Dove	RB
Little Stint	PV	Cuckoo	MB
Dunlin	WV	Barn Owl	RB

Little Owl	RB	Fieldfare	WV
Tawny Owl	RB	Song Thrush	RB
Short-eared Owl	WV	Redwing	WV
Nightjar	MB	Ring Ouzel	MB
Swift	MB	Blackbird	RB
Kingfisher	RB	Wheatear	MB
Green Woodpecker	RB	Stonechat	RB
Great Spotted Wood-pecker	RB	Whinchat	MB
		Redstart	MB
Lesser Spotted Wood-pecker	RB	Black Redstart	WV
		Robin	RB
Skylark	RB	Grasshopper Warbler	MB
Swallow	MB	Sedge Warbler	MB
House Martin	MB	Blackcap	MB
Sand Martin	MB	Garden Warbler	MB
Raven	RB	Whitethroat	MB
Carrion Crow	RB	Lesser Whitethroat	MB
Rook	RB	Willow Warbler	MB
Jackdaw	RB	Chiffchaff	MB
Magpie	RB	Wood Warbler	MB
Jay	RB	Goldcrest	RB
Chough	RB	Spotted Flycatcher	MB
Great Tit	RB	Pied Flycatcher	MB
Blue Tit	RB	Dunnock	RB
Coal Tit	RB	Meadow Pipit	RB
Marsh Tit	RB	Tree Pipit	MB
Willow Tit	RB	Rock Pipit	RB
Long-tailed Tit	RB	Water Pipit	V
Nuthatch	RB	Pied Wagtail	RB
Treecreeper	RB	White Wagtail	PV
Wren	RB	Grey Wagtail	RB
Dipper	RB	Yellow Wagtail	PV
Mistle Thrush	RB	Starling	RB

Hawfinch	RB	Chaffinch	RB
Greenfinch	RB	Brambling	WV
Goldfinch	RB	Yellowhammer	RB
Siskin	RB	Reed Bunting	RB
Linnet	RB	Snow Bunting	V
Redpoll	RB	House Sparrow	RB
Bullfinch	RB	Tree Sparrow	RB

CARDIGANSHIRE

CARDIGAN
BAY

N

Aberystwyth •
1

10
5

4
• Tregaron

Aberaron •

2 •
New
Quay

7

Lampeter •

8 Cardigan
9

Newcastle
Emlyn

6
11
12

0   5   10
miles

Chapter 7

Cardiganshire

Cardiganshire, with its sweeping fifty miles of coastline encompassing nearly half Cardigan Bay occupies virtually the same area as when it was ruled by Celtic chieftains during the period that the Romans were leaving Britain. One Ceredig, son of Cunedda, gave his name to this kingdom—Ceredigion—the land of Ceredig—and this forms the present day Cardiganshire. In the north the Dyfi estuary divides the county from Merioneth, while in the south the Teifi forms a natural boundary with Pembrokeshire and western Carmarthenshire, the Tywi continues the boundary eastwards. In the east Cardiganshire is separated from Breconshire, Radnorshire and Montgomeryshire by a boundary wandering over some of the loneliest uplands of central Wales, passing close to Plynlimon, 2,470 feet, the highest point in the county, before descending to the Dyfi estuary.

The town of Cardigan with its castle built in the turbulent times of Richard I sleeps at a strategic point on the lower Teifi. However, Aberystwyth on the northern coastal section and with an equally long history has developed into the main county centre. Besides administrative offices there are national institutions here like the University College, the oldest of the University Colleges of Wales, and the National Library of Wales. Between these two ancient towns, there are other smaller communities on the Cardiganshire Bay coast like Aberayron, New Quay and Aberporth. These are now holiday centres, but during the seventeenth, eighteenth and nineteenth centuries each was an important harbour for coastal traffic with some ships plying farther afield. This

was the time when lead, zinc and silver were mined in
north Cardiganshire to such an extent that rivers were
heavily polluted and the countryside in parts scarred by
spoil heaps like those still visible in the upper Rheidol
valley. After about 1870 the mining boom declined and
activities gradually ceased during the early years of this
century, though there have been recent suggestions that
the mines, or at least some of them should be re-opened.
Despite this early brush with industry, Cardiganshire
has remained for the most part an agricultural county,
nine-tenths of its total land area being devoted to such
activities.

The sea coast, with Cardigan Island at the mouth of
the Teifi its south-western bastion, is mainly unspoiled;
industry has not intruded here and holiday caravan and
camping places are modest by most standards. For much
of its length this is a cliff coast backed by steep sidings
which rise, bracken-clothed, above the more precipitous faces. At one or two points there are coastal oakwoods whose windswept trees are the remnants of much
larger areas which once covered much of this countryside.
Steep-sided valleys run down to the shore in many places,
forming at their mouths small coves and occasionally
larger bays. The only major area of sand is in the extreme
north beyond Borth. Access to the cliff tops away from
coastal towns and villages is often difficult; there is no
cliff path like that in neighbouring Pembrokeshire. However, from an ornithological view this means less disturbance in the breeding season to sensitive species like
the buzzard, peregrine and raven.

South of Aberystwyth, and extending inland a dozen
miles or so to the Teifi valley, is an agricultural area,
mainly dairy farming. Intersected by the fertile valley of

the Afon Aeron, the highest point is reached on the Mynydd Bach, 1,183 feet, south-east of Aberystwyth.

North-east of the county town the ground rises considerably higher, reaching 1,700 feet at Moel-y-llyn with numerous surrounding peaks approaching this height. This region was the scene of Cardiganshire's mineral exploitation; a glance at the map soon reveals the site of many a disused mine. Rivers like the Rheidol, Stewy and Leri with their tributaries plunge rapidly towards the valley floor on their short journey to the sea. The high rainfall together with suitable natural contours has attracted the attention of water engineers, the result being reservoirs like those at Nant-y-Moch and Dinas. Forestry

Greenshank

has taken place on many slopes with particularly large areas planted like the Rheidol Forest 1,480 hectares (3,690 acres), and Taliesin 1,750 hectares (4,331 acres).

More high ground lies to the east of the Teifi valley extending to the county border and beyond, forming the western marches of the Cambrian Mountains. Much of the land here is above 1,000 feet, rising northwards to Plynlimon, 2,470 feet, birthplace of the rivers Severn and Wye, though both commence their eastward journeys just outside Cardiganshire.

Some parts of Cardiganshire have received much ornithological attention in recent years, among them Tregaron Bog and the Dyfi estuary. Most ornithologists have been based in or close to Aberystwyth, often as students at the University and this has led to a greater amount of information being available concerning the northern habitats. A lack of ornithological observation away from these well-watched areas has meant that information from parts of the county, in particular the southern and eastern border regions is even at the present time sparse. Although discoveries may not be spectacular, there is a great need for more information concerning the status of resident species in the east and south. Another aspect which has received virtually no attention is bird migration. The position in Cardiganshire is briefly but concisely summed up in *The Birds of Cardiganshire*—'There are bird observatories on islands to the south, on Skokholm, and to the north, on Bardsey, from which much knowledge has been gained, but from the county coastline, in between, we know little of any consequence. That there is considerable passage of many species in spring and in autumn is undoubted; that weather movements of some species occur from time to time is well known; that pas-

sages of some species are to be observed inland; but none
of these has been studied and recorded in detail so that
there is little or nothing we can usefully write about
them.' One hopes that when this avifauna is revised, work
will have already commenced on the migration of birds
through the county.

Information

County Avifaunas
Ingram, Geoffrey C. S., Salmon, H. Morrey and Condry,
W. M., *The Birds of Cardiganshire*, West Wales National
Trust 1966.

Bird Report
No county bird report is available, but a joint report with
Carmarthenshire and Pembrokeshire, known as the *Dyfed
Bird Report* is published by the West Wales Naturalists'
Trust, price 20p.

County Bird Recorder
Peter Davis, Ty Coed, Tregaron.

Ornithological Society
No society as such, but the West Wales Naturalists' Trust
(see Naturalists' Trust) has an active branch in Aberystwyth with a varied programme of field meetings and

overleaf – *Short-eared owl*

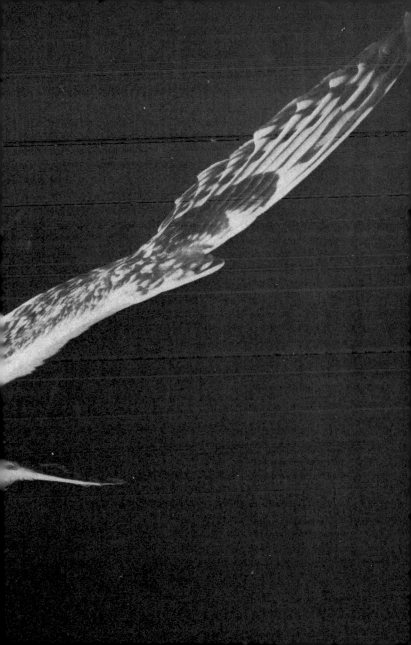

lectures. Secretary: John Hedger, Gweithdy'r Crydd, Ffair Rhos, Ystrad Meurig.

Naturalists' Trust
The West Wales Naturalists' Trust (see also Ornithological Society) covers the counties of Cardiganshire, Carmarthenshire and Pembrokeshire. Formerly the West Wales Naturalists' Society it changed to a Trust in 1961 and now owns or leases six reserves in Cardiganshire. Members receive the journal *Nature in Wales* and a quarterly bulletin, while there are field meetings and winter lectures. Subscription £2.00 (adults), 50p (children and students). Hon. Gen. Sec. Dillwyn Miles, 4 Victoria Place, Haverfordwest.

Royal Society for the Protection of Birds Representative
Not appointed.

British Trust for Ornithology Representative
As for County Bird Recorder.

Tourist Information
Information Officer, Cardiganshire County Council, Swyddfa'r Sir, Aberystwyth and from Cardiganshire Bay Resorts Association, Town Hall, Aberystwyth.

1. ABERYSTWYTH HARBOUR SN580810: Situated on the southern side of the town the harbour is easily accessible at several points. The main ornithological interests are the wintering (September until April) purple sandpipers which feed on the rock areas exposed at low tide. Numbers are never large, up to about twenty seems about the maximum of this so frequently-overlooked wader. Should

investigation of the harbour area prove fruitless, the observer may well find the birds on rocks off the promenade a little to the north. Other species likely to be encountered are oystercatchers, turnstone, redshank and the commoner gulls.

2. BIRD ROCK SN377601: This, the most important seabird site on the Cardiganshire coast lies nearly a mile south-west of New Quay Head. The best view of the cliffs with their sea birds is obtained from a view point about 100 yards east of the coastguard lookout, which is reached by the unclassified road through Penrhyn Farm at SN379597. Kittiwakes first nested here in 1962 and now number over 100 pairs. About forty pairs of razorbills occupy crevices in the cliff, while up to 350 pairs of guillemots use more exposed ledges. Other species include fulmars (they first prospected here in 1945, breeding two years later), shags, great black-backed and herring gulls, and possibly lesser black-backed gulls.

3. CARDIGAN ISLAND SN1651: This 16 hectare (40 acre) island rising to 172 feet a mile north of the Teifi mouth on the southern border of the county is a reserve of the West Wales Naturalists' Trust. Permission to visit the island should be obtained from the Trust and boatmen may be hired in St Dogmaels or at Gwbert. Boats from both places take occasional parties round the island during the summer months.

There is a large herring gull colony along with smaller numbers of fulmars, shags, oystercatchers, great black-backed and lesser black-backed gulls and usually a pair of ravens. Razorbills are often seen close inshore and could possibly breed, as could kittiwakes which now

seem content to gather in a large noisy 'club' on the
north-west shore, though two pairs nested in 1961.
Puffins nested, but disappeared it is said after brown rats
landed from the wrecked liner *Herefordshire* in 1934.
Recent and most laudable efforts by the North Pembrokeshire section of the Trust seem to have sucessfully
eradicated the rats, though in view of the general decline
in the British and Irish puffin population, it seems unlikely that the birds will return at present. Manx shearwaters have been heard flighting over the island at night
and it has been suggested that this bird could now be
induced to establish a colony in the absence of rats.
Chicks, deserted just before fledging by their parents at
the major Pembrokeshire colonies could be placed in
artificial tunnel systems on Cardigan Island. When
making their way naturally to sea they might become
orientated towards their new home, to which it is hoped
they would return to breed after several juvenile years at
sea. One looks forward to hearing that this imaginative
project is under way. The prominent position of Cardigan
Island leads one to suppose it might prove a good vantage point for observing seabird passage in St George's
Channel. This seems worthy of further investigation.

4. CORS TREGARON SN6863: Fifteen miles south-east of
Aberystwyth lies Cors Goch Glan Teifi 'The Red Bog
beside the Teifi', which to quote from the Nature Conservancy Reserve leaflet (available free from the South
Wales Regional Office) 'is a great, sodden, miry carpet
spread over the floor of the upper Teifii valley in Cardiganshire. Dying sedges turn the peat bogs and marshes indian
red in autumn'. Some 770 hectares (1,898 acres) are
managed as a National Nature Reserve by agreement

with the owner Lord Lisburne and the co-operation of his tenant farmers. Ten thousand years ago glacial action deposited a moraine of rocks and soil across the valley; behind this a shallow lake filled, later passing through transitional stages until the present *Sphagnum* peat-bog formed. The western section of which is one of Britain's best developed and best preserved raised bogs. Due to its relative inaccessibility only a limited amount of peat cutting and drainage has taken place, so there have been few changes during historical times.

The reserve may be viewed from vantage points along the B4343 Ponthydfendigaid to Tregaron road, or for the northern section, the disused railway line which forms the eastern boundary. Permits to enter the reserve may be obtained from the Regional Officer for South Wales, The Nature Conservancy, Plas Gogerddan, Aberystwyth, or from the Assistant Regional Officer, Ty-Coed, Tregaron.

Besides having a high physiographical and botanical importance, the reserve is the most southerly known station for the large heath butterfly in Britain. Otters and polecats are among the animals which frequent the reserve, while the Teifi provides fine opportunities for the fisherman. Mallard and curlew are common breeding species on the bog, while teal, red and black grouse also occur. Montagu's harrier, quail and corncrake have occasionally nested during recent years on the reserve.

The winter visitors include wigeon, whooper and Bewick's swans, hen harrier, merlin, kite, golden plover and great grey shrike. The bog was formerly a regular winter haunt of Greenland white-fronted geese, but these are now scarce and irregular visitors. More unusual species noted in recent years have included white stork, purple heron, American green-winged teal and Richard's pipit.

5. DEVIL'S BRIDGE SN7477: One of the most popular tourist attractions in Cardiganshire is the gorge below Devil's Bridge where the River Rheidol, rising at 1,750 feet on Plynlimon some seven miles away, plunges 200 feet in about a mile. Adding further to the spectacle is the 400-foot cascade of the smaller Mynach River. From near the car park above the gorge a path descends through mixed woodland, where nestboxes have been erected at various points. These are normally occupied by great and blue tits and pied flycatchers, while other woodland species which may be seen include buzzard, jay, redstart and wood warbler. Occasionally kites soar over the wooded valley slopes and should always be looked for.

A leaflet describing features on the path may be obtained from the Hafod Arms, Devil's Bridge, price 2½p (postage extra).

6. DYFI ESTUARY SN69: This estuary, ornithologically the most important on the west coast of Wales, forms the Cardiganshire–Merionethshire border. The main section runs east for about four and a half miles from the sea with a maximum width of just over one and a half miles, before narrowing rapidly to continue upstream for a further three miles. Some 1,428 hectares (3,525 acres) of the saltings and foreshore comprise the Dyfi Estuary National Nature Reserve, a National Wildfowl Refuge, and next to Snowdon the largest reserve in Wales. Permits from the Regional Officer for South Wales, The Nature Conservancy, Plas Gogerddan, Aberystwyth, are required

if one wishes to visit parts of the estuary away from the foreshore. Access to the eastern section is by arrangement with the Royal Society for the Protection of Birds (see Ynyshir). The most convenient access points are from the Ynyslas Dunes car park sn608943 (see also Ynyslas), and on the bridge on the B4353 over the Afon Leri sn616932. Sunday shooting is prohibited on the Dyfi so that during the wildfowling season this is the best day for visiting the area.

Ornithologically the estuary is most important during the winter months or during the spring and autumn wader passages. Wigeon are the most numerous of the wintering duck with up to 2,500 being present in some years, smaller numbers of mallard, teal, pintail, shoveler and shelduck are also present, while whooper and Bewick's swans occur most winters. Grey plover winter on the estuary, but dunlin are the most numerous wader at that season with up to 4,000 having been estimated. Ringed plover are especially numerous on autumn passage, a time when most of the waders regularly occurring in Britain may be seen. The estuary is the roosting place for a small flock of Greenland white-fronted geese (about seventy-five in the 1971–2 season) which feeds on the nearby bog of Cors Fochno and in the upland region of the Plynlimon massif. More unusual visitors to the Dyfi Estuary have included little egret, osprey, Kentish plover, dotterel and lesser yellowlegs.

7. LOCHTYN sn3155: This peninsular National Trust property just north of Llangranog is freely accessible and provides a good vantage point for viewing the high steep cliff slopes which run some four miles north-east to New Quay Head. Razorbills and guillemots nest on the

cliffs to the east of the peninsula where herring gulls are the main species. Ravens and choughs frequent the area and pairs of stonechats are usually to be seen. The narrow steep-sided valleys which divide the cliff line to the north and south of Lochtyn are rarely visited by ornithologists though they are worthy of exploration.

8. TEIFI ESTUARY SN1646 TO 1548: Except for the smaller Nevern (Pembrokeshire) this is the only estuary in south-west Wales between those around Milford Haven and the Dyfi. However, its small size and restricted area of mud flats, sand banks and spartina salting means that wader and wildfowl numbers are not high. Access is easy, leaving Cardigan and running along or close to the south side is the B4546, while on the north side the B4548 provides similar opportunities.

Shelduck breed in the vicinity of the estuary and during the winter about thirty are resident, being joined by small numbers of mallard, teal and wigeon, with some diving duck like tufted duck, goldeneye and red breasted merganser also being present. Lapwing, ringed plover, curlew, redshank and dunlin are the most numerous waders being joined, particularly in the autumn, by grey plover, whimbrel, black-tailed and bar-tailed godwits, greenshank and spotted redshank.

9. TEIFI VALLEY RESERVE SN1845: Still on the tidal reaches of the Teifi but upstream from Cardigan is a reserve leased by the West Wales Naturalists' Trust from the Coedmore Estate and the Crown Commissioners. Access is restricted to Trust members, but it is well worth paying the subscription if only to obtain a permit to visit this, one of the most exciting small nature re-

serves in Wales. The narrow strip of mud flats is backed
by a reed bed and alder carr above which rises the now
overgrown spoil heaps of long disused slate quarries. Upstream the river narrows between steep wooded slopes as
one approaches Cilgerran. Adjacent to the lower section
are Pentoed Meadows which when partially flooded in
winter prove most attractive to wildfowl and waders, and
should, if possible, be included in the reserve at the first
opportunity.

Mallard, teal and wigeon are the main duck seen on
the reserve, though goldeneye are usually present on the
open river and early in 1972 an American green-winged
teal was seen. Bewick's swans spend their time on
Pentoed Meadows with large flocks of lapwing, golden
plover and curlew. Sedge warblers breed and reed
warblers have been heard in recent summers; does this
species breed? Its nearest known regular site is on the
Gower peninsula some forty miles to the south-east
though there are several recent records from Carmarthenshire. Most woodland species which occur in western
Britain may be seen in the valley and a number of boxes
have been provided for hole-nesting species.

10. VALE OF RHEIDOL SN5980 TO 7376: Running almost
due east for some twelve miles from Aberystwyth is the
Vale of Rheidol. At first the river is wide and meandering, with oxbow lagoons on the flood plain, but later it
narrows to the dramatic gorge at Devil's Bridge. In 1902
a narrow gauge railway was completed for the transport
of lead and zinc ores from the now deserted mines near
Devil's Bridge to the coast. Since 1931 the line has only
been operational during the summer months, carrying
an ever increasing number of tourists. A visitor is

strongly advised to take one of the trains (depart from Aberystwyth main line station), the outward journey taking about an hour, the return (downhill) a little less.

The river proves attractive to birds like the grey heron, common sandpiper, black-headed gull, kingfisher, sand martin and grey wagtail. Redstarts and pied flycatchers are summer visitors to the woods towards the valley head. Any large raptor soaring in up currents along the escarpment should be carefully scrutinised; most will be identified as buzzards, but occasionally the fortunate observer will locate a kite. As a contribution to European Conservation Year 1970 the Cardiganshire Branch of the West Wales Naturalists' Trust produced a most attractive booklet 'What you will see in the Vale of Rheidol'. This is available from the Aberystwyth Station bookstall, price 15p, or from the Trust Office, 18p (post included).

11. YNYS-HIR SN6896: This reserve of the Royal Society for the Protection of Birds is situated at the head of the broad, lower section of the Dyfi estuary (see Dyfi estuary). It is a rich area of diverse habitats including saltings, marshes, woods and farmland. The reserve, which may be reached from the A487 Aberystwyth to Machynlleth road in Eglwysfach SN686955, is open to the public on Saturdays, Sundays, Wednesdays and Thursdays, April to September inclusive. Permits 50p, (25p for children) may be obtained from the Reserves Department, Royal Society for the Protection of Birds, The Lodge, Sandy, Beds.

There is a heronry, while among species of special interest which breed on or close to the reserve are shelduck, red-breasted merganser, buzzard, nightjar, lesser spotted woodpecker, willow tit, whinchat, pied flycatcher and redpoll. During the autumn and winter wigeon, golden-eye, hen harrier, bar-tailed godwit, turnstone and curlew are among birds which visit the area. White-fronted geese come to feed on the reserve wetlands and are occasionally joined by pink-footed geese. More unusual visitors to the reserve in recent years have included little egret, goosander, goshawk, hobby, lesser yellowlegs, spotted redshank, black tern and Richard's pipit.

12. YNYSLAS DUNES SN6094: These, the only large sand dunes in Cardiganshire—they rise to sixty feet—are highly attractive to both naturalists and holidaymakers. The many facets of human pressure in such an attractive area have led to serious erosion problems and dune degradation. This has been combatted with the aid of board walks and the control of cars, chiefly preventing their access into the dunes and on to the beach. To help the visitor a manned information kiosk has been established in an adapted ex-W.D. building near the road at SN608943 and a leaflet produced by the Nature Conservancy describing a trail through the dunes is available. A number of information sheets to various aspects of the reserve have also been published by the Nature Conservancy, including Mammals, Field Studies, Jellyfish and Pebbles. The one entitled 'Summer Birds at Ynyslas' describes species one might encounter not only among the dunes, but also along the foreshore and up the estuary.

Ynyslas is a good starting point for exploration of the Dyfi Estuary (see Dyfi Estuary) but turning one's back and searching out to sea can be productive. Cormorants and the ubiquitous herring gull can always be seen, while during both the spring and autumn passage flocks of terns gather to feed. Little gulls are becoming frequent visitors in spring with up to six in April 1973. Occasionally groups of Manx shearwaters, common scoter and passing gannets may be observed in flight offshore. In winter scaup are often present. Stonechats and reed buntings breed among the dunes, which offer shelter to passing migrants like wheatears and the occasional 'fall' of small warblers and, in winter, finch and thrush flocks.

Check list

RB   Resident Breeder   MB   Migrant Breeder
WV   Winter Visitor   PV   Passage Visitor
             V   Vagrant

Black-throated Diver	V	Bittern	V
Great Northern Diver	WV	Mallard	RB
Red-throated Diver	WV	Teal	RB
Great Crested Grebe	WV	Garganey	PV
	Has bred		Has bred
Black-necked Grebe	V	Gadwall	PV
Little Grebe	RB	Wigeon	WV
Fulmar	RB	Pintail	WV
Manx Shearwater	PV	Shoveler	WV
British Storm Petrel	V		Has bred
Leach's Petrel	V	Scaup	WV
Gannet	PV	Tufted Duck	WV
Cormorant	RB	Pochard	WV
Shag	RB	Goldeneye	WV
Grey Heron	RB	Long-tailed Duck	WV

Velvet Scoter	V	Corncrake	PV
Common Scoter	WV		Has bred
Eider	V	Moorhen	RB
Red-breasted Merganser		Coot	RB
	RB	Oystercatcher	RB
Goosander	WV	Lapwing	RB
Smew	V	Ringed Plover	MB
Shelduck	RB	Grey Plover	WV
White-fronted Goose	WV	Golden Plover	RB
Pink-footed Goose	WV	Turnstone	WV
Brent Goose	PV	Snipe	RB
Barnacle Goose	V	Jack Snipe	WV
Canada Goose	V	Woodcock	RB
Mute Swan	RB	Curlew	RB
Whooper Swan	WV	Whimbrel	PV
Bewick's Swan	WV	Black-tailed Godwit	PV
Buzzard	RB	Bar-tailed Godwit	PV
Sparrowhawk	RB	Green Sandpiper	PV
Red Kite	RB	Wood Sandpiper	PV
Marsh Harrier	V	Common Sandpiper	MB
Hen Harrier	WV	Redshank	RB
Montagu's Harrier	PV	Spotted Redshank	PV
	Has bred	Greenshank	PV
Peregrine	RB	Knot	WV
Merlin	MB	Purple Sandpiper	WV
Kestrel	RB	Little Stint	PV
Red Grouse	RB	Dunlin	MB
Black Grouse	RB	Curlew Sandpiper	PV
Partridge	RB	Sanderling	PV
Quail	PV	Ruff	PV
	Has bred	Grey Phalarope	PV
Pheasant	RB	Great Skua	V
Water Rail	RB	Arctic Skua	PV

Great Black-backed Gull	RB	Lesser Spotted Wood-	
Lesser Black-backed Gull		pecker	RB
	MB	Skylark	RB
Herring Gull	RB	Swallow	MB
Common Gull	WV	House Martin	MB
Little Gull	PV	Sand Martin	MB
Black-headed Gull	RB	Raven	RB
Kittiwake	RB	Carrion Crow	RB
Black Tern	PV	Rook	RB
Common Tern	PV	Jackdaw	RB
Arctic Tern	PV	Magpie	RB
Little Tern	PV	Jay	RB
Sandwich Tern	PV	Chough	RB
Razorbill	RB	Great Tit	RB
Guillemot	RB	Blue Tit	RB
Puffin	V	Coal Tit	RB
Stock Dove	RB	Marsh Tit	RB
Woodpigeon	RB	Willow Tit	RB
Turtle Dove	PV	Nuthatch	RB
Collared Dove	RB	Treecreeper	RB
Cuckoo	MB	Wren	RB
Barn Owl	RB	Dipper	RB
Little Owl	RB	Mistle Thrush	RB
Tawny Owl	RB	Fieldfare	WV
Long-eared Owl	WV	Song Thrush	RB
Short-eared Owl	RB	Redwing	WV
Nightjar	MB	Ring Ouzel	MB
Swift	MB	Blackbird	RB
Kingfisher	RB	Wheatear	MB
Hoopoe	V	Stonechat	RB
Green Woodpecker	RB	Whinchat	MB
Great Spotter Wood-		Redstart	MB
pecker	RB	Black Redstart	PV

Robin	RB	White Wagtail	WV
Grasshopper Warbler	MB	Grey Wagtail	RB
Sedge Warbler	MB	Yellow Wagtail	PV
Blackcap	MB	Great Grey Shrike	V
Garden Warbler	MB	Starling	RB
Whitethroat	MB	Greenfinch	RB
Lesser Whitethroat	MB	Goldfinch	RB
Willow Warbler	MB	Siskin	WV
Chiffchaff	MB	Linnet	RB
Wood Warbler	MB	Redpoll	RB
Goldcrest	RB	Bullfinch	RB
Spotted Flycatcher	MB	Crossbill	V
Pied Flycatcher	MB	Chaffinch	RB
Dunnock	RB	Brambling	WV
Meadow Pipit	RB	Yellowhammer	RB
Tree Pipit	MB	Reed Bunting	RB
Rock Pipit	RB	Snow Bunting	WV
Water Pipit	WV	House Sparrow	RB
Pied Wagtail	RB	Tree Sparrow	WV

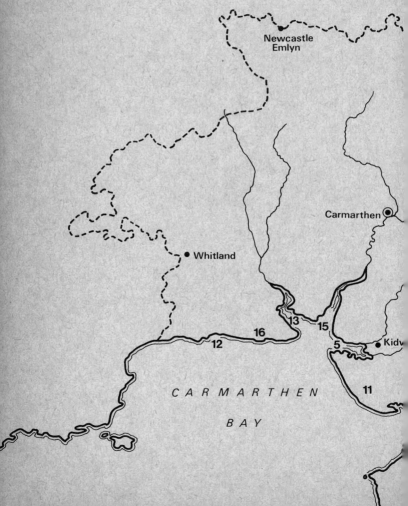

CARMARTHENSHIRE

Newcastle
Emlyn

Carmarthen

● Whitland

13
15
16
12
5
● Kidv

11

CARMARTHEN

BAY

Lampeter

10

14

Llandovery

Llandeilo

9

4

Ammanford

Llanelli

7

6 3 8

0   5   10
miles

Chapter 8

Carmarthenshire

Although Carmarthen, the largest county in Wales with 920 square miles, is situated in the south-western peninsula, it has only a short sea coast of about twenty-five miles as the gull flies, between the Crunwear stream and the Loughor estuary. This is mainly a low coast of sandy beaches and muddy foreshores, backed in several places by rolling sand dune systems rich in botanical and entomological importance. There are cliffs of no great height west of Pendine and also near the mouth of the Taf. Half way along the coastline three river systems enter the Carmarthen Bay together forming a vast estuarine complex of oystercatcher-haunted cockle beds and sand banks. Inland, except for a long section on the Teifi in the north, the county boundary dividing Carmarthenshire from Breconshire, Cardiganshire, Glamorgan and Pembrokeshire straggles along more modest waterways or over the watersheds of higher ground.

One of the main features of Carmarthenshire is a broad vale extending all the way from Whitland, on the Pembrokeshire border, through Carmarthen then north-east to Llandovery and beyond. East from Carmarthen the Tywi meanders through its broad flood plain. In summer at low level it exposes gravel spits where the common sandpiper and nimble grey wagtail search out choice invertebrates. In winter, silt-laden and forboding, it washes in times of flood over the water meadows forcing lapwing and golden plover flocks to higher ground. Climb any of the roads leading up the southern flank of the valley and you will be rewarded with one of the finest views, almost aerial in its magnificence, in

south-west Wales: the valley below, a patchwork of small
fields and twisted river banks, then beyond, the hills of
north Carmarthenshire.

The uplands north-west of the vale rise to about 900
feet and are deeply dissected by narrow valleys, often
wooded like those of the Cynin, Dewi Fawr and Gronw.
North and north-east of Brechfa and the Afon Cothi the
land rises considerably higher, reaching nearly 1,700 feet
on the Breconshire border beyond Ystradffin. The highest
ground in Carmarthenshire lies more to the east where
the Carmarthen Van, the western extension of the Black
Mountains reaches 2,460 feet near Fan Foel. Deservedly
this area with its cliff line of Bannau Sir Gaer forms part
of the Brecon Beacons National Park.

Although Carmarthenshire is interlaced by rivers, both
fast flowing, and on lower ground the more leisurely,
with some like the Teifi and Tywi of considerable importance, the county is rather poorly endowed with
standing freshwater. There are few pools and lakes of any
size and those which do occur tend to be in upland
regions, only the Witchett near the coast at Pendine being
at low altitude. The much opposed new reservoir of Llyn
Brianne, built to supply the ever-increasing water requirements of Swansea and west Glamorgan has yet to be
evaluated as a site for waterfowl.

Early man found the lowland area west from Carmarthen an ideal route, as his successors do at the present
time, to Pembrokeshire and the Irish Sea. There are
many traces of his presence in this region with standing
and inscribed stones, one of the finest examples of the
latter having been transported to Carmarthen Museum.
The higher ground northwards is characterised by numerous hill forts of Iron Age man. The Romans came this

way and indeed were the first to exploit the mineral resources of Wales when they mined for gold at Dolaucothi
in north Carmarthenshire. To guard their crossing point
at the head of the Tywi estuary, they built a fort—
Moridvnvm—for here ancient routes across south-west
Wales converged, and these had to be controlled by any
occupying force. Later, in the Dark Ages this spot was
known as Caerfyrddin (Merlin's Fortress) and this in
turn became the name for the county—Sir Caerfyrddin.
Henry I built a castle at Carmarthen while the Norman
masons were also active at other strategic points like
Dryslwyn, Kidwelly and Laugharne. In 1284 virtually
all the land which now comprises Carmarthenshire was
established as a shire by Edward I, the only later addi-
tions being some small western areas in the sixteenth
century.

Carmarthenshire is mainly an agricultural county
with about 85 per cent of its surface being so devoted in
one form or another. The numerous milk churn stands
where farm lanes meet main highways, the continual
passage of bulk tankers and churn lorries to the dairies at
Carmarthen and Whitland provide ready evidence that
dairy farming is dominant. Indeed this is one of its most
important areas in Britain. On the higher ground sheep
farming takes over and afforestation particularly in the
Brechfa region, where plantations cover 6,500 hectares
(15,000 acres), is an important source of employment.

Industrial Carmarthenshire is mainly concentrated in
the south-east where the anthracite seams of the west
Glamorgan coal field penetrate to the Gwendraeth Fawr
valley. Coal was mined in the county about 1500, but it
was not until the coming of iron smelting in the latter
part of the eighteenth century that this fuel came into its

own. Llanelli, the largest town in Carmarthenshire, owed its importance initially to copper smelting, then to sheet steel and finally to tin plate factories. Other industrial towns include Ammanford and Burry Port.

The large size of the county—one prospective parliamentary candidate described it as being more like a continent than a constituency plus its small resident population of ornithologists means plenty of opportunities for adding to our knowledge of the county's avifauna. Even such exciting areas as the Taf estuary, the Pendine area and the upper reaches of the Burry Inlet (north bank) receive comparatively little attention. Inland, particularly in the north and north-west, and in the border regions adjacent to Brecon and Glamorgan, much work remains to be done before really full information is available concerning breeding birds. That exciting discoveries await the observer is evidenced by such recent events as reed warblers being discovered at several sites, while other possible species to be looked for in suitable areas include the long-eared owl and lesser whitethroat. The late summer gatherings of terns in Carmarthen Bay are only now being documented, while the large autum/winter flock of common scoter in the same area is of international importance.

Information

County Avifaunas
Barker, T. W., *Handbook of the Natural History of Car-*

marthenshire (Carmarthen, 1905). This contains the first
list of Carmarthenshire birds.
Ingram, Geoffrey C. S., and Salmon, H. Morrey, *A Hand
List of the Birds of Carmarthenshire* (Haverfordwest, 1954).
   Much new information on the birds of Carmarthenshire has been gathered during the two decades since the
publication of this work. This, in amalgamation with the
previously published records, forms the basis of a new
avifauna now in the course of preparation by D. H. V.
Roberts, the County Bird Recorder.

Bird Report
No county bird report is available, but a joint report with
Cardiganshire and Pembrokeshire, known as the *Dyfed
Bird Report*, is published by the West Wales Naturalists'
Trust, price 20p.

County Bird Recorder
D. H. V. Roberts, Gwynfryn C.P. School, Pontiets,
Llanelli.

Ornithological Society
No society as such, but the West Wales Naturalists' Trust
(see Naturalists' Trust) has two active branches in the
county which arrange varied programmes of lectures
and field meetings, of which many have an ornithological
interest.

Naturalists' Trust
The West Wales Naturalists' Trust (see also Ornitho-
logical Society) covers the counties of Cardiganshire,
Carmarthenshire and Pembrokeshire. Formerly the West

Wales Field Society it changed to a Trust in 1961 and now leases two Reserves in the county. An important development initiated by the Carmarthenshire Branch of the Trust has been the Farm Nature Reserve, where the Trust advises and assists farmers in the maintenance of agricultural land of natural history interest. Members receive the quarterly Trust bulletin and the journal *Nature in Wales*, while there are frequent lectures and field meetings. Subscription £2.00 (adults), 50p (children and students). Hon. Gen. Sec. Dillwyn Miles, 4 Victoria Place, Haverfordwest, Pembs.

Royal Society for the Protection of Birds Representative
J. Humphrey, Troedrhiwgelynen, Rhandirmwyn, Llandovery, Carms.

British Trust for Ornithology Representative
As for County Bird Recorder.

Tourist Information
Wales Tourist Board Office, Guildhall Square, Carmarthen. Brecon Beacons National Park Information Office, 8 Broad Street, Llandovery.

1. BISHOP'S POND, ABERGWILI SN4420: This oxbow lake near Carmarthen is accessible by a footpath from the A40 at SN443210.
   Small numbers of mallard, teal and wigeon winter here while both whooper and Bewick's swans are seen almost annually. Redstarts are seen in summer at this their most southerly location in Carmarthenshire.

2. CARMARTHEN BAY POWER STATION SN4600: The warm

water outfalls from the station are proving increasingly attractive to birds such as terns and gulls making this a site not to be missed by the ornithologist. This is also one of the best areas on the north side of the Burry Inlet (see Glamorgan) to watch birds. Common, Arctic and Sandwich terns are regularly seen here while on autumn passage; rarer visitors have included roseate tern, little and Sabine's gull. Up to 400 turnstone may be seen along the shoreline with small numbers spending the summer here. More occasional waders have included purple sandpiper, little stint and curlew sandpiper. Great northern and red-throated divers, great crested grebe with duck like the eider and red-breasted merganser which occur on the Burry Inlet, occasionally enter the harbours of Burry Port and Pembrey, so that these sites should also be included in the itinerary of anyone visiting this area.

3. DINAS SN7846: An area of some 49 hectares (120 acres) rising to over 1,000 feet has been a reserve of the Royal Society for the Protection of Birds since 1963. Sessile oak is the predominant tree of the area and the reserve is bounded on two sides by the Tywi in its turbulent infancy. A Nature Trail extends over a circuit of a mile and a half from the entrance near Ystradffin. Summer visitors breeding on the reserve include ring ouzel, redstart, wood warbler and pied flycatcher, while along the river common sandpiper, dipper and grey wagtail may be seen. Although kites do not nest on the reserve, they occasionally soar overhead, but the raptor more likely to be encountered is the buzzard.

A Nature Trail leaflet is available from the R.S.P.B. post at the entrance.

4. DRYSLWYN SN5620: The Tywi water meadows at Dryslwyn are one of the most important inland wildfowl wintering grounds in south-west Wales. Although the land is privately owned and the shooting rights are let, good views of both geese and duck may be obtained from the B4300 which follows the south bank from Carmarthen to Llandeilo. Even if the birds are not visible, the journey along the almost deserted road, in contrast to the busy A40 a mile away on the north bank, is something to be savoured. Most winters at least one field meeting is arranged by sections of the West Wales Naturalists' Trust, so that there are opportunities for members to walk the disused railway line to watch the flocks at relatively close quarters. The main interest centres around the white-fronted geese (the European form *Anser a. albifrons*) which winter there; numbers sometimes reach 2,000, though about 1,000 seems more normal. Wigeon are also numerous, flocks of up to 3,000 strong having been recorded. Smaller numbers of mallard and teal frequent the meadows as do parties of shoveler and pintail. Flocks of lapwing, golden plover and curlew usually number some hundreds, while rarer visitors have included lesser white-fronted goose, pink-footed goose, barnacle goose, red kite, hen harrier, grey plover and great grey shrike.

5. GWENDRAETH ESTUARY SN3506 TO 3906: The rivers Gwendraeth Fach and Gwendraeth Fawr converge near the ancient harbour of Kidwelly, whose ruined thirteenth-century castle is all that reminds the traveller of the town's former importance. From just below Kidwelly the estuary extends some two and a half miles before merging, together with those of the Taf and Tywi, into Carmarthen Bay. Towyn Burrows form the southern shore;

some 2,025 hectares (5,000 acres) in extent, this is one of the last great coastal wildernesses remaining in Wales. Perhaps the only reason for this situation being the various service activities which have taken place over the past forty years (part is still a bombing range), which have greatly restricted public access. While such restrictions have ensured the high botanical importance of the dunes and saltings, the military disturbance and afforestation in some parts has at least been partly detrimental to the avifauna, chiefly white-fronted geese; up to 500 wintered at one time, but now are rarely seen. Nowadays the visitor seeking birds on the Gwendraeth works the north side of the estuary; this is easily accessible from the minor road that runs from Ferryside to Kidwelly via the hamlet of Tan-y-lan SN374076. The best point is probably Salmon Scar Point where the Gwendraeth meets the Tywi and this is accessible from the road at SN365078.

Oystercatchers and curlew are typical waders with mallard, wigeon and shelduck typical wildfowl which occur on the estuary. Turnstones are practically resident at Salmon Scar Point. Eider from the Burry Inlet flock sometimes move into the Gwendraeth. Velvet scoter, spotted redshank and purple sandpiper are more sporadic visitors to this area.

6. GWENFFRWD SN7546: This reserve of the Royal Society for the Protection of Birds is situated about ten miles north of Llandovery. Covering some 446 hectares (1,100 acres) near the confluence of the Gwenffrwd and Tywi valleys there is a range of habitats from hanging oak woods to moorland rising to 1,343 feet at Cefn Gwenffrwd. Travel north from Llandovery along unclassified roads to the village of Rhandirmwyn and then follow

the Pumpsaint road which keeps to the west flank of the Gwenffrwd valley. The Reserve is open Mondays, Wednesdays and Saturdays, mid-April to August inclusive. Permits (50p, 25p for children) may be obtained from the Reserves Department, Royal Society for the Protection of Birds, The Lodge, Sandy, Beds.

Birds which may be observed at the reserve include buzzard, red kite, merlin, common sandpiper, short-eared owl, dipper, ring ouzel, redstart, wood warbler and pied flycatcher. In 1972 pied flycatchers occupied 119 of the 227 nest boxes on the reserve. Occasional visitors to the area include hen harrier, peregrine (it once bred) and black grouse; among rare species recorded, honey buzzard and hobby are outstanding.

7. LLANELLI ss5099: Not at first sight an ideal bird-watching haunt, but close to this, the largest town in Carmarthenshire, are several interesting areas at present little watched. The upper reaches of the Burry Inlet receive little attention from the north bank, yet it is probable that similar species occur there as do on the south side (see page 201). The docks at Llanelli and the point at Penrhyn Gwyn ss515974 to the south are both excellent vantage points. On the western outskirts Stradey Woods are bisected by an unclassified road which leaves the A484 at Pwll, sn484011. To the north of the town is Swiss Valley with its twin reservoirs of Cwm Lledi, the upper pool being particularly attractive to winter wildfowl. This area is reached from the A476 at sn523037, and a permit to enter must be obtained from the West Glamorgan Water Board, 15 Maesyrhaf, Pwll, Llanelli. Detailed watching at all three sites is most desirable and here are opportunities for ornithologists in east Car-

marthenshire to increase our knowledge of this little
known region.

8. LLYN BRIANNE SN8049: This deep, steep-sided reservoir
on the border with Breconshire and Cardiganshire was
completed in 1972 so it is too early to assess its value
ornithologically. The reservoir is close to the Dinas
serve (see page 140) and a scenic road follows the east
bank, eventually joining the mountain road from Aber-
gwesyn to Tregaron.

An enterprising cormorant visited the reservoir in
February 1972, one hopes that equally enterprising
ornithologists will make observations there, they may be
well rewarded.

9. LLYN Y FAN FACH SN8021: In the shadow of the
highest ground in Carmarthenshire (2,460 feet at Bannau Sir Gaer) is the small lake of Llyn y Fan Fach
(1,700 feet), drained by the Afon Sawdde which flows
seven miles westwards to join the Tywi. Above the lake
is a line of Old Red Sandstone cliffs nearly two miles in
length. Although of greatest interest to botanists for the
plants they harbour, they are nevertheless attractive to
certain birds including buzzard, peregrine, merlin, ring
ouzel and wheatear. Red grouse and golden plover occur
on the tops, the former breeding. The lake attracts common sandpiper during the summer and the occasional
pair probably breeds, but records of wildfowl are few,
probably because of the altitude and because visits by
ornithologists have been infrequent.

10. LLYN PENCARREG SN5345: A kettle hole lake near the
Teify between Llanybydder and Lampeter, which is
reached from the A485 at Pencarreg village SN535450.

Although the numbers of waterfowl occurring here are not large, it is, nevertheless, of local importance in Carmarthenshire, and in hard weather provides a refuge for birds arriving from farther east. Mallard, tufted duck and pochard breed and all are numerous in winter, while less regular visitors include goldeneye, goosander, whooper and Bewick's swans with smew and black tern particularly noteworthy occurrences. The first twite to be recorded in Carmarthenshire was seen here in January 1962.

11. PEMBREY BURROWS SN4200: (see also Gwendraeth Estuary page 141, the Towyn Burrows being the nothern section of this area.) The future of the Burrows is at present unresolved since the proposed transfer of the gunnery range from Shoeburyness was rejected at a public enquiry. The now disused Royal Ordnance Factory covers a large area and has roof-nesting herring gulls; at one time it also had a few pairs of lesser black-backed gulls. There is a large intensive poultry unit at the end of the Burrows which have considerable conifer plantations. The southern side may be approached across the golf course from Burry Port but access to the central and northern areas is restricted.

There is a large starling roost here in the winter months, but the main interest seems to be birds of prey which visit the area on passage such as Montagu's harrier, or winter here like merlin and great grey shrike. The shore has the usual estuary birds, while rare visitors in recent years have included blue-winged teal and cream-coloured courser.

12. PENDINE SN2307: The area of Carmarthen Bay off Pendine extending west to Amroth in Pembrokeshire

holds a large flock—up to 25,000 have been estimated in winter—of common scoter. Even in mid-summer small parties can usually be seen flighting low over the water. Possibly due to a lack of observers, records of other sea duck, divers and grebes are rather few, nevertheless, great northern diver, red-throated diver, great crested grebe and velvet scoter have all been noted. In late summer, parties of migrating terns—common, Arctic, little and Sandwich—gather in the bay at times fishing close inshore off the beach. The cliffs west from Pendine to Ragwen Point sn2207 have a small number of breeding herring gulls, while cormorants are seen ashore, though it seems, only to roost. Fulmars have prospected the cliffs since the early 1960s and now occupy a number of ledges; breeding was confirmed near Telpyn Point in 1971. Telpyn Point is an ideal place to observe seabird movements in the bay, including shearwaters and gannets, and would repay those able to make regular observations. Look for nightjars in the wooded cwms running back from the coast.

13. TAF ESTUARY SN3010 TO 3208: The estuary downstream from Laugharne is important for wildfowl and waders, and is best viewed during periods of neap tides, particularly following high water. There are two main access points, both on the west bank. A footpath runs south from opposite Laugharne Castle, along the estuary or through the woods, but later along a seawall which one can follow for about one and a half miles to Ginst Point sn325081. When the Ministry of Defence Proof and Experimental Establishment at Laugharne Burrows is engaged in firing, red flags indicate that entry as far as the Point is prohibited. Nevertheless, good view

of the estuary may be obtained from the seawall nearer Laugharne. At weekends and in the evenings it is generally possible to drive to Ginst Point by following the unclassified road from SN287096 on the A4066 west of Laugharne. Once at the Point a visitor is advised to move up river and, if necessary, walk out across the *Spartina* saltings and cockle beds to the water's edge. Caution should be exercised when the tide is rising as the many channels fill quickly and one could easily become trapped.

Large numbers of oystercatchers feed on the cockle beds throughout the winter months. Other waders which appear in good numbers include dunlin, ringed plover and redshank, the latter seeming to be especially frequent in the narrower muddy section near to Laugharne. Shelduck are present virtually throughout the year, while during the winter mallard and teal are especially numerous. There are also small numbers of other duck like wigeon, pintail, shoveler, goldeneye and red-breasted merganser, the latter lingering well into the spring and may possibly breed shortly. Cormorants, probably from the large colony on St Margaret's Island, Pembrokeshire, can always be seen feeding in the estuary, while some roost on the cliffs below Craig Ddu SN3210 and on the sand banks at Ginst Point. Unusual visitors recorded on or close to the Taf estuary have included bittern, spoonbill, surf scoter, Bewick's swan, Montagu's harrier and avocet. A snow goose in September 1972 was probably an escape.

14. TALLEY LAKES SN6333: Just to the north of the village of Talley SN635320 are two small lakes which may be seen either from the B4302 Llanbyther to Llandeilo road,

or from an unclassified road from Talley which joins the
B4302 just north of the lakes. Although small they are one
of the few areas of open fresh water in north-west Carmarthenshire and, as a private bird sanctuary prove most
attractive to wildfowl.

The lakes are a breeding place for great crested grebe,
mallard, coot, and quite possibly tufted duck, pochard
and little grebe. Winter visitors include goldeneye, goosander and wild swans. The pied flycatchers which breed
nearby are at the southerly edge of their breeding range
in Carmarthenshire. Black grouse breed in the coniferous
plantations with red grouse on the hill tops and there is
always a chance of seeing a passing red kite.

15. TYWI ESTUARY SN3713 TO 3509: This, the largest of
the Carmarthenshire estuaries, extends some fifteen
meandering miles southwards to the sea from a point two
miles above Carmarthen. The tortuous upper reaches are
extremely narrow with steep high banks having only
small numbers of waders together with the occasional
heron or pair of shelduck. Visitors are advised to concen-
trate on the lower section downstream from near the
saltings of Morfa Uchaf SN3712. At low tide wide expanses
of sand and mud flats are exposed which attract wader
flocks. The two small estuary-side towns, Llanstephan on
the west bank and Ferryside on the east with their approach roads provide numerous access points.

There is a winter flock of about 150 wigeon, while
other regular visitors include great crested grebe, great
northern diver, curlew, redshank and dunlin, with occasional greenshank, spotted redshank and ruff.

16. WITCHETT SN2807: Although access to the pool is restricted, due to the presence of a Ministry of Defence

Proof and Experimental range on Laugharne Burrows, occasional organised parties of naturalists, usually members of the West Wales Naturalists' Trust, make arrangements with the range commandant to visit during the winter months. The reed fringed pool which can be viewed from vantage points on the surrounding dunes is probably the most important area of fresh water in the county. Although observations in recent years have been sporadic, many years of watching between the two world wars by the late J. F. Thomas of Laugharne indicated its true potential. Should the range ever be closed, then the Witchett along with its surrounding reed beds, dune slacks and scrub must surely be declared a Nature Reserve.

Black-headed gulls bred at the pool in the past, but now are only visitors, however it is for duck and other water birds that the main interest lies. Resident breeders in recent years include great crested and little grebe, teal and pochard. Reed warblers were discovered nesting in 1971, so extending their known range farther west in Wales than previously thought. Birds possibly breeding at the pool include shoveler, tufted duck, water rail, oystercatcher and redshank. In winter, mixed flocks of duck usually number over 100 while unusual visitors have included red-throated diver, bittern, gadwall, hen harrier and great grey shrike.

Check list

RB   Resident Breeder   MB   Migrant Breeder
WV   Winter Visitor   PV   Passage Visitor
                    V   Vagrant

Great Northern Diver	WV	Smew	V
Red-throated Diver	WV	Shelduck	RB
Great Crested Grebe	RB	Greylag Goose	V
Little Grebe	RB	White-fronted Goose	WV
Fulmar	RB	Pink-footed Goose	V
Manx Shearwater	PV	Brent Goose	V
British Storm Petrel	V	Barnacle Goose	V
Gannet	PV	Canada Goose	V
Cormorant	PV	Mute Swan	RB
Shag	PV	Whooper Swan	WV
Grey Heron	RB	Bewick's Swan	WV
Bittern	V	Buzzard	RB
Mallard	RB	Sparrowhawk	RB
Teal	WV	Red Kite	RB
	Has bred	Hen Harrier	WV
Garganey	V	Montagu's Harrier	PV
Gadwall	WV	Peregrine	WV
Wigeon	WV	Merlin	RB
Pintail	WV	Kestrel	RB
Shoveler	WV	Red Grouse	RB
Scaup	WV	Black Grouse	RB
Tufted Duck	WV	Partridge	RB
	Has bred	Quail	V
Pochard	WV	Pheasant	RB
	Has bred	Water Rail	RB
Goldeneye	WV	Corncrake	MB
Long-tailed Duck	V	Moorhen	RB
Velvet Scoter	V	Coot	RB
Common Scoter	WV	Oystercatcher	WV
Eider	WV		Has bred
Red-breasted Merganser		Lapwing	RB
	WV	Ringed Plover	WV
Goosander	WV	Grey Plover	WV

Golden Plover	WV	Common Tern	PV
Turnstone	WV	Arctic Tern	PV
Snipe	RB	Little Tern	PV
Jack Snipe	WV	Sandwich Tern	PV
Woodcock	RB	Razorbill	PV
Curlew	RB	Guillemot	PV
Whimbrel	PV	Puffin	V
Black-tailed Godwit	PV	Stock Dove	RB
Bar-tailed Godwit	PV	Woodpigeon	RB
Green Sandpiper	PV	Turtle Dove	PV
Common Sandpiper	MB	Collared Dove	RB
Redshank	WV	Cuckoo	MB
	Has bred	Barn Owl	RB
Spotted Redshank	V	Little Owl	RB
Greenshank	PV	Tawny Owl	RB
Knot	WV	Long-eared Owl	V
Purple Sandpiper	V	Short-eared Owl	RB
Little Stint	PV	Nightjar	PV
Dunlin	WV		May breed
Curlew Sandpiper	V	Swift	MB
Sanderling	PV	Kingfisher	RB
Ruff	V	Hoopoe	V
Great Black-backed Gull		Green Woodpecker	RB
	PV	Great Spotted Wood-	
Lesser Black-backed Gull		pecker	RB
	PV	Lesser Spotted Wood-	
	Has bred	pecker	RB
Herring Gull	RB	Woodlark	V
Common Gull	WV		May breed
Little Gull	V	Skylark	RB
Black-headed Gull	RB	Swallow	MB
Kittiwake	PV	House Martin	MB
Black Tern	PV	Sand Martin	MB

Raven	RB	Garden Warbler	MB
Carrion Crow	RB	Whitethroat	MB
Rook	RB	Lesser Whitethroat	MB
Jackdaw	RB	Willow Warbler	MB
Magpie	RB	Chiffchaff	MB
Jay	RB	Wood Warbler	MB
Great Tit	RB	Goldcrest	RB
Blue Tit	RB	Spotted Flycatcher	MB
Coal Tit	RB	Pied Flycatcher	MB
Marsh Tit	RB	Dunnock	RB
Willow Tit	RB	Meadow Pipit	RB
Long-tailed Tit	RB	Tree Pipit	MB
Nuthatch	RB	Rock Pipit	RB
Treecreeper	RB	Pied Wagtail	RB
Wren	RB	White Wagtail	PV
Dipper	RB	Grey Wagtail	RB
Mistle Thrush	RB	Yellow Wagtail	MB
Fieldfare	WV	Waxwing	V
Song Thrush	RB	Great Grey Shrike	WV
Redwing	WV	Starling	RB
Ring Ouzel	MB	Hawfinch	V
Blackbird	RB	Greenfinch	RB
Wheatear	MB	Goldfinch	RB
Stonechat	RB	Siskin	RB
Whinchat	MB	Linnet	RB
Redstart	MB	Twite	V
Black Redstart	V	Redpoll	RB
Nightingale	V	Bullfinch	RB
Robin	RB	Crossbill	V
Grasshopper Warbler	MB	Chaffinch	RB
Reed Warbler	MB	Brambling	WV
Sedge Warbler	MB	Corn Bunting	V
Blackcap	MB	Yellowhammer	RB

Reed Bunting	RB	House Sparrow	RB
Snow Bunting	V	Tree Sparrow	RB

DENBIGHSHIRE

6

Colwyn
Bay   4

Llanwrst

Denbigh ●

5

2

● Ruthin

3

9

Wrexham ◉

8

Llangollen ●

1

7

0   5   10
 miles

Chapter 9

Denbighshire

Although a large county occupying a central position in North Wales, Denbighshire has but a short coastline of some twelve miles bounded by Liverpool Bay. With its low shore lands and extensive sands this is very much an area for the holidaymaker; numerous caravan and camping sites have been established as well as larger resorts like Abergele and Colwyn Bay. Little Terns once nested on the beaches but now disturbance is too great even for this determined seabird, so that Denbighshire's few seabird colonies are all away from the coast. Black-headed gulls nest beside moorland pools, but more interesting are the fulmars and herring gulls which occupy the cliffs—some man-made by quarrying—on the limestone escarpment within a mile or two of the coast.

The western boundary leaves the coast at Penrhyn Bay, cutting across the Llandudno peninsula to the river Conway which is followed almost to its source on the Migneint, aptly described as 'one of the boggiest stretches of high moorland in Wales'. From here it wends eastwards across high ground and the upper reaches of rivers like the Ceirw and Alwen to reach the Dee just west of Llangollen. Now the course is southwards, crossing the Berwyns to reach 2,713 feet at that most remote of spots where the borders of Denbighshire, Merioneth and Montgomeryshire meet. There are still several more miles of southern uplands to be encompassed before the Afon Tanat is crossed and the Shropshire border met. The Dee is rejoined at Chirk and from there forms a goodly sector of the eastern border, twisting and turning across the English plain to about five miles from Chester. From

here the border swings back north-west across the Clwy-
dian Range before descending into the lovely tree-fringed
Vale of Clwyd, and thence to the sea not far from the
Flintshire town of Rhyl.

Denbighshire may be divided into three main areas.
Firstly, the coastal hinterland bounded in the east by the
lowlands of the Vale of Clwyd and in the west by those of
the Conway valley. Secondly, the central moorlands extending to the very south of the county, and thirdly the
Vale of Maelor in the south-east.

Two of the most important towns are situated in
the Vale of Clwyd—Denbigh and Ruthin. The latter,
the county's main administrative centre, sits astride the
Clwyd not far south of where its valley narrows among
the lower slopes of the moorland interior. Both towns are
at strategic points on routes from England into North
Wales. The Romans had a settlement at Denbigh, and
various Welsh chieftains, among them Dafydd ap
Gruffydd, brother of the only native Prince of Wales had
fortified dwellings at both places. After Edward I had
conquered this region strong castles were built which saw
much service during the numerous Welsh uprisings, the
Wars of the Roses and the Civil War. In the latter campaign both were held at first for the King and suffered
for this later at the hands of the Parliamentarians who
left considerable sections in ruins.

The Conway valley is narrower. The lower section extending inland about thirteen miles to Betws-y-Coed consists of winter-flooded water meadows up to a mile wide,
through which the river, tidal to Llanwrst, meanders.
This small town is superbly situated for exploring the
moorland interior of west Denbigh or for those wishing
to stray across the border into Caernarvonshire and the

Snowdonia National Park. It was about here in 954 that the warring princes of North and South Wales met in battle. Farther downstream where the estuary begins to widen to the sea is the National Trust property of Bodnant. Some 70 acres in extent the gardens, especially when the magnolia and rhododendrons are in bloom, are among the loveliest in Britain and should not be missed by the visitor to these parts, or indeed the resident.

The central moorlands of Denbighshire generally lie below the 2,000-foot contour except where they extend onto the Berwyn ridge. Unlike many other parts of inland Wales the hand of the water engineer has passed lightly with only one reservoir of any size being constructed. This is the Alwen on Mynydd Hiraethog completed in 1921 in order to supply water to Birkenhead. Two spots of particular interest should be sought by the traveller in the southern part of the county. For those with historical inclinations Owain Glyndwr had a wooden castle at Sycharth, not far from Llansilan. This was burnt in 1403 by an English raiding party led by the future Henry V; the motte still remains, as do hollows where there were once ponds supplying the garrison with fish, and the moat which proved of no avail against the final attackers. A little farther east in the Rhaeadr valley a series of waterfalls cascade for about 240 feet and are the highest in southern Britain.

The most rugged of the moorland areas is that north of the Dee near Llangollen. The Horseshoe Pass is a favourite tourist attraction in summer and a hazard to motorists in winter when it is one of the first main roads in North Wales to be closed because of snow and ice. The Dee valley about Llangollen is narrow but engineers have found room for two trunk roads, a railway, and an extension of the Shropshire Union Canal. The latter is of especial interest where it crosses from the southern to the northern bank at Pont Cysyllt on a splendid sandstone aqueduct just over 1,000 feet long and at its highest point 120 feet above the rock-split Dee.

The Dee valley begins to widen north-east of Chirk and within a mile or two the countryside becomes very English in character; a rich land of dairy farming and stock raising, this is the Vale of Maelor. Indeed most of Denbighshire is an agricultural county, with sheep and forestry on the hill lands. Industry of any note is confined to the Wrexham area fringing the Vale of Maelor and the hill lands farther west. Coal, iron, lead and limestone have all been quarried here, though neither of the metals are sought these days. This in turn led to other industrial developments so that Wrexham is the largest town in North Wales and together with its associated communities has a population of nearly 100,000.

Most ornithological observation in Denbighshire seems to be concentrated towards the northern coastal zone, in particular Colwyn Bay with its wildfowl stocks and the Conway and Clwyd estuaries. The upland areas are often overlooked though it is here that discoveries await the keen observer—certainly we require to know more concerning local species like the golden plover and dunlin and even common species like the black-headed gull. The southern valleys are relatively little known, and the possibility that hawfinches bred in the Tanat in 1971 seems to indicate the sort of surprises that await unveiling. The Vale of Maelor, in a strictly Welsh context, is a restricted habitat, certainly the distribution there of birds like the yellow wagtail and corn bunting is of special importance.

Information

County Avifaunas
Forrest, H. E., *The Vertebrate Fauna of North Wales* (London, 1907). This, together with a supplement published in 1919, is the only avifauna available, though is long out of date.

Bird Report
Records of birds in Denbighshire are published annually in the *Cambrian Bird Report* by the Cambrian Ornithological Society. Price 30p plus postage from the Hon. Sec.

County Bird Recorder
Dr P. J. Dare, Tan-yr-allt, Trefriw, Caerns.

Ornithological Society
The Cambrian Ornithological Society covers the counties of Anglesey, Caernarvonshire, Denbighshire and Merioneth. Indoor meetings are held during the winter months at Bangor, Colwyn Bay and Llandudno. Field meetings are arranged throughout the year, mainly in the Society's area, but occasionally farther afield. Special help is available for beginners attending meetings. Besides the Cambrian Bird Report a cyclostyled newsletter is circulated to members five times a year. Subscription £1.00 per annum for adults, 50p for juniors. Hon. Sec. E. G. Griffiths, Longleat House, Longleat Avenue, Craigside, Llandudno, Caerns.

Naturalists' Trust
The North Wales Naturalists' Trust covers the counties of
Anglesey, Caernarvonshire, Denbighshire, Flintshire,
Merioneth and Montgomeryshire. Founded in 1963 the
Trust at the moment has only one reserve in Denbigh-
shire, 10 acres of mixed hardwoods in the Vale of Clwyd
near Ruthin. There are two active branches of the Trust
in Denbighshire, one in the Vale of Clwyd, the other at
Wrexham. Hon. Gen. Sec. Mrs M. J. Morgan, 154 High
Street, Bangor. Subscription £2.00 per annum, students
£1.00, juniors 50p.

British Trust for Ornithology Representative
J. M. Harrop, Ty Derwen, Llanfair, D.C., Ruthin.

Royal Society for the Protection of Birds Representative
W. G. Roberts, Ty'r Ysgol, Tan-y-fron, Llansannan,
Denbigh.

Tourist Information
The Official Guide is available (price 15p) from the
Clerk's Department, County Offices, Ruthin. There is an
Information Centre of the Snowdonia National Park in
Llanrwst.

1. CEIRIOG VALLEY SJ2037: The Afon Ceiriog rises in the
Berwyns and runs east to join the Dee near Chirk, forming for part of its course the boundary with Shropshire.
The B4500 follows the river from Chirk to Llanarmon
Dyffryn Ceiriog SJ158328, beyond which an unclassified
road and then tracks lead on to the Berwyns and across
into Merioneth. North of the valley, and best reached
from Glyn Ceiriog, is the Ceiriog Forest area.

   Typical valley birds include kingfisher, dipper, redstart, wood warbler, pied flycatcher and grey wagtail,
while the forestry areas and open moorland have attracted both red and black grouse, long-eared and short-
eared owls.

2. CLOCAENOG FOREST SJ0152: On the hills south-west of
Ruthin lies one of the largest forestry areas in North
Wales, the Clocaenog Forest 6,000 hectares (15,000
acres). The B5105 from Ruthin to Cerrigydrudion skirts
the southern edge of the forest and from this a number of
unclassified roads and forest tracks run north into the
plantations, providing easy access.
   This area is very good for black grouse while other
species include buzzard, sparrowhawk, red grouse, tawny
owl, great spotted woodpecker, raven, whinchat, redstart, tree pipit and redpoll.

3. LLYN GWERYD SJ1755: This lake lies at nearly 1,100 feet
towards the southern end of the Clwyd Hills. The Offa's
Dyke walk passes close by, or the unclassified road which
leaves the B5431 at SJ183526, about three miles south of
Llanarmon-yn-Ial, takes one to the southern edge of the
plantations which partly surround the lake.
   There is a black-headed gull colony, and great crested
grebe, mallard, teal and tufted duck may also be seen at
the lake.

4. LLANDDULAS QUARRIES SH8978: These quarries, either
side of the A55 between Llanddulas and Colwyn Bay, are
the sites of one of the few seabird colonies in Denbighshire (the others are also in quarries).
   The most numerous species present is the herring gull,

but there are also small numbers of lesser black-backed gulls and about fifty pairs of fulmars, the latter nesting above the Dulas valley at SH908766.

5. MYNYDD HIRAETHOG SH9256: About eight miles south-west of Denbigh is a large area of moorland, boggy in places with a number of pools and lakes, together with the conifer-surrounded Alwen Reservoir. Both the A543 and B4501 from Denbigh cross the moors and there are several unclassified roads and tracks.

Dunlin nest in this area and small though fluctuating numbers of black-headed gulls breed at some of the pools. Other species include great crested grebe, teal, merlin, red grouse, curlew, short-eared owl, ring ouzel, whinchat and wheatear.

6. RHOS-ON-SEA SH8481: This point at the western side of Colwyn Bay is the best vantage point for observing autumn seabird passage in this area and for watching the winter congregations of wildfowl in the Bay.

Species noted here include red-throated diver, great crested grebe, Manx shearwater, common scoter, oyster-catcher, redshank, knot, purple sandpiper, Arctic skua and all our breeding terns.
Machin, E. H., 'Winter Counts of Birds at Rhos Point, Denbighshire', Cambrian Orn. Soc. Rep. (1965).

7. TANAT VALLEY SJ1524: The Afon Tanat, a tributary of the Severn runs through the most southerly sector of Denbighshire. The B4396 which leaves the A495 about six miles west of Oswestry follows the north bank of the river.

Birds which may be seen in this region include common sandpiper, buzzard, kingfisher, dipper, raven, red-start, wood warbler and pied flycatcher. The hawfinch, a bird of extremely local distribution in Wales probably bred in the valley in 1971 and this warrants further investigation.

8. WORLD'S END MOORS SJ2349: North of Llangollen and the Dee Valley is an extensive area of moorland rising to 1,844 feet at Cyrn y Brain. The western edge of the moors is skirted by the A542 through the famous Horseshoe Pass; however, a better route for the ornithologist is to leave Llangollen by the unclassified road at SJ215423 near the Dee Bridge. This road runs beneath the crags to World's End and thence across the moors to Minera about four miles from Wrexham. For several years the North Wales Naturalists' Trust, in conjunction with Shell, have operated a Nature Trail at World's End during June and July. Leaflets are available from Shell garages in the area or from the Trust Office.

This is one of the best moors in Wales for red grouse, while other notable species include short-eared owl, raven and ring ouzel.

9. WREXHAM GRAVEL PITS SJ3453: On the edge of the Dee Valley, a wide area of rich agricultural land close to the northern outskirts of Wrexham includes a small area of gravel pits. These are best seen from the unclassified road which leaves the A483 at SJ337518 in Acton Park and continues through Little Acton to Gresford.

Canada geese occasionally nest in this area which is the only location in Denbighshire for yellow wagtail and corn bunting. It certainly warrants detailed watching.

Check list

RB	Resident Breeder	MB	Migrant Breeder
WV	Winter Visitor	PV	Passage Visitor
	V	Vagrant	

Great Northern Diver	V	Red-breasted Merganser	
Red-throated Diver	WV		WV
Great Crested Grebe	RB	Goosander	V
Little Grebe	RB	Shelduck	RB
Fulmar	RB	Greylag Goose	V
Manx Shearwater	PV	White-fronted Goose	WV
British Storm Petrel	PV	Canada Goose	WV
Leach's Petrel	V	Mute Swan	RB
Gannet	PV	Whooper Swan	WV
Cormorant	PV	Bewick's Swan	WV
Shag	PV	Buzzard	RB
Grey Heron	RB	Sparrowhawk	RB
Mallard	RB	Hen Harrier	RB
Teal	RB	Peregrine	PV
Gadwall	V	Merlin	RB
Wigeon	WV	Kestrel	RB
Pintail	WV	Red Grouse	RB
Shoveler	WV	Black Grouse	RB
Scaup	V	Partridge	RB
Tufted Duck	WV	Quail	PV
Pochard	WV		Has bred
Goldeneye	WV	Pheasant	RB
Long-tailed Duck	WV	Water Rail	WV
Velvet Scoter	V		Has bred
Common Scoter	WV	Corncrake	PV
Eider	V	Moorhen	RB

Coot	RB	Herring Gull	RB
Oystercatcher	RB	Common Gull	WV
Lapwing	RB	Black-headed Gull	RB
Ringed Plover	RB	Kittiwake	PV
Grey Plover	WV	Black Tern	V
Golden Plover	RB	Common Tern	PV
Turnstone	WV	Arctic Tern	PV
Snipe	RB	Roseate Tern	V
Jack Snipe	WV	Little Tern	PV
Woodcock	RB	Sandwich Tern	PV
Curlew	RB	Razorbill	WV
Whimbrel	PV	Guillemot	WV
Black-tailed Godwit	PV	Puffin	PV
Bar-tailed Godwit	PV	Stock Dove	RB
Green Sandpiper	PV	Woodpigeon	RB
Has wintered		Turtle Dove	MB
Wood Sandpiper	V	Collared Dove	RB
Common Sandpiper	MB	Cuckoo	MB
Redshank	WV	Barn Owl	RB
Has bred		Little Owl	RB
Spotted Redshank	V	Tawny Owl	RB
Greenshank	PV	Short-eared Owl	RB
Knot	WV	Nightjar	MB
Purple Sandpiper	WV	Swift	MB
Dunlin	WV	Kingfisher	RB
Has bred		Green Woodpecker	RB
Sanderling	PV	Great Spotted Wood-	
Great Skua	V	pecker	RB
Arctic Skua	PV	Lesser Spotted Wood-	
Great Black-backed Gull		pecker	RB
	WV	Skylark	RB
Lesser Black-backed Gull		Swallow	MB
	MB	House Martin	MB

Sand Martin	MB	Garden Warbler	MB
Raven	RB	Whitethroat	MB
Carrion Crow	RB	Lesser Whitethroat	MB
Rook	RB	Willow Warbler	MB
Jackdaw	RB	Chiffchaff	MB
Magpie	RB	Wood Warbler	MB
Jay	RB	Goldcrest	RB
Chough	RB	Spotted Flycatcher	MB
Great Tit	RB	Pied Flycatcher	MB
Blue Tit	RB	Dunnock	RB
Coal Tit	RB	Meadow Pipit	RB
Marsh Tit	RB	Tree Pipit	MB
Willow Tit	RB	Rock Pipit	WV
Long-tailed Tit	RB	Pied Wagtail	RB
Nuthatch	RB	White Wagtail	PV
Treecreeper	RB	Grey Wagtail	RB
Wren	RB	Yellow Wagtail	MB
Dipper	RB	Starling	RB
Mistle Thrush	RB	Hawfinch	RB
Fieldfare	WV	Greenfinch	RB
Song Thrush	RB	Goldfinch	RB
Redwing	WV	Siskin	WV
Ring Ouzel	MB	Linnet	RB
Blackbird	RB	Redpoll	RB
Wheatear	MB	Bullfinch	RB
Stonechat	RB	Chaffinch	RB
Whinchat	MB	Brambling	WV
Redstart	MB	Yellowhammer	RB
Black Redstart	V	Corn Bunting	RB
Robin	RB	Reed Bunting	RB
Grasshopper Warbler	MB	House Sparrow	RB
Sedge Warbler	MB	Tree Sparrow	RB
Blackcap	MB		

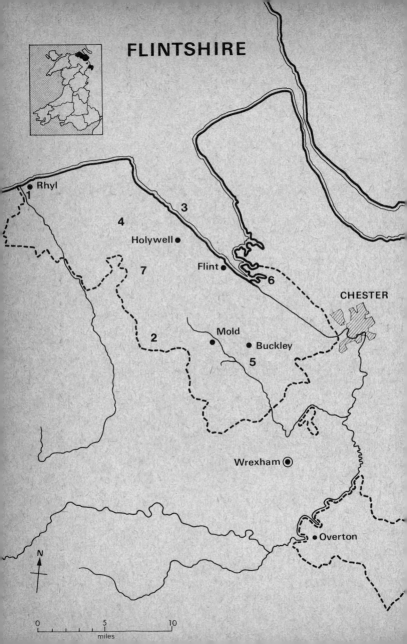

FLINTSHIRE

- Rhyl
- 1
- 3
- 4
- Holywell •
- 7
- Flint •
- 6
- CHESTER
- 2
- Mold •
- Buckley •
- 5
- Wrexham ◉
- Overton •

N

0   5   10
miles

Chapter 10

Flintshire

Flintshire, the smallest county in Wales with 255 square miles, lies in the extreme north-east of the Principality, and indeed includes its most easterly point, a spot some two miles south-west of the Shropshire market town of Whitchurch. A curious feature of the county is its division into three sections. The largest is bounded on the north by Liverpool Bay between the holiday centres of Rhyl and Point of Air. Thence the Dee estuary, haunt of almost countless winter waders, runs south-east for nearly fifteen miles, dividing Flintshire from Cheshire. The boundary continues almost to the outskirts of Chester before the Dee is crossed and a south-westerly course pursued. At the Nant-y-Ffrith Reservoir high on the Esclusham Moors the boundary direction turns northwards again, for a while following the River Terrig, a tributary of the larger Alyn which eventually joins the Dee near Holt (Denbighshire). The Clwyd Hills are climbed to their summit—Moel Fammau (1,820 feet)—with its ruined Jubilee Tower. These same hills are followed north, the boundary intersecting Iron Age hill forts, like those of Moel Arthur and then Penycladdiau, the latter, covering 50 acres, being the largest single hill fort in the whole of Wales. Modern man has also left his mark on the uplands, though doubtless it will be less permanent than those of earlier peoples—a television station high above the Wheeler valley. The boundary descends this same valley to join the Clwyd near Broadford, though this is left after several miles to meander

overleaf – *Oystercatcher*

eastwards across the coastal plain before rejoining its
estuary a mile from the sea at Rhyl.

So much for the main section of the county. A little
way north out of Wrexham the parishes of Marford and
Hosely, close to Gresford belong to Flintshire. Four miles
south-east of Wrexham is the larger of the two detached
sections, the Hundred of Maelor with the village of Overton at its centre. What, one is intrigued to ask, is responsible for this curious division, without parallel elsewhere
in the United Kingdom? The two detached sections were
Norman Marcher Lordships before Edward I established
the present main county of Flintshire by his Statute of
Rhuddlan in 1284, and they remained separate entities
until transferred by a Special Act of Henry VIII to the
main county.

Flintshire is a hilly county. The Clwyd hills, a western
backbone of Silurian sandstone extend for over twenty
miles between Prestatyn and their most southerly peak,
Moel y Waun (1,351 feet), near the hamlet of Llandegla.
To the east and four miles inland from the Dee, part of
the limestone arc which encompasses North Wales forms
the Halkyn Mountain, though its highest point is a bare
964 feet. This region was once the most important lead-
producing region in Wales. The now silent subterranean
galleries are mostly flooded, while above ground the
spoil heaps and old pit head workings are a rich hunting
ground for the botanist and industrial archaeologist. The
coastal plain extends up to five miles inland from Liverpool Bay along the Vale of Clwyd, though elsewhere it is
a good deal narrower. At its north-eastern point the once
fine sandhills of Point of Air are now much ruined by a
huge holiday encampment, though this remains a fine
vantage point for those seeking waders on the Dee, and

in summer a few pairs of little terns manage to nest.

The two detached sections are unlike the main county. The smaller, that north of Wrexham, lies on the edge of the Dee plain. The Hundred of Maelor is on slightly higher ground to the east of the Dee and is typically English in character. Interesting features of this area are the meres at Hanmer and Llyn Bedydd, smaller versions of those near the Shropshire town of Ellsmere to the south-west. The great peat moss of Whixall is now eroded by peat digging, more for use by the gardener than for fuel. Crossing the moss and forming part of the boundary with Shropshire is the Llangollen Branch of the Shropshire Union Canal, a favourite boating holiday area.

The Flintshire county handbook describes the county as a link between old and new: 'On one side there lie the unchangeable mountains of North Wales, cradle of an ancient society and important sector of the Welsh nation. On the other side, marching along the shore of the River Dee, stretches Flintshire's industrial belt, cradle of the Industrial Revolution in North Wales.'

This industrial aspect of the county includes a wide range of manufacturing and service concerns, large as well as small. Near Point of Air man still tunnels for coal at the county's only active mine, the workings of which extend far beneath the Dee estuary. At the head of the same estuary the first steel mills came into operation at Shotton as far back as 1896; since then the plant has considerably expanded and adapted to the changes that two world wars and changing markets have dictated. Now management and workers face their biggest test, for early in 1973 it was announced that the factory is to close. Other well-known industrial undertakings include Courtaulds which have one of their largest concerns close by

the castle in Flint, chemical, paper and glass factories.
Away from the industrial region on Deeside the countryside is mainly agricultural in character; dairy farming is
predominant in the lowlands, while on the hills there is
sheep farming as well as extensive forestry plantations.

The Coat of Arms of the Flintshire County Council includes four choughs, yet it is many years since the bird
was recorded in the county and there is some doubt as to
whether it has ever nested during historical times. Although this species, one of the rarest to breed in Wales, is
absent, and despite the county's small size and lack of
certain habitats Flintshire nevertheless remains one of the
most important ornithological areas in Wales. This is
chiefly due to the Dee estuary and its associated marsh-

Little Tern

lands and lagoons where most bird-watching is carried out in Flintshire. In view of possible changes to the Dee, should road crossings be constructed, it is important that great efforts be made to learn all about the waders and wildfowl which use this area. The knowledge gained can then be applied to establish reserves if such developments take place affecting the rich mud and sand bank feeding zones. At Shotton Pools the example of what can be achieved when a large landowner—in this case the British Steel Corporation—and an enthusiastic group of amateur ornithologists—the Merseyside Ringing Group —work together to establish and manage a Nature Reserve, is something which deserves the widest recognition and emulation. On the sea coast near Prestatyn the Flintshire Ornithologists Society and the North Wales Naturalists' Trust co-operate to provide protection for one of the few colonies of little terns surviving in Wales. Without question it is only by their long hours of vigil that this small group of terns still flourishes. Flintshire, then, is very active ornithologically, but it is a pity no annual report is published, something which might be remedied if bird-watchers submitted records from inland as well as from coastal regions.

Information

County Avifaunas
Forrest, H. E., *The Vertebrate Fauna of North Wales* (London, 1907) together with the supplement published in 1919 included records from Flintshire.
Done, C., *The Birds of Flintshire* (Flint Orn. Soc., 1968).

This, the only recent avifauna for any North Wales
county was prepared by members of the Flintshire Ornithological Society under the chairmanship of C. Done.

Some Flintshire records for the 13 square miles of the
county which lie north of the River Dee between Chester
and Connah's Quay are included in: Bell, T. H., *The
Birds of Cheshire* (Altrincham, 1962).

Records for the detached Hundred of Maelor about
Overton have been included with those of Shropshire in:
Rutter, E. M., Gribble, F. C. and Pemberyon, T. W.,
A Handlist of the Birds of Shropshire (1964).

Bird Report
Despite its fine lead in respect of a modern county avifauna the Flintshire Ornithological Society does not yet
publish a Bird Report. Records for the Shotton Pools area
are included in the *Cheshire Bird Report* 25p from Dr
R. J. Raines, 34 Beryl Road, Nactorum, Birkenhead.

County Bird Recorder
R. R. Birch, 8 Thornberry Close, Saughall, Chester.

Ornithological Society
The Flintshire Ornithological Society. Mrs M. Bogguley,
1 Gareth Close, Rhyl.

Naturalists' Trust
The North Wales Naturalists' Trust covers the counties
of Anglesey, Caernarvonshire, Denbighshire, Flintshire,
Merioneth and Montgomeryshire. Founded in 1963 the
Trust owns or leases a number of reserves of which one, a
long-disused marl pit is in Flintshire. The Clwyd and
Wrexham branches of the Trust cover sections of Flint-

shire; both arrange comprehensive series of field meetings and lectures. Members receive the journal *Nature in Wales* twice a year together with their own duplicated newsletters. Subscription £1.00 per annum (adults), 50p (students), 25p (juniors). Hon. Gen. Sec. Dr W. S. Lacey, School of Plant Biology, U.C.N.W., Bangor, Caerns.

Royal Society for the Protection of Birds Representative
Not yet appointed.

British Trust for Ornithology Representative
E. J. Stokes, Glan-yr-Afon House, Brook Street, Mold.

Tourist Information
The County Handbook, price 15p is available from Flintshire County Council, Shire Hall, Mold.

1. CLWYD ESTUARY SJ0079: Rising in the Clocaenog Forest on the borders of Denbighshire and Merioneth, the River Clwyd enters the sea at Rhyl. For the last three miles of its journey it forms a narrow estuary, being tidal to just above Rhuddlan. Access is probably best from this latter point, footpaths running from the town north along the east and west banks.

The Clwyd is one of the more important of the small North Wales estuaries with maximum numbers of waders occurring in mid-winter when up to 5,000 birds gather on the mud flats. Dunlin are the most numerous wader but small numbers of all regular species—oystercatcher, curlew and redshank in particular—occur. Less common species which may also be seen on the Clwyd include spotted redshank and ruff.

2. CILCAIN RESERVOIRS SJ1664: These small reservoirs on the northern slopes of Moel Famau, (1,820 feet) the highest point on the Clwydian range in Flintshire are the only areas of open water in this section of the county. A bridleway runs to the reservoirs from Cilcain village which is reached by a maze of unclassified roads running west from Mold.

Small parties of duck—usually mallard and teal—frequent the reservoirs in winter, being joined occasionally by other species. Buzzards, merlin, red grouse and ring ouzel all breed on the Clwydian hills and there are past records of black grouse from the vicinity of Moel Famau. The reservoirs seem to be an ideal point to commence exploration of this whole upland region.

A Nature Trail commences from the car park at SJ172611 and a leaflet is available price 2p from the Forestry Commission, North Wales Office.

3. DEE ESTUARY SJ1285 TO 2873: Although Cheshire (The Wirral) forms the east bank of the Dee and Flintshire the west, I am treating the estuary as a whole, for birds seen on one shore, ignoring man's artificial boundaries, can, with but a few wing-beats, cross from one side to the other.

In the Middle Ages the Dee was navigable right up to Chester, twenty-two miles from the open sea. Since then six centuries of silting has resulted in a vast complex of sand and mud banks being uncovered as the tide recedes, while sea-borne traffic has long since moved to the nearby Mersey. As far back as ornithological records go the importance of the Dee for waders and, to a lesser extent wildfowl, has been appreciated. Some of the finest photographs of massed wader flocks have been obtained on

Hilbre Island off West Kirby (Cheshire). Since 1969 regular counts of the waders and wildfowl on the estuary have been made as part of the Birds of Estuaries Enquiry organised jointly by the British Trust for Ornithology and the Royal Society for the Protection of Birds. The results, obtained from the activities of some thirty observers show that the Dee is the third most important estuary in Britain after Morecambe Bay and the Wash.

Like all our major estuaries various schemes have been proposed for the 'development' of the Dee. All involve motorway crossings, the embankments formed producing a system of freshwater lakes which will become focal points for greatly increased leisure use of the whole region. The decision to build a barrage and roads rests largely with the Water Resources Board and their assessment of future water requirements. What will be the quality of water from the newly formed lakes, for these will no doubt become favourite roosting places for a large proportion of the gulls which inhabit north-west England? Naturalists intend to play a constructive role in any scheme involving changes in the estuary. It is hoped that some areas can be saved, while the provision of mud banks in or beside some of the newly formed lakes, and the establishment of reserve areas may go some way towards mitigation for the losses which will undoubtedly occur. Meanwhile investigations by ornithologists continue and our store of knowledge, which can be put to practical use should developments take place, increases. For those who have yet to visit the Dee the message is clear. Do so now, for once changes commence the estuary and its tens of thousands of waders will never be the same.

The vast size of the Dee—it is up to fifteen miles long and five wide—together with a substantial tidal range means that at low water a vast area of sand and mud banks are exposed over which the birds disperse. The best time for an observer to visit the area seems to be at the time of medium spring tides (27.5 to 30.0 feet. Liverpool height), when the flocks assemble on 'roosts' close to the shore. At neap tides the waders are dispersed and at extreme high tide they forsake the estuary altogether and seek roosting places in fields, mainly on the Cheshire bank.

On the Flintshire side Mostyn Bank sj1482 is an important wader feeding area and when this is covered by the tide the birds congregate at Point of Air sj1284 and at Tan Lan sj1383. An unclassified road for the former leaves the A548 at sj114834 while the latter is accessible by means of the sea wall leaving Tan Lan at sj132824. Waders from the Bagillt Bank midway up the estuary seem to 'roost' on North Flint marsh sj2374; this area is reached from the A548 just north of Flint. These are the most important wader areas on the west bank of the Dee, there are other equally important sites on the east.

The period August to May is best for waders with numbers reaching a peak of between 80,000 and 90,000 birds in November, while in most months at least 50,000 are present. The most numerous species are dunlin and knot, the numbers of both reaching about 50,000 at some times —in fact the Dee is the most important estuary in Europe for the latter species. Although the numbers of bar-tailed godwits, up to 6,000, may seem small by comparison, about half the world population winters in Britain, the Dee being a major site for this bird. Oystercatcher, lapwing, ringed plover, curlew, redshank, and sanderling all occur in numbers exceeding 1,000 at some time or other during the winter months, while less usual waders include jack snipe, green sandpiper, spotted redshank, greenshank, little stint and curlew sandpiper. Rare species which have occurred in recent years include Kentish plover, buff-breasted sandpiper and Baird's sandpiper.

4. LLYN HELYG SJ1177: This lake three miles inland from the Dee estuary at Mostyn is the most important inland freshwater habitat for birds in Flintshire. Its attractiveness is enhanced by the surrounding woodland, mainly deciduous with a small area of conifers. Leave the B5332, which runs from Rhuddlan to the A55 west of Holywell, at Tan-yr-allt crossroads, SJ123774, and follow the unclassified road west for nearly half a mile. Several tracks and footpaths may be followed through the woods to the eastern end of the lake, while a little farther on access is possible at the western end.

Llyn Helyg is the only breeding site in Flint for the great crested grebe, and two or three pairs are normally present with some over-wintering. Little grebes also breed here, as do moorhen and coot, the latter increasing dramatically in winter with flocks of up to 300 being noted. A pair or two of shelduck usually nest in the surrounding woods, as do mallard and in most years shoveler, flocks of up to eighty of the latter species having been recorded in winter. Other winter wildfowl include wigeon (160 in December 1968), scaup, tufted duck, pochard and goldeneye; less frequently, long-tailed duck, whooper and Bewick's swans are encountered.

5. PADESWOOD SJ2762: A small pool about a mile and a half south of Buckley. Leave the town on an unclassified road from SJ278640, after about a mile cross the A5118

then within a short distance the southern edge of the pool
is passed.

The pool attracts small numbers of wintering duck,
with dabbling species—mallard, teal, shoveler, and,
diving duck—tufted duck and pochard.

6. SHOTTON POOLS SJ2971: Within the perimeter of the
British Steel Corporation Shotton Works lies an interesting area of lagoons, cooling pools and reedbeds, part of
which was was declared a Nature Reserve in 1970 as a
contribution to European Conservation Year. Bird-
watchers may obtain permission to visit the Reserve and
adjacent areas by applying to the Works Relations
Manager, Shotton Works, Deeside, Flintshire, CH5 2NH.
Full access details are provided with the pass.

Since 1957 the Merseyside Ringing Group (D. Okill,
78 Woolacombe Road, Liverpool 16) have been ringing
birds at Shotton and have been closely involved with the
management of the Nature Reserve. They have planted
over three hundred trees around the pools and also introduced various plants to the area which provide food
for waterfowl. Several areas of reed have been cleared
and a hide constructed. Their most rewarding work has
undoubtedly been the provision of nesting rafts which
have attracted common terns to nest. In 1970 13 pairs
nested on the first raft; with a further two rafts in 1971
40 pairs nested, and in 1972 91 pairs which reared 152
young. This imaginative scheme which one hopes can be
adopted elsewhere, has justly received a Prince of Wales
Award. A further project which should improve this, one
of the richest ornithological areas in Wales, is to flood a
further area of marsh so creating more open shallow
water to encourage waders and surface-feeding duck.

Some forty-four species of birds breed in the Shotton Pools area, including several of restricted distribution in Wales—reed warbler, yellow wagtail and corn bunting. Other notable breeding species include little grebe, shoveler, kestrel, redshank, black-headed gull, whinchat and redpoll. Regular visitors include garganey, tufted duck, hen harrier, water rail, jack snipe, green sandpiper, spotted redshank (up to five, usually winter), black tern and short-eared owl. The following rare visitors have been noted since 1969—black-necked grebe, long-tailed duck, spotted crake, Temminck's stint, white-winged black tern, roseate tern, great grey shrike, woodchat shrike and red spotted bluethroat.

7. YSCEIFIOG SJ1471: Like Llyn Helyg this pool in a steep-sided valley below Ysceifiog hamlet is also surrounded by woodland. Situated just north of the A541 in the upper reaches of the Wheeler valley, the pool is reached by a footpath leaving the road opposite Ysceifiog Church.

Small numbers of diving duck—tufted duck, pochard and goldeneye—winter here, being joined occasionally by less common species such as goosander.

Check list

RB	Resident Breeder	MB	Migrant Breeder
WV	Winter Visitor	PV	Passage Visitor
		V	Vagrant

Black-throated Diver	v	Bewick's Swan	wv
Great Northern Diver	wv	Buzzard	RB
Red-throated Diver	wv	Sparrowhawk	RB
Great Crested Grebe	RB	Peregrine	wv
Little Grebe	RB	Merlin	RB
Fulmar	RB	Kestrel	RB
Manx Shearwater	PV	Red Grouse	RB
Gannet	PV	Black Grouse	v
Cormorant	PV	Partridge	RB
Shag	v	Quail	v
Grey Heron	PV	Pheasant	RB
Mallard	RB	Water Rail	RB
Teal	RB	Corncrake	v
Garganey	PV	Moorhen	RB
Gadwall	v	Coot	RB
Wigeon	wv	Oystercatcher	RB
Pintail	wv	Lapwing	RB
Shoveler	RB	Ringed Plover	RB
Scaup	wv	Little Ringed Plover	MB
Tufted Duck	wv	Grey Plover	wv
Pochard	wv	Golden Plover	wv
Goldeneye	wv	Turnstone	wv
Long-tailed Duck	v	Snipe	RB
Velvet Scoter	v	Jack Snipe	wv
Common Scoter	wv	Woodcock	RB
Red-breasted Merganser		Curlew	RB
	wv	Whimbrel	PV
Shelduck	RB	Black-tailed Godwit	wv
White-fronted Goose	wv	Bar-tailed Godwit	wv
Pink-footed Goose	wv	Green Sandpiper	PV
Canada Goose	PV	Wood Sandpiper	PV
Mute Swan	RB	Common Sandpiper	MB
Whooper Swan	wv	Redshank	RB

Spotted Redshank	PV	Barn Owl	RB
Greenshank	PV	Little Owl	RB
Knot	WV	Tawny Owl	RB
Purple Sandpiper	V	Short-eared Owl	WV
Little Stint	PV	Nightjar	MB
Dunlin	WV	Swift	MB
Curlew Sandpiper	PV	Kingfisher	RB
Sanderling	PV	Green Woodpecker	RB
Ruff	V	Great Spotted Wood-	
Great Skua	V	pecker	RB
Arctic Skua	PV	Lesser Spotted Wood-	
Great Black-backed Gull		pecker	RB
	PV	Skylark	RB
Lesser Black-backed Gull		Shorelark	WV
	PV	Swallow	MB
Herring Gull	PV	House Martin	MB
Common Gull	WV	Sand Martin	MB
Little Gull	V	Raven	RB
Black-headed Gull	RB	Carrion Crow	RB
Kittiwake	PV	Rook	RB
Common Tern	MB	Jackdaw	RB
Arctic Tern	PV	Magpie	RB
Roseate Tern	PV	Jay	RB
Little Tern	MB	Great Tit	RB
Sandwich Tern	PV	Blue Tit	RB
Razorbill	V	Coal Tit	RB
Guillemot	V	Marsh Tit	RB
Puffin	V	Willow Tit	RB
Stock Dove	RB	Long-tailed Tit	RB
Woodpigeon	RB	Nuthatch	RB
Turtle Dove	MB	Treecreeper	RB
Collared Dove	RB	Wren	RB
Cuckoo	MB	Dipper	RB

Mistle Thrush	RB	Water Pipit	WV
Fieldfare	WV	Rock Pipit	WV
Song Thrush	RB	Pied Wagtail	RB
Redwing	WV	White Wagtail	PV
Ring Ouzel	MB	Grey Wagtail	RB
Blackbird	RB	Yellow Wagtail	MB
Wheatear	MB	Waxwing	V
Stonechat	RB	Starling	RB
Whinchat	MB	Hawfinch	RB
Redstart	MB	Greenfinch	RB
Robin	RB	Goldfinch	RB
Grasshopper Warbler	MB	Siskin	WV
Reed Warbler	MB	Linnet	RB
Sedge Warbler	MB	Twite	WV
Blackcap	MB	Redpoll	RB
Garden Warbler	MB	Bullfinch	RB
Whitethroat	MB	Crossbill	V
Lesser Whitethroat	MB	Chaffinch	RB
Willow Warbler	MB	Brambling	WV
Chiffchaff	MB	Yellowhammer	RB
Wood Warbler	MB	Corn Bunting	RB
Goldcrest	RB	Reed Bunting	RB
Spotted Flycatcher	MB	Lapland Bunting	V
Pied Flycatcher	MB	Snow Bunting	WV
Dunnock	RB	House Sparrow	RB
Meadow Pipit	RB	Tree Sparrow	RB
Tree Pipit	MB		

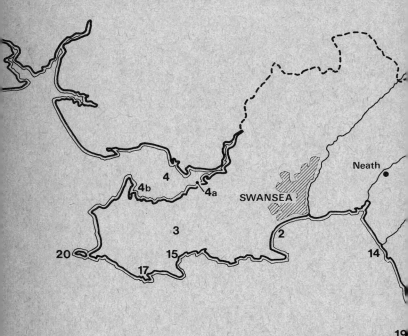

Neath

SWANSEA

4

4b

4a

3

2

20

15

14

17

19

BRISTOL   CHANNEL

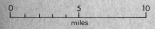
0   5   10
miles

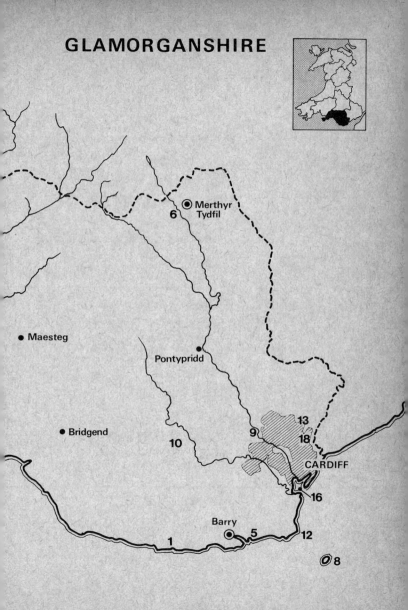

GLAMORGANSHIRE

Merthyr
Tydfil

6

● Maesteg

Pontypridd

● Bridgend

10

13

9

18

CARDIFF

16

Barry

1

5

12

8

Chapter 11

Glamorgan

Thoughts of a pulsating industrial and commercial Wales immediately turn to Glamorgan with cities and towns like Bridgend, Cardiff, Merthyr Tydfil, Neath and Swansea. The county is the most populous in Wales; in 1971 1,255,374 people lived in its 818 square miles. Some eighty miles of coastline bordering the Bristol Channel, a rich agricultural hinterland and farther north vast mineral wealth have combined to give the county pre-eminence in Wales. Even so, and the traveller may be forgiven for thinking otherwise, only one-fifth of Glamorgan is occupied by industrial concerns and human habitation.

Man has a long history in Glamorgan. Old Stone Age peoples, wrapped in animal skins against the Arctic cold, hunted the lowlands of this part of Wales between 18,000 and 50,000 years ago. At Paviland, Gower, one of the oldest burial sites in Britain was discovered. At first the remains were thought to be female, hence the name 'Red Lady of Paviland' given to the skeleton, but it has since been identified as that of a man about 25 years old. There are many other traces of early man, including megalithic tombs like those at Arthur's Stone, Parc le Breos and Tinkinswood and hill forts like Caerau, Llanbleddian and Cil Ifor. Following the departure of the Romans—whose occupation in these parts was mainly military, few civilian remains having been discovered—Glamorgan, like the rest of Britain, slipped into the Dark Ages. In the tenth century, Morgan, a Welsh prince, ruled over all the

Stonechat

land between the Tawe and Wye and gave his name to this part of Wales—Morgannwg. By Norman times the eastern boundary had shifted west to the Rhymney and almost four centuries of Marcher rule commenced with its conquest in 1090 by Robert Fitzhamon. However, the Marcher writ did not extend into the hills, and even in the lowlands the many castles whose remains now stand in various states of repair are mute evidence of the conflicts of that time. There were numerous uprisings and skirmishes, including, in 1158, one of the most daring commando raids of all time when Ifor Bach led his men into Cardiff Castle at night and captured Earl William, his wife and son.

Such changes which took place in Glamorgan during Norman times and the following more peaceful centuries were leisurely indeed when compared to the industrial revolution which commenced in Glamorgan during the second half of the eighteenth century. Although copper and lead smelting had been practised around Swansea during the early 1700s, the main impact occurred when the northern uplands and valleys revealed their treasure of coal, iron ore, limestone plus a superabundant water supply. Iron works soon opened at Dowlais, Cyfarthfa and Hiwaun and above all Merthyr Tydfil, which during the latter half of the eighteenth century grew from a small village to become the largest town in Wales with about 17,000 inhabitants. In valleys like the Aberdare, Llynfi, Merthyr, Rhondda and Ogmore coal mining was carried on to such an extent that by the end of the nineteenth century the South Wales coalfield was the most extensively worked in the world. On the coast further explosive growth was taking place as harbours were built, connected by railway to the valley towns so that the industrial wealth of Glamorgan could be exploited to the full.

Glamorgan may be divided into two main regions, the northern uplands—Blaenau Morgannwg, and a southern area—Bro Morgannwg comprising the Vale of Glamorgan and the Gower peninsula.

The main body of the county is the northern uplands which extend in a great sweep from north of Swansea east to the Monmouthshire border on the Rhymney River. Much of this region is an irregular plateau of between 1,000 and almost 2,000 feet, the highest point being Craig-y-llyn, 1,969 feet, near the head of the Rhondda Fawr valley. There are three distinct valley systems, each between 500 and 800 feet below the plateau level. The rivers Cynon, Ely, Rhondda and Taff all flow south-east. The Ogmore and tributaries flow south and the western rivers of Avan, Neath and Tawe south-west. These are short and fast flowing streams, only the Tawe exceeding 40 miles in length.

The Vale of Glamorgan is mainly agricultural, rising to about 400 feet in places with numerous villages and small towns, some whose names show the early non-Welsh influence which followed the Norman conquest—Colwinston, Flemingston and English St Donats. The Vale is flanked on the east by Cardiff and Barry and in the west by Port Talbot. Westwards still, beyond Swansea, lies the relatively unspoilt Gower Peninsula, bounded on the north by the Burry Inlet with its saltings and lonely mud flats, and on the south by a cliff line extending from Mumbles to Worms Head. This is a region of small villages and hamlets which, except for the rush of summer

overleaf – *Kittiwake*

G

holiday traffic, remain havens of rest and quiet, yet are within such a short distance of the Swansea conurbation.

Besides inland industrialisation in the valleys the most serious change to the habitats found in Glamorgan is that which has occurred on the sea coast east from Swansea Bay. Dockland facilities, cement works, steel plants, power stations and holiday areas, all most necessary, have combined to alter the coastal fringe in less than fifty years. Except possibly for the herring gull, most shore-breeding species have diminished in numbers; some like the oystercatcher and ringed plover are now reduced to a few pairs breeding, while others like the merlin and little tern have long ceased to occur except as occasional passage birds. On the other hand some changes are beneficial, like the construction of reservoirs particularly those at lowland sites. That at Eglwys Nunydd has greatly enhanced the bird life of the county. Large areas in upland regions, as with other parts of Wales, have been extensively planted with conifers, and Coed Morgannwg, an amalgamation of several forest areas north-east of Neath totalling 15,000 hectares (38,000 acres) is the largest in Wales.

With a high population and two active ornithological societies based on the main centres of Cardiff and Swansea, it is hardly surprising that Glamorgan is perhaps the ornithologically best known county in Wales. Nevertheless some parts are rarely visited, in particular the region north of Neath and Swansea including the Loughor estuary on the Carmarthenshire border. The forestry areas north-east of Neath would repay scrutiny, such areas elsewhere in Wales have been colonised by black grouse, short-eared owl and siskin. On the coast, concentrated watching from Lavernock Point during the 1960s revealed its importance as a site for observing both land and seabird passage. Similar observations certainly require to be made at the possibly more interesting vantage points along the south side of Gower. Some individual species like water rail, woodlark and hawfinch are probably under recorded as breeding species and should be looked for in suitable habitats. There remain many opportunities for the ornithologist to make discoveries even in well-watched Glamorgan.

Information

County Avifaunas
'The Birds of Glamorgan', *Trans. Cardiff Nats. Soc.* Vol. xxxi (1900). 'The Birds of Glamorgan', *Trans. Cardiff Nats. Soc.* Vol. lviii (1927). Both these early works were compiled by committees.
Ingram, Geoffrey C. S. and Salmon, H. Morrey, 1936 *Glamorgan County History* I: 267–287.
Heathcote, A., Griffin, D., and Salmon, H. Morrey, 'The Birds of Glamorgan'. *Trans. Cardiff Nats. Soc. Annex to Vol. XCIV* (1967).
    Although not a county avifauna *Gower Birds* Vol. 1: No. 4 1971 gives an assessment of the status of all species recorded in Gower between 1957 and 1969.

Bird Report
Annual report covering whole of Glamorgan (including Gower) published by the Ornithological Section of the Cardiff Naturalists' Society and available from Mrs A.

Heathcote (see County Bird Recorder) price 25p (postage included).

Gower Birds—an annual report covering Gower east to a line from Pontardualais at the head of the Loughor Estuary, south-east to Neath and then down the River Neath to Swansea Bay. Price 25p (postage extra) from R. Tallack, (see Ornithological Societies).

County Bird Recorder
Mrs A. Heathcote, 140 Ty Glas Road, Llanishen, Cardiff CF4 5EH. Records for the Gower Peninsula should be sent to the Bird Recorder for the Gower Ornithological Society:

H. E. Grenfell, 14 Bryn Terrace, Mumbles, Swansea.

Ornithological Societies
The Cardiff Naturalists' Society has an active Ornithological Section which holds meetings on the second Tuesday of each month from October to March in the Zoology Lecture Theatre of the University College, Cardiff. Field meetings are held in every month except August. Subscription 75p per annum, Juniors (between 12 and 18) 25p. Hon. Sec. P. Hughes, 6 Carshalton Road, Gwaun Meisgyn, Beddau, Pontypridd.

The Gower Ornithological Society (see Bird Report for area covered) also has a full programme of lectures and field meetings, the former held at the Royal Institution, Swansea. Subscription 75p per annum. Hon. Sec. R. Tallack, 69 Maesygwernan Road, Morriston, Swansea.

Naturalists' Trust
The first Trust to be established in Wales was Glamorgan in 1961 which now manages a total of twenty-nine re-

serves. Newsletters are circulated to members each March and September and there is an annual Bulletin. Other publications include a *Handbook of Nature Reserves*, and *Naturalists' Trust Reserves in Gower*. Meetings at about monthly intervals are held between September and March in centres like Cardiff, Swansea, Bridgend and Merthyr Tydfil, while outdoor activities include visits to nature reserves and conservation work. Subscription £1.05 per annum (adults), 50p (associate) and 25p (students). Hon. Membership Sec. Mrs C. Kwantes, Tavistock House, 76 Parc Wern Road, Sketty, Swansea. Hon. Sec. Group Capt. E. F. Campbell-Smith, 12 Caswell Drive, Swansea SA3 4RJ.

Royal Society for the Protection of Birds Representative
G. Hearl, 110 Wenallt Road, Rhiwbina, Cardiff and J. C. W. Lewis, 58 Southgate, Pennard, Nr. Swansea.

British Trust for Ornithology Representative
R. J. Howells, 'Ynys Enlli', 14 Dolgoy Close, West Cross, Swansea.

Tourist Information
Wales Tourist Board, Welcome House, High Street, Llandaff, Cardiff CF5 2YZ.

1. ABERTHAW ST0366: This area on the most southerly section of the Glamorgan coast was formerly a Site of Special Scientific Interest comprising the Thaw estuary and its adjacent shingle banks. Following the construction of two South Wales Electricity Generating Board power stations the estuary was used as a dump for ash so that rapid changes began to take place in its ecology and

attractiveness to wildlife. More recently the demand for ash has meant that dumping here has ceased and the lagoon has remained static. It is hoped that an agreement can be reached between the Glamorgan Naturalists' Trust and the SWEGB for the establishment of a Trust reserve at this potentially interesting site. Access is best achieved from East Aberthaw where tracks cross the railway at two points.

Oystercatcher and ringed plover still attempt to breed here despite considerable disturbance. Both are now very much reduced in numbers as breeding species in Glamorgan. Interesting waders seen on passage have included grey plover, green and wood sandpipers, greenshank, little stint, pectoral sandpiper and curlew sandpiper.

2. BLACKPILL ss6290: Approximately mid-way along the mud and sand flats which stretch for some four miles between Swansea Docks and The Mumbles, and easily accessible from the A4067 which follows the shore, is Blackpill. Here the Clyne River, though little more than a stream, enters the sea after its short journey from the Gower hinterland.

Blackpill seems the most attractive section of the bay for waders and wildfowl, and a wide variety of species, some occurring in high numbers, may be observed there at the appropriate season. In mid-winter the oyster-catcher and ringed plover flocks rise to approximately 1,000 each. The flats are the most important site in South Wales for sanderling; up to 500 are recorded during autumn passage with smaller numbers in all other months. Bar-tailed godwits and grey plover overwinter, the number of the former reaching a peak of about 200, the latter about 40. Little gulls are now regular visitors to

Blackpill between March and June, with monthly maximum of up to 15. More unusual visitors recorded in the area include great northern diver, long-tailed duck, red-breasted merganser, Kentish plover, spotted redshank, ruff, Arctic skua and Mediterranean Gull.

3. BROAD POOL, CILLIBION SS510910: This small pool, situated beside the minor road that crosses Cefn Bryn from Reynoldston ss483900 to Cillibion ss515914, was acquired in 1962 as the first reserve of the Glamorgan County Naturalists' Trust. Standing in common land it has free public access, though most birds can easily be observed from the road where a car makes an ideal hide. Lapwing, snipe, curlew and redshank breed in the vicinity while Bewick's swans have been noted in winter.

4. BURRY INLET SS5596 TO 4498: This large intertidal area, bordered on the south bank by the Gower Peninsula, Glamorgan and on the north by Carmarthenshire is the most important estuary area in Wales. A large section is now designated a National Wildfowl Refuge.

The two most important areas of the Inlet are as follows:

4a. PENCLAWDD SS5496: The B4295 Llanrhidian to Swansea road follows the shore between Penclawdd and Crofty villages while west of the latter an unclassified road meanders along the saltings' edge.

Pintail are the most numerous wintering duck in the area; the majority occurring early in the year when generally over 1,000 are present. Oystercatchers, although not occurring in such high numbers as at Whiteford, may, nevertheless, be counted in several thousands during the

winter months off Penclawdd. This seems the most fav-
oured spot on the Burry Inlet for wintering black-tailed
godwits; there are sixty to seventy most years. Several
hundred redshanks also winter here while both spotted
redshank and greenshank occur in small numbers during
the autumn.

4b. WHITEFORD POINT ss4496: This National Nature
Reserve on the north-west coast of Gower was the first
property in Wales to be acquired by the National Trust
(1965) as a result of Enterprise Neptune, the Trust's
campaign to safeguard the coast. It is leased to the Nature
Conservancy. The most prominent feature of the Reserve
is the well developed ridge of sand dunes running north
for some two miles from Cwm Ivy to Whiteford Point. To
the west and exposed to the Atlantic surf is Whiteford
Beach (bathing is *dangerous* at all times) while on the
sheltered eastern side an expanse of saltings eventually
give way to the mud and sand banks of Llanrhidian
Sands. Visitors should leave Swansea on the A4118 turning right at Fairwood Common on the B4271 for Llanrhidian, after which minor roads should be followed to
Llanmadoc. Most ornithologists will visit the reserve in
winter when it is possible to park with consideration in
the village; this often becomes congested during the summer holiday months. From Cwm Ivy at the road's end
follow the National Trust signs reading 'To Whiteford
Burrows', the track leading first through conifer plantations then along the edge of the West Marsh to Berges
Island and Whiteford Point. Just east of the Point there
are two small hides constructed by members of the
Glamorgan Naturalists' Trust and the Gower Ornitho-

logical Society, these are excellent vantage points besides providing shelter for the observer. Access away from the footpaths is by permit only. Do not touch suspicious objects—unexploded shells are found from time to time on the beach and among the dunes. A leaflet describing the Whiteford National Nature Reserve is published by the Nature Conservancy and is available free from the South Wales Regional Office.

Whiteford Point is the best place in Gower, indeed in South Wales, to see wintering divers and grebes, all the regular occurring British species being noted annually. Although there is no evidence to suggest breeding, there has been a resident flock of eider ducks on the Burry Inlet, particularly in the Whiteford area, for as long as can be remembered, though ornithologists did not become aware of this fact until 1917. The maximum count seems to have been about eighty, but in recent years the flock has been somewhat smaller than this. The nearest known breeding places on the west coast of Britain are on Walney Island (Lancashire), Wigtownshire and in Ireland from Co. Down to Co. Sligo. Red-breasted mergansers have nested at Whiteford for several years, flightless immatures being noted on several occasions. This represents a considerable southward extension from the nearest known breeding sites in north Cardiganshire.

Whiteford and the oystercatcher are indisputably linked; the Point provides a resting place for vast flocks of this bird when high water covers its Burry Inlet feeding grounds. In 1969 the monthly maxima in the Burry Inlet reached nearly 18,000 in mid-winter. Knot and dunlin occur in flocks of several thousands, while waders which may be seen in hundreds include turnstone, curlew, black-tailed and bar-tailed godwits.

5. CADOXTON PONDS ST1368: These ponds are inside the dock area at Barry and permission to enter should be obtained from the office of the British Transport Docks Board. There is considerable disturbance, particularly from anglers, but even so the site is well worth a visit. Access is from the A4055 at ST140689.

Reed and sedge warblers breed, this being one of the few known sites for the former in east Glamorgan. There is a winter flock of coot and these are usually joined by small parties of tufted duck, pochard and sometimes goldeneye. Red-necked grebe, whooper and Bewick's swan have also been recorded.

6. CYFARTHFA CASTLE LAKE SO0407: In the north of the county there is a scarcity of suitable areas of open water, however small. This lake is one of these scarce areas. Now a municipal park situated on the western outskirts of Merthyr Tydfil, it is on the A470 Merthyr Tydfil to Brecon road at SO040072.

Little grebes have nested here though chiefly they are winter visitors along with small numbers of tufted duck, pochard and coot which have been joined occasionally by goldeneye.

7. EGLWYS NUNYDD RESERVOIR SS7984: This, the largest sheet of fresh water 81 hectares (200 acres) in Glamorgan, was created around a small pool to the north of Kenfig Burrows, and provides cooling water for the British Steel Corporation, Margam site. The average depth when construction work is completed will be 14 feet, the reservoir being fed by the Kenfig River Springs and the Castle Stream, the only outlet being to the former reen system thence to the steel works. Besides its industrial use it

serves as a multi-purpose recreational area—sailing, fishing and a model boat club—while in 1968 a Nature Reserve Agreement was signed between the then Steel Company of Wales and the Glamorgan Naturalists' Trust. It is hoped that one section together with an adjacent reed bed will be set aside for wildlife conservation. Permits are required to visit the reservoir and these are available to members of the two ornithological societies and the Glamorgan County Naturalists' Trust and may be obtained from the Trust secretary. Access is by means of a lane leaving the B4283 at ss802847.

The reservoir is an important ornithological site, particularly for wintering wildfowl. Tufted duck and pochard are most numerous with up to 400 of each in mid-winter. Goldeneye are regular visitors with up to thirty occurring. Long-tailed duck are seen most winters and have remained until April, while scaup, red-breasted merganser, goosander and smew have also been recorded. Teal are the most numerous dabbling duck, the maximum number being 160; up to fifty shoveler along with smaller numbers of mallard, gadwall and wigeon winter, while garganey appear in spring. All three divers have been recorded; great crested and little grebes breed, with both Slavonian and black-necked sometimes occurring in winter. There is a large winter flock of coot, of which a few pairs remain to breed.

At passage times little gull, black, common and Arctic terns are all regularly seen. The high water level on to a concrete facing means that there is little area suitable to passing waders though a few call briefly, the common sandpiper being most frequent, with occasional individuals overwintering. There is a regular mid-April passage of wagtails with pied and white predominating.

Small parties of yellow wagtails, several pairs of which breed nearby, and the occasional blue-headed wagtail have been noted. Rarer species seen include bittern, purple heron, spoonbill, little ringed plover and white-winged black tern.

Raum, J., 'Eglwys Nunydd Reservoir' *Glam. County Nats. Trust Bull.* 10 (1971): 22–3.

8. FLAT HOLM ST2265: Some $2\frac{3}{4}$ miles off Lavernock Point is the 21 hectare (52 acre) Carboniferous Limestone island of Flat Holm, owned by Trinity House. Along with Steep Holm (Somerset) it occupies a strategic position at the head of the Bristol Channel, having been occupied by military garrisons in time of war, or threat of war, for over a century. The island has also been farmed and at one time had a public house and an isolation hospital, but at the present time, except for the lighthouse-keepers, the only occupation is intermittent, the lessee living on the mainland. Enquire at Penarth or Weston-super-Mare regarding boats to Flat Holm.

Although Flat Holm has low cliffs on the east and south sides, the only breeding seabirds are gulls. Lesser black-backed gulls totalled about 100 pairs in 1956 and had increased to 1,100 pairs by 1969. A similar large increase has been noted in the herring gull population; they first nested in 1954, ten years later there were 381 pairs and in 1969 920 pairs. A pair of great black-backed gulls nest from time to time, shelduck (probably as many as ten pairs in 1969) breed, as do a pair of kestrels, a few rock pipits and possibly a pair of oystercatchers.

9. GLAMORGANSHIRE CANAL, WHITCHURCH ST1480: The Glamorganshire Canal once carried traffic 25 miles be-

tween Cardiff and Merthyr Tydfil, but the last barge ceased operating in 1943. Unfortunately the waterway is now mainly dry or filled in, and the only section with permanent water is for about one mile on the north-west outskirts of Cardiff. Extending from Melingriffith to Tongwynlais the canal, with its adjacent strip of mixed woodland, was designated a Nature Reserve by Cardiff City Council in 1967 after consultation with the Cardiff Naturalists' Society and the Glamorgan County Naturalists' Trust. Beside the towpath a footpath runs the length of the woodland. Access to the southern end is by way of Velindre Road from the Whitchurch roundabout at ST152804, and to the northern end by Ironbridge Road from Tongwynlais village ST153820; this latter route will be altered when the M4 is built west of Cardiff.

Over seventy species of birds have been recorded in the area, of which thirty-two have bred. Kingfisher and water rail are regular winter residents, while other species noted include tawny owl, great spotted woodpecker, jay, nuthatch and treecreeper.

10. HENSOL LAKE ST0478: The lake in Hensol Park was a sanctuary for wildfowl when in private ownership during the early part of this century, but a change to public ownership as a mental hospital in the late 1920s resulted in considerable disturbance, while in 1963 the water level was reduced. Nevertheless, the lake still proves attractive to birds and may be reached by turning north off the A48 at ST074742, or south from the A4119 at ST061810. Permission to visit must be obtained from the Hospital Authorities, Hensol Hospital, Pontyclun.

Great crested grebes nested in 1969, the first time since 1950, though formerly several pairs nested annually,

with eight in 1922. Little grebe, coot and moorhen all
nest, while herons from the nearby heronry are often seen
fishing at the water's edge or flying overhead. There is a
small reed warbler colony. Tufted duck have nested since
the first occurrence in 1963, and in winter a flock of between forty and fifty is usually present with a smaller
number of pochard. Small numbers of mallard, teal, gadwall and wigeon are present in winter while a ferruginous
duck, the sixth to be sighted in Glamorgan this century
stayed from 3 November 1965 until 29 January 1966.

11. KENFIG POOL ss7981 : This, the largest natural lake, 28
hectares (70 acres) in Glamorgan, together with its surrounding dunes, is the most important natural history area
in South Wales yet to be designated a nature reserve, despite two decades of effort. The pool is freely accessible from
the car park at the village of Kenfig ss8081 which is
reached by a minor road leaving the B4283 at either
ss811822 or ss820799.

Although disturbance, formerly shooting but now
mainly sailing, greatly reduced the ornithological attractiveness of Kenfig Pool it has now largely recovered
and the list of rare birds recorded there in recent years is
comparable to any other mainland site in Wales. Red-
necked grebe, bittern, little bittern, red-crested pochard,
Montagu's and hen harrier, spotted crake, red-necked
phalarope, glaucous gull, little gull, white-winged black
tern, bluethroat, aquatic warbler, firecrest and great grey
shrike having all been noted. Many species of wildfowl
use the pool regularly in winter including the commoner
dabbling and diving duck and all three swans.

12. LAVERNOCK POINT st1868: In the extreme south-east

where the Bristol Channel coast makes a right-angle turn
from a north–south to an east–west axis is Lavernock
Point. The Liassic Limestone cliffs, though only about 50
feet high, provide an excellent vantage point for viewing
the Bristol Channel out to Flat Holm two and three-
quarter miles away and beyond. Some $14\frac{1}{2}$ acres of scrub
grassland on the cliff top is a reserve of the Glamorgan
County Naturalists' Trust for the point has botanical and
geological as well as ornithological interest. Access is by
means of an unclassified road from the B4267 Penarth to
Barry road at st178686, or by a footpath along the coast
from Penarth.

Regular watches during the 1960s, mainly by W. E.
Jones, indicated the importance of the Point during the
spring and autumn migration periods with 149 species
recorded between 1962 and 1965. More unusual land
birds seen include black redstart, Bonelli's warbler, pied
flycatcher, Richard's pipit, red-backed shrike and wax-
wing. Seabird movement has greatly exceeded expecta-
tions for a site so far towards the head of an estuary, with
the period late July to October being particularly interesting. Manx and sooty shearwaters, gannet, Arctic skua,
pomarine skua, great skua, Sabine's gull, black tern,
razorbill and guillemot all having been noted.

Jones, W. E., 'Migration at Lavernock Point', *Glamorgan
Bird Report* 1 (1965): 139–41.
Jones, W. E., 'Sea-watching in Glamorgan', *Seabird Bull.*
2 (1966): 18–20.

13. LISVANE AND LLANISHEN RESERVOIRS ss1881 AND 1882:
These two reservoirs on the northern outskirts of Cardiff
were constructed in the latter half of the last century. The
land around the reservoirs is private, but members of the

Ornithological section of the Cardiff Naturalists' Society
may apply to the Water Engineer, Cardiff City Council
for permits. Llanishen reservoir is used for sailing, but an
informal agreement between the Cardiff Naturalists'
Society and the Cardiff City Council ensures that Lisvane
reservoir is a sanctuary. The reservoirs and the land immediately adjacent prove attractive to migrants in both
spring and autumn with good passages of hirundines,
warblers, wagtails and pipits. More unusual visitors
during recent years have included ferruginous and long-
tailed duck, velvet scoter, smew, little ringed plover, grey
phalarope, little gull, white-winged black tern, reed·
warbler and snow bunting.
Cox, J. E. and Young, S. F., 'Migration at Llanishen/
Lisvane Reservoirs', *Glamorgan Bird Report* 2 (1968): 6–8.

14. MARGAM BREAKWATER ss7488: This new breakwater
was built to create a deep-water harbour for Port Talbot
in order to accommodate large iron-ore carriers carrying
material for the steel works. It is reached by a lane
leaving the A48 at ss796862 near Margam and then crossing the railway lines. For part of its length the road is
private and a toll may be charged.

There is a small spring passage of terns, but in autumn
up to 1,500 may be involved, chiefly common and Arctic
with small numbers of black, little and Sandwich terns.
Many gulls are usually present and both little gull and
kittiwake have been seen.

15. OXWICH ss5087: In 1963 as the result of an agreement
between the Nature Conservancy and the owner, Mr
C. P. M. Methuen-Campbell, a National Nature Reserve totalling 220 hectares (542 acres) was established at

Oxwich. This includes a rich variety of habitats—mixed woodland, salt and fresh marsh lagoons, sand dunes and foreshore. Access to parts of the reserve is restricted to permit holders, but a minor road leaving the A4118 Port Eynon to Swansea road at ss502884 crosses the reserve to a car park in Oxwich village. Much can be seen by walking this road, or by following the marked footpaths through those sections of the reserve open to the public.

An information leaflet to the Reserve along with a Nature Trail leaflet published by the Nature Conservancy are available from the South Wales Regional Office, or the Gower Countryside Centre situated in Oxwich village.

Oxwich is the most westerly regular breeding site in Britain for the reed warbler while those other passerines of marshy areas—the sedge warbler and reed bunting abound. Shoveler are usually present during the breeding season and have certainly nested in the past. Small numbers of other duck winter at Oxwich and bitterns occur regularly at this time. Rarer visitors have included little egret, little bittern and marsh harrier.

16. PENARTH FLATS ST1873: Although surrounded by Cardiff and Penarth docks with their associated industrial developments, roads and railways, the estuaries of the rivers Ely and Taff open on to the mile-wide Penarth Flats to provide an attractive area for winter wildfowl flocks. Access points at this, the largest centre of human population in Wales, are too numerous to mention, but the most advantageous areas to watch are from Ferry Road ST181734 and Windsor Esplanade ST187743.

Mid-winter seems the best time with up to 6,000 dunlin, 1,000 redshank and 150 curlew normally present, together with smaller numbers of other waders including grey plover, turnstone and knot. Up to 200 shelduck usually feed on the flats throughout the winter, while in July broods that have been hatched farther up the rivers are led by their parents to the comparative safety of the open shore. Unusual birds seen in the area have included whimbrel, snowy owl and black redstart.

17. PORT EYNON ss4684: There are two Nature Reserves of the Glamorgan County Naturalists' Trust at the small seaside village of Port Eynon. The first is a section of the limestone cliffs running westwards towards Overton, an area of outstanding scenic, geological and botanical importance. The second, known as Sedgers Bank, consists of nearly 29 hectares (87 acres) of low lying tidal rocks; only a small area being above high-water mark. Access from Port Eynon village is by means of a footpath close to the Youth Hostel.

On and above the cliffs, birds like the raven, stonechat and linnet breed, while Sedgers Bank provides a rich feeding ground for rocky shore waders like the oyster-catcher, turnstone and purple sandpiper, and there are always rock pipits present. Port Eynon Point is the most southerly point on the Gower coast and in August and September coasting movements of seabirds may be observed, including gannet, Manx and sooty shearwater, common scoter, kittiwake, razorbill and guillemot, though this is an aspect of Gower ornithology yet to be fully explored.

18. ROATH LAKE st1879: In 1887 some 42 hectares (103 acres) of boggy ground was given by the Marquis of Bute to Cardiff Corporation and three other neighbouring

landowners gave an additional 18 acres, which later be-·
came Roath Park. It was opened to the public by the Earl
of Dumfries on 20 June 1894. A dam thrown across the
Nant Fawr brook in 1895 flooded 30 acres and formed
what is now Roath Lake. Being long and narrow, the
birds on it are never at any great distance from the observer. Although the lake is used for various water sports,
the presence of semi-domesticated duck at least partly
accounts for the variety of other wildfowl attracted there,
particularly in winter. Up to 300 mallard have been
recorded along with smaller numbers of teal, wigeon, pintail, shoveler, tufted duck and pochard, which alternate
between here and the Lisvane and Llanishen Reservoirs.
Occasional visitors have included great crested grebe,
gadwall, goosander and glaucous gull.

19. SKER POINT ss7879 : This rocky headland nearly three
miles north of Porthcawl may be reached either by walking from Porthcawl golf links, or by the minor road which
runs right to the Point from Parc Newydd, ss809795, on
the unclassified road between Porthcawl and Kenfig.

Oystercatcher, ringed plover and redshank may breed
in the vicinity and all can be seen along the shore where
small parties of sanderling are often seen. Look carefully
at the rocky sections, for turnstone and purple sandpiper
are present throughout much of the year. Up to 3,000
golden plover and up to twenty ruff winter on farmland
adjacent to the Point. Sea-watching in the right season
enables the observer to watch small passages of Manx
shearwaters, gannets and terns.

20. WORMS HEAD ss3887 : The Head, together with a
small section of mainland coast was declared the Gower

Coast National Nature Reserve in 1958. The main ornithological interest—seabirds—is on Worms Head, rather
than the mainland. Follow the A4118 and the B4247
west from Swansea to Rhossili; from the village a footpath leads to a Coastguard Station overlooking the Head.
A rocky causeway, uncovered for about 2½ hours either
side of low water (tide tables at the Coastguard Station),
provides access and this should be crossed on its northern
flank.

   Puffins once nested on Worms Head, but there seems
to have been no suggestion of breeding since 1963 when
a bird was noted carrying fish ashore. However, this is a
species to be looked for, a few being seen most summers.
Much diminished numbers of razorbill and guillemot
still breed on the north cliffs of the Outer Head and although the colony is not easily seen from the land, both
species can be observed flying back and forth. Kittiwakes
have nested since 1943 and in 1970 the colony numbered
about 345 occupied nests. Fulmars do not nest, but often
patrol the cliffs, presumably from their small colony just
south of Rhossili. Although little explored as a sea-
watching site, Worms Head seems to offer excellent opportunities for the enthusiast in this field of ornithology.
Manx and sooty shearwater, gannet, common and velvet
scoter, and terns of several species have all been observed.

Check list

RB   Resident Breeder   MB   Migrant Breeder
WV   Winter Visitor   PV   Passage Visitor
                 V   Vagrant

Black-throated Diver	V	Common Scoter	WV
Great Northern Diver	WV	Eider Non-breeding	
Red-throated Diver	WV	resident Burry Estuary	
Great Crested Grebe	RB	Red-breasted Merganser	
Red-necked Grebe	V		WV
Slavonian Grebe	WV		Has bred
Black-necked Grebe	WV	Goosander	WV
Little Grebe	RB	Smew	WV
Fulmar	RB	Shelduck	RB
Manx Shearwater	PV	White-fronted Goose	WV
British Storm Petrel	V	Brent Goose	WV
Leach's Petrel	V	Canada Goose	PV
Gannet	PV	Mute Swan	RB
Cormorant	RB	Whooper Swan	WV
Shag	RB	Bewick's Swan	WV
Grey Heron	RB	Buzzard	RB
Bittern	WV	Sparrowhawk	RB
Breeds at one locality		Marsh Harrier	V
Mallard	RB	Hen Harrier	WV
Teal	RB	Montagu's Harrier	PV
Garganey	PV	Peregrine	WV
Gadwall	WV		Has bred
	Has bred	Merlin	WV
Wigeon	WV	Kestrel	RB
Pintail	WV	Red Grouse	V
Shoveler	WV	Partridge	RB
	Has bred	Quail	V
Scaup	WV	Pheasant	RB
Tufted Duck	RB	Water Rail	RB
Pochard	WV	Corncrake	PV
Goldeneye	WV		Has bred
Long-tailed Duck	WV	Moorhen	RB
Velvet Scoter	WV	Coot	RB

Oystercatcher	RB	Common Gull	WV
Lapwing	RB	Little Gull	PV
Ringed Plover	RB	Black-headed Gull	RB
Grey Plover	WV	Kittiwake	MB
Golden Plover	WV	Black Tern	PV
Turnstone	WV	Common Tern	PV
Snipe	RB	Arctic Tern	PV
Jack Snipe	WV	Little Tern	PV
Woodcock	RB	Sandwich Tern	PV
Curlew	RB	Razorbill	MB
Whimbrel	PV	Guillemot	MB
Black-tailed Godwit	PV	Puffin	PV
Bar-tailed Godwit	WV	Stock Dove	RB
Green Sandpiper	PV	Feral Rock Dove	RB
Wood Sandpiper	PV	Woodpigeon	RB
Common Sandpiper	MB	Turtle Dove	MB
Redshank	RB	Collared Dove	RB
Spotted Redshank	WV	Cuckoo	MB
Greenshank	PV	Barn Owl	RB
Knot	WV	Little Owl	RB
Purple Sandpiper	WV	Tawny Owl	RB
Little Stint	PV	Short-eared Owl	WV
Dunlin	WV	Nightjar	MB
Curlew Sandpiper	PV	Swift	MB
Sanderling	WV	Kingfisher	RB
Ruff	WV	Hoopoe	V
Grey Phalarope	V	Green Woodpecker	RB
Great Skua	V	Great Spotted Wood-	
Arctic Skua	PV	pecker	RB
Great Black-backed Gull		Lesser Spotted Wood-	
	RB	pecker	RB
Lesser Black-backed Gull		Skylark	RB
	MB	Swallow	MB
Herring Gull	RB	House Martin	MB

Sand Martin	MB	Garden Warbler	MB
Raven	RB	Whitethroat	MB
Carrion Crow	RB	Lesser Whitethroat	MB
Rook	RB	Willow Warbler	MB
Jackdaw	RB	Chiffchaff	MB
Magpie	RB	Wood Warbler	MB
Jay	RB	Goldcrest	RB
Great Tit	RB	Spotted Flycatcher	MB
Blue Tit	RB	Pied Flycatcher	MB
Coal Tit	RB	Dunnock	RB
Marsh Tit	RB	Meadow Pipit	RB
Willow Tit	RB	Tree Pipit	MB
Long-tailed Tit	RB	Rock Pipit	RB
Nuthatch	RB	Pied Wagtail	RB
Treecreeper	RB	White Wagtail	PV
Wren	RB	Grey Wagtail	RB
Dipper	RB	Yellow Wagtail	MB
Mistle Thrush	RB	Waxwing	V
Fieldfare	WV	Starling	RB
Song Thrush	RB	Hawfinch	RB
Redwing	WV	Greenfinch	RB
Ring Ouzel	MB	Goldfinch	RB
Blackbird	RB	Siskin	WV
Wheatear	MB	Linnet	RB
Stonechat	RB	Redpoll	RB
Whinchat	MB	Bullfinch	RB
Redstart	MB	Crossbill	V
Black Redstart	WV	Chaffinch	RB
Nightingale	V	Brambling	WV
Robin	RB	Yellowhammer	RB
Grasshopper Warbler	MB	Reed Bunting	RB
Reed Warbler	MB	Snow Bunting	WV
Sedge Warbler	MB	House Sparrow	RB
Blackcap	MB	Tree Sparrow	RB

MERIONETHSHIRE

Blaenau ● Ffestiniog

3

Corwen ●

13

9

Bala ●

8

2

11

12

10

● Dolgellau

7

4

6

1

● Towyn

5

0   5   10
miles

Chapter 12

Merioneth

Merioneth is a medium-sized county, roughly triangular in shape, situated in north-west Wales. The northern section of Cardigan Bay washes its mainly low and sandy shoreline which extends for about 22 miles (excluding estuaries) between the Dyfi and Glaslyn. From the latter river the boundary travels inland and eastwards with first Caernarvonshire, and then Denbighshire to the north, its most distant point from the sea being reached on the Dee five miles downstream from the market town of Corwen. The other boundary axis of Merioneth runs south-west from here for about 45 miles, first crossing the Berwyns, then skirting the Arans before descending to the Dyfi and hence to the sea by way of the Dulas valley.

Merioneth is one of the most rugged and mountainous counties in Wales, only Breconshire exceeding it, with the proportion of its total area over 1,500 feet, 18 per cent compared to 16.8 per cent. The most outstanding upland feature, though not the highest, is the Harlech dome, described as the key to the whole structure of Snowdonia. This section of high ground of just over 2,000 feet in west Merioneth lies between the Vale of Ffestiniog and the Mawddach Valley. Here, on the Rhinog range erosion has been complete so that the Silurian and Ordovician rocks have now disappeared, only the Cambrian remaining. Surrounding the dome higher ground still remains, to the north across the border into Caernarvonshire Snowdon itself. Within Merioneth there are numerous peaks—Cader Idris, Aran Benllyn, Arennig Fawr, Moel Llyfnant and the highest of them all Aran Fawddwy 2,970 feet.

About the time the last legions of Rome were leaving Britain, Meirion one of Cunedda's many sons, conquered much of the land which is now present-day Merioneth. Bronze and Iron Age remains, as well as Roman, together with ancient trackways and paths across high ground indicate that even in this mountainous region man was an active settler and traveller in early times. The harsh terrain proved advantageous to the Welsh when the Normans pressed into Wales, but following a major encounter in the shadows of Cader Idris in 1283 Edward I divided north-west Wales into the counties of Anglesey, Caernarvonshire and Merioneth administered from Caernarvon by the Justice of North Wales. To enforce the English rule Harlech Castle was built, Harlech then being a small port. For seven centuries sand-laden currents have deposited their sediments along these shores and now the castle stands half a mile inland from the sea. Just north of the town the sand accumulation is even greater and Morfa Harlech is one of the richest natural history habitats in Wales, while to the south Morfa Dyffryn is similarly of great interest to the naturalist.

Although visitors to this maritime section may turn towards Snowdonia, the uplands that brood over this coast —the Rhinogs—are among the most fascinating in Wales. This almost rectangular tract of country stretches for approximately twelve miles from the Mawddach estuary north to the Vale of Ffestiniog, its eastern extremity being marked by the route of the A487 which follows the Afon Eden for part of the way. The highest point in the Rhinogs is Y Llethr, 2,475 feet. No modern roads traverse this region, though several minor routes penetrate along

Siskin   overleaf – *Golden Plover*

valleys like those of the Afon Artro and Afon Ysgethin. Ancient and not so ancient trackways do however cross so that for those properly equipped this is very much an area for the hill walker. Progress away from tracks is arduous, the terrain contrasting between bare rocks and deep heather. Look out for the herds of 'wild' goats for which the Rhinogs are renowned.

Southwards, across the Mawddach estuary lies Cader Idris (2,927 feet) with cliffs and crags on its north side and also overlooking Tal-y-llyn Pass. No motorist should travel through the Pass without stopping in the summit lay-by to take deep breaths of the panorama. The whole region is a must for the geologist, naturalist, especially botanists, and hill walkers. Cader Idris is separated from other high ground to the east by the greatest geological fault in Wales, that which runs from Llyn Tegid (Bala Lake) to the sea near Towyn. North-east lies Aran Fawddy and then the Berwyns, north Rhobell Fawr, Arennig Fawr and Arennig Fach which finally drop away to the Migneint and the Denbighshire moors.

Except in the coastal zone and the wider valley systems the soil cover in Merioneth is generally thin, this coupled with the altitude means that most farming revolves around sheep. Forestry operations are extensive, Coed-y-Brenin being the largest planted area, though other important plantations are those in the Dyfi valley, Cynwyd, Hafod Fawr and in the Bala region. Although Dolgellau is the county town, Blaenau Ffestiniog in the north is the largest population centre due entirely to the slate mining and quarrying industry of which this is one of North Wales' centres. A more modern development has been the construction of the Trawsfynydd Nuclear Power Station on the shores of Llyn Trawsfynydd. Merioneth is not without a large reservoir—Llyn Clelyn between the Arrenig peaks supplies water to Liverpool. Mineral prospecting has been carried out in Merioneth literally for centuries with varying success—copper, lead, silver, gold and manganese have all been sought. There are plans afoot at the present time to mine copper if trial borings indicate a sufficient quantity of ore, and one recent suggestion, at present shelved, is to dredge for gold in the Mawddach estuary.

The estuary and sea coasts of Merioneth are proving more interesting for birds like divers, grebes and sea duck than previously realised. Further watching in such areas is certainly desirable. Inland the forestry areas have already been shown to be important for black grouse, redpoll and siskin, all presently expanding their range in Wales. Plantations at present unoccupied should be examined regularly for signs of colonisation. Because of its vastness and small numbers of birds the upland region is passed by in most parts with few observations by ornithologists. Nevertheless the status of species like golden plover and dunlin which breed locally on the high ground requires investigation.

Information

County Avifaunas
Forrest, H. E., *The Vertebrate Fauna of North Wales* (London, 1907). This, together with a supplement published in 1919 is the only avifauna available though it is long out of date. A current avifauna is at present being compiled.

H

Condry, W. M., *The Snowdonia National Park* (London, 1966). Includes a list of the birds of Snowdonia, together with brief notes concerning their present status.

Bird Report
Records of birds in Merioneth are published annually in the *Cambrian Bird Report*, published by the Cambrian Ornithological Society. Price 30p plus postage from the Hon. Sec.

County Bird Recorder
Dr P. J. Dare, Tan-yr-allt, Trefriw, Caerns.

Ornithological Society
The Cambrian Ornithological Society covers the counties of Anglesey, Caernarvonshire, Denbighshire and Merioneth. Indoor meetings are held during the winter months at Colwyn Bay, Llandudno and Bangor. Field meetings are arranged throughout the year, mainly in the Society's area, but occasionally farther afield. Special help is available for beginners attending meetings. Besides the Cambrian Bird Report a cyclostyled newsletter is circulated to members five times a year. Subscription £1.00 per annum (adults), 50p (juniors). Hon. Sec. E. G. Griffiths, Longleat House, Longleat Avenue, Craigside, Llandudno, Caerns.

Naturalists' Trust
The North Wales Naturalists' Trust covers the counties of Anglesey, Caernarvonshire, Denbighshire, Flintshire, Merioneth and Montgomeryshire. Founded in 1963 the Trust owns or leases a number of reserves of which five are in Merioneth. Members receive the journal *Nature in*

Wales twice a year, together with their own duplicated newsletters. Subscription £1.00 per annum (adults), 50p (students), 25p (juniors). Hon. Gen. Sec. Mrs. M. J. Morgan, 154 High Street, Bangor, Caerns.

British Trust for Ornithology Representative
P. Hope Jones, Bedwen, Bro Enddwyn, Dffryn Ardudwy, Merioneth.

Royal Society for the Protection of Birds Representative
Not yet appointed.

Tourist Information
The Official Guide to Merioneth is available from the Information Officer, Dolgellau (price 20p).

For information and a list of publications concerning the Snowdonia National Park write to the National Park Information Officer, Plas Tanybwlch, Maentwrog, Blaenau Ffestiniog, Merioneth. There are National Park countryside centres in Aberdovey, Bala, Blaenau Ffestiniog, Dolgellau and Harlech.

1. AFON DYSYNNI SH5702: A peninsula of sand and shingle extending north-westwards almost blocks the Afon Dysynni from the sea two miles north of Towyn. Behind this natural embankment a large tidal pool known as Broad Water has formed, beyond which are low lying meadows. An unclassified road runs north beside the railway from Towyn and from the bridge over the Dysynni at SH567029 a footpath follows the south side of Broad Water until the estuary narrows near Bryncrug SH6003.

In winter small numbers of the usual wildfowl occur here—mallard, teal and wigeon—with pintail, goldeneye and red-breasted merganser less frequently. Eiders occasionally occur offshore. Waders occurring regularly, particularly on passage include oystercatcher, ringed plover, curlew, greenshank and dunlin. More regular watching, however, is required at this potentially interesting site.

2. COED-Y-BRENIN SH7326: One of the largest forest areas in North Wales, Coed-y-Brenin (King's Forest) covers some 36 square miles, of which 25 are planted with trees, mainly conifers. The A487 Dolgellau to Portmadoc road follows the valley of the Afon Eden through the forest; there are also several unclassified roads and nearly 100 miles of forest track.

The Forestry Commission have established two Forest Walks and these provide an excellent introduction to the area. That at Tyn-y-Groes about three miles north of Llanelltyd commences at a car park at SH729235 just off the A487 north of Tyn-y-Groes Hotel and runs for just over two miles. Farther north where the A487 crosses the Afon Eden, Dolgefeiliau Forest Trail commences from the picnic area close to the bridge at SH722269. Here the visitor has a choice of routes between one-half and two miles duration. Trail leaflets (price 5p) are available from the Forestry Commission (North Wales) or National Park Information Centres.

Common sandpiper, kingfisher, dipper and grey wagtail are typical species which may be observed along the fast-flowing Afon Eden and Mawddach or their tributaries. The woodlands, being mainly conifers, tend to have a more restricted bird population than mixed or purely deciduous woods, but several species are of special interest. Black grouse may be found while two finches of

changing status breed. The redpoll is now numerous and
has increased in recent years finding the developing
plantations highly suitable. The siskin, which first nested
in Snowdonia in the 1940s, was located in Coed-y-Brenin
in the 1960s and there are now a scattering of pairs
throughout the forest. Experience gained with this species
in a known breeding area will prove invaluable in locat-
ing it elsewhere in Wales as it continues to expand its
range.

3. COEDYDD MAENTWROG SH6641 : These oak woods in the
Vale of Ffestiniog are remnants of much larger areas of
woodland which flourished at one time in the North
Wales valleys. In 1963 some 169 acres were purchased by
the National Trust in conjunction with the then newly-
formed North Wales Naturalists' Trust. The area was
leased to the Nature Conservancy who in 1966 declared
it a National Nature Reserve. Access to the larger section
is best achieved by means of a gate fifty yards from the
Oakeley Arms Hotel on the B4410 Maentwrog to Rhyd
road. Another part of the reserve overlooks Llyn Mair,
an artificial lake; here there is a Nature Trail which
should not be missed by the visitor. Leaflet (price 3p)
from the Nature Conservancy (North Wales). The Trail
can be reached from Tan-y-bwlch station SH650415 or
from the car park at SH653414 beside Llyn Mair. An interesting feature at Point C of the Trail is the display of
nestboxes used to attract hole-nesting species in woodland. This must surely interest some visitors enough for
them to erect similar boxes in their own gardens. Woodland birds which may be seen in the Maentwrog woods
include green and great spotted woodpecker, redstart,
wood warbler and pied flycatcher. Llyn Mair is visited

in winter by little grebe, coot, tufted duck, pochard and goldeneye and occasionally by rarer species like the whooper swan.

4. CRAIG YR ADERYN (BIRD ROCK) SH6406: This precipitous site is situated on the south side of the Dyffryn Dysynni about six miles from the sea near Towyn. Although past records are vague, it seems most probable that cormorants have nested here for several centuries. At the present time about fifty pairs occupy ledges on the north-west face. There are now few inland cormorant colonies in Britain save for several in trees on Irish loughs and two on freshwater lochs within two miles of the sea in Scotland. Good views of the colony, which is now a reserve of the North Wales Naturalists' Trust, may be obtained from the unclassified road which follows the Afon Dysynni from Bryncrug SH608034. A pair of choughs nest at an inaccessible crevice high on the rock, this being their only natural inland site in Wales.

5. DYFI ESTUARY SH6596: See Cardiganshire (page 122).

6. DYFI FOREST SH8010: Bounded on the east and south by the Afon Dyfi, and on the north and west by the A458 and A487 is a vast area of hill land intersected by narrow valleys extensively planted in the southern sector with conifers. The boundary with Montgomeryshire bisects the forest. The plantations rise to about 1,300 feet, while to the north of these the summit is reached at 2,213 feet on Maesglasau. The main roads already mentioned provide basic access to this region which has few unclassified roads; there are however many footpaths and tracks waiting to be explored by the visitor.

Red grouse, merlin, snipe, ring ouzel and wheatear are all birds of high ground which the visitor might expect to encounter. Keep a look out for the occasional pair of golden plover or dunlin, birds of high-altitude breeding grounds in Wales having a very patchy distribution. The valleys and woodlands are the haunt of birds like the buzzard, black grouse, common sandpiper, dipper, redstart, wood warbler, pied flycatcher, redpoll and siskin, the latter, as in Coed-y-Brenin, being a relative newcomer to the forest.

7. LLYN MWYNGIL (TAL-Y-LLYN LAKE) SH7109: Lying on the same fault line as Llyn Tegid that at Tal-y-llyn is dominated by the impressive pass rising to nearly 1,000 feet above which is the Cader Idris (2,927 feet) range. The lake only reaches a maximum width of 400 yards and any birds can easily be observed from the B4405 which skirts the eastern shore or from a track on the western side.

Great crested grebe nested here in 1971 and mallard, mute swan and coot do so annually. In winter there are good numbers of tufted duck and pochard with an influx of coot to swell the resident flock. Other visitors in small numbers include little grebe, goldeneye and red-breasted merganser.

8. LLYN TEGID (BALA LAKE) SH9234: At the eastern end of an impressive geological fault running south-west to reach the sea near Towyn is Llyn Tegid. Four miles long and with a maximum width of nearly three-quarters of a mile the lake is the largest natural sheet of fresh water in Wales. From the town of Bala close to the northern shore the A494 runs along or close to the western bank, while

on the east the B4403 and a now disused railway line provide equally convenient access.

Despite its size Llyn Tegid attracts only small numbers of wildfowl whether in the breeding season or as winter visitors. Birds breeding along the shore include mallard, curlew, common sandpiper, whinchat, sedge warbler, grey wagtail and reed bunting. Terns are occasionally seen on passage, particularly during the late summer. In winter the lake is frequented by such species as little grebe, mallard, teal, tufted duck, pochard, goldeneye and coot. A lack of regular observation prevents a proper assessment being made concerning the true status of many species at the lake. It could well prove to be an important point for waders and terns on passage through inland Wales.

9. LLYN TRAWSFYNYDD SH6936: Although an artificial lake it has a more irregular shape than most of those which have drowned Welsh valleys, and this, together with several small islands, has no doubt been responsible for the establishment of a rich and varied fauna. A recent and most questionable development, seeing that the lake is in the middle of the Snowdonia National Park, has been the construction of a nuclear power station close to the shore. What effect this will have on bird life is still too early to be judged, but the raising of the lake temperature, at least in the vicinity of the station, may prove attractive. The A487 passes close to the eastern side and from this unclassified roads or footpaths run along both the northern and southern shores.

Great crested grebe and little grebe occur in winter while tufted duck and pochard are numerous as winter visitors, when up to 100 may be seen. Other duck recorded include mallard, teal, pintail, wigeon and goldeneye. Common sandpipers breed around the shore and for the past few years there has been at least one pair of oystercatchers; their first inland breeding site in Wales other than Anglesey. The possibility of this habit extending, as it has done in northern England and Scotland, should be borne in mind wherever a pair is encountered inland during the breeding season. Another recent development has been the establishment of a gull colony, mainly herring gulls with a small number of lesser black-backed gulls and usually a pair of great black-backed gulls. Common and Arctic terns often occur on passage.

10. MAWDDACH ESTUARY SH6416: The longest river wholly within the Snowdonia National Park is the Afon Mawddach. Rising on open boggy moorland it plunges through the Coed-y-Brenin forest before entering Cardigan Bay at Barmouth after a journey of some twenty-two miles. For the last seven miles the river is tidal, and with its surrounding mountains, clothed in woodland on the lower slopes, justifies the many claims that the Mawddach Estuary is the most beautiful in Wales. Recent proposals by Rio Tinto Zinc to dredge for gold in the estuary fortunately seem to have been shelved, at least for the time being. The best views of the estuary are obtained from the A496 which runs close to the northern shore, the footbridge at Barmouth or the golf links at Fairbourne at its extreme south-west point.

Red-breasted merganser and shelduck breed as do a few pairs of common sandpiper. Mallard and wigeon, up to about 100 of each, are the most numerous wintering duck. Small numbers of all the regular waders are usually to be seen.

11. MORFA DYFFRYN SH5625 : One of the largest sand dune areas in Merioneth is Morfa Dyffryn where both perm- anent and mobile dunes have accumulated over shingle banks protruding from an ancient coastline now up to two miles inland. The dunes extend, basically as two parallel ridges, from the Ysgethin Estuary SH5722 north to the Artro Estuary SH5727. Both estuary mouths are nearly blocked by spits behind which, in the case of the Artro, a tidal pool one-and-a-half miles by half a mile has formed. The whole dune area is of great physiographical and botanical interest and in 1962 some 203 hectares (500 acres) were declared a National Nature Reserve. Permits are required to visit parts of the reserve away from rights of way. Access to Morfa Dyffryn is best by way of Llanbedr SH5826, taking the unclassified road which leaves the A496 immediately south of the bridge over the river. This follows the perimeter of Llanbedr airfield then except for a period of about two hours either side of high water, across the tidal pool to Mochras, better known as Shell Island. Several paths strike south from this road into the dunes.

Birds breeding in the area include shelduck, oyster- catcher, lapwing, ringed plover, snipe, redshank, stone- chat, grasshopper warbler and reed bunting. Regular winter visitors include golden plover, dunlin and sander- ling, while casual visitors seen in recent years have been jack snipe, greenshank and little stint. Offshore, Manx shearwater, gannet, Arctic skua, kittiwake and terns are seen in the late summer.

12. PRECIPICE WALK NATURE TRAIL SH7321 : High on the Nannau Estate above the Mawddach Valley is the ridge of Foel Cynwch rising to 1,068 feet with Llyn Cynwch

sheltering on its eastern slopes. The famous Precipice
Walk of nearly three miles encircles the ridge at about
750 feet providing quite remarkable views north across
Coed-y-Brenin to Snowdonia, west down the Mawddach
Estuary and south to Cader Idris. Leave the A494 Bala
road on the outskirts of Dolgellau and follow the unclassified road towards Llanfachreth. After about two
miles a small car park is reached beside the turning for
Ty'n-y-Groes at SH746212. About 150 yards down this
latter road a sign marks the access point to the Nature
Trail. A brief leaflet concerning the Trail is available
from Snowdonia National Park Information Centres
(price 2p).

   In the wooded areas of the lower slopes typical birds
are members of the tit family, green and great spotted
woodpeckers, redstart, wood warbler, and pied flycatcher. On the higher ground ring ouzel and meadow
pipit may be seen, while buzzards and ravens often soar
along the escarpment.

13. TRAETH BACH SH5736: In the extreme north-west of
the county the Afon Glaslyn and Afon Dwyryd unite
near Portmadoc to form the estuarine basin of Traeth
Bach. Some five miles in length and reaching a maximum
width of two miles, its narrow entrance is flanked on the
south side by the vast sand dune expanse of Morfa
Harlech and on the north by the very much smaller
Morfa Bychan. An attempt was made during the early
nineteenth century to reclaim land at the mouth of the
Afon Glaslyn, an embankment which now carries the
A497 being constructed. This provides an excellent view-
ing point overlooking the marshes and pools of the
Glaslyn. Portmeirion peninsula SH5837 with its maze of

footpaths leaving the A497 is the best point on the north side to watch birds on the estuary. For the south bank there is a footpath leaving Talsarnau sh612360 on the A496 and several from the vicinity of Llanfihangel-y-traethau sh597354 on the B4573, all of which approach the shore.

Duck breeding in the area include mallard, teal, shoveler, red-breasted merganser and shelduck. In winter wigeon numbers rise to about 1,000 while the mallard flock approaches 500, with teal and pintail usually reaching about 100, all these species feeding on the open flats. The river channels attract small numbers of tufted duck, goldeneye and red-breasted merganser. Oystercatcher and lapwing are the most numerous waders, up to 300 of each being present in mid-winter, together with about 200 curlew. Occurring regularly, though in much smaller numbers, are grey and golden plover, whimbrel, bar-tailed godwit and greenshank; spotted redshank are occasionally seen and the little gull is one of the rarer species to have been noted in this area.

Gough, R. E. J., 'Wildfowl counting in north-west Merioneth', *Camb. Bird Rep.* 1969: 28–32.

Check list

RB	Resident Breeder	MB Migrant Breeder
WV	Winter Visitor	PV Passage Visitor
	V Vagrant	

Black-throated Diver	V	Whooper Swan	WV
Great Northern Diver	V	Bewick's Swan	WV
Red-throated Diver	WV	Buzzard	RB
Great Crested Grebe	RB	Sparrowhawk	RB
Slavonian Grebe	V	Hen Harrier	RB
Little Grebe	RB	Peregrine	RB
Fulmar	PV	Merlin	RB
Manx Shearwater	PV	Kestrel	RB
Gannet	PV	Red Grouse	RB
Cormorant	RB	Black Grouse	RB
Shag	PV	Partridge	RB
Grey Heron	RB	Pheasant	RB
Mallard	RB	Water Rail	WV
Teal	RB	Corncrake	V
Gadwall	WV	Moorhen	RB
Wigeon	WV	Coot	RB
Pintail	WV	Oystercatcher	RB
Shoveler	WV	Lapwing	RB
Scaup	WV	Ringed Plover	RB
Tufted Duck	WV	Grey Plover	WV
Pochard	WV	Golden Plover	RB
Goldeneye	WV	Turnstone	WV
Long-tailed Duck	V	Snipe	RB
Common Scoter	WV	Jack Snipe	WV
Eider	WV	Woodcock	RB
Red-breasted Merganser		Curlew	RB
	RB	Whimbrel	PV
Goosander	V	Black-tailed Godwit	PV
Shelduck	RB	Bar-tailed Godwit	WV
White-fronted Goose	WV	Green Sandpiper	PV
Barnacle Goose	V	Common Sandpiper	MB
Canada Goose	WV	Redshank	RB
Mute Swan	RB	Spotted Redshank	WV

Greenshank	PV	Short-eared Owl	WV
Knot	WV	Nightjar	MB
Purple Sandpiper	WV	Swift	MB
Little Stint	PV	Kingfisher	RB
Dunlin	RB	Green Woodpecker	RB
Curlew Sandpiper	V	Great Spotted Wood-	
Sanderling	PV	pecker	RB
Ruff	V	Lesser Spotted Wood-	
Arctic Skua	V	pecker	RB
Great Black-backed Gull		Skylark	RB
	RB	Swallow	MB
Lesser Black-backed Gull		House Martin	MB
	PV	Sand Martin	MB
Herring Gull	RB	Raven	RB
Common Gull	WV	Carrion Crow	RB
Little Gull	WV	Rook	RB
Black-headed Gull	RB	Jackdaw	RB
Kittiwake	PV	Magpie	RB
Black Tern	V	Jay	RB
Common Tern	PV	Chough	RB
Arctic Tern	PV	Great Tit	RB
Little Tern	MB	Blue Tit	RB
Sandwich Tern	PV	Coal Tit	RB
Razorbill	WV	Marsh Tit	RB
Guillemot	WV	Willow Tit	RB
Stock Dove	RB	Long-tailed Tit	RB
Woodpigeon	RB	Nuthatch	RB
Turtle Dove	MB	Treecreeper	RB
Collared Dove	RB	Wren	RB
Cuckoo	MB	Dipper	RB
Barn Owl	RB	Mistle Thrush	RB
Little Owl	RB	Fieldfare	WV
Tawny Owl	RB	Song Thrush	RB

Redwing	WV	Meadow Pipit	RB
Ring Ouzel	MB	Tree Pipit	MB
Blackbird	RB	Rock Pipit	RB
Wheatear	MB	Pied Wagtail	RB
Stonechat	RB	White Wagtail	PV
Whinchat	MB	Grey Wagtail	RB
Redstart	MB	Yellow Wagtail	PV
Black Redstart	V	Starling	RB
Robin	RB	Hawfinch	RB
Grasshopper Warbler	MB	Greenfinch	RB
Sedge Warbler	MB	Goldfinch	RB
Blackcap	MB	Siskin	RB
Garden Warbler	MB	Linnet	RB
Whitethroat	MB	Redpoll	RB
Willow Warbler	MB	Bullfinch	RB
Chiffchaff	MB	Chaffinch	RB
Wood Warbler	MB	Brambling	WV
Goldcrest	RB	Yellowhammer	RB
Spotted Flycatcher	MB	Reed Bunting	RB
Pied Flycatcher	MB	House Sparrow	RB
Dunnock	RB	Tree Sparrow	RB

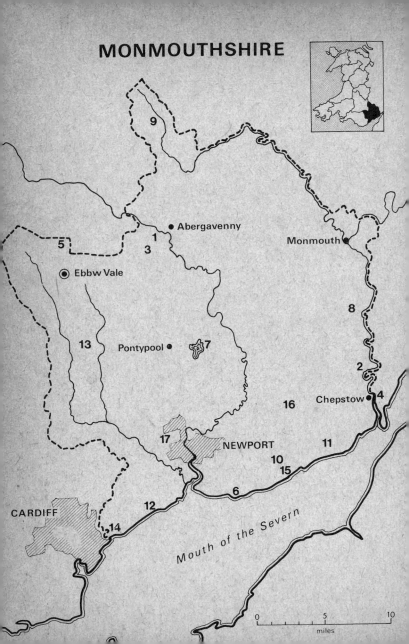

MONMOUTHSHIRE

9

5

● Abergavenny

1

3

◉ Ebbw Vale

Monmouth ●

8

13

Pontypool ● 7

2

16

Chepstow ● 4

17

NEWPORT

11

10

15

6

12

CARDIFF

14

Mouth of the Severn

0   5   10
         miles

Chapter 13

Monmouthshire

Monmouthshire, one of the smaller counties in Wales, covers 524 square miles and is roughly 27 miles north to south and 22 miles east to west. This border county has long been the southern gateway to Wales, a place where races from pre-Roman times met and often fought. The Normans, to keep the Welsh at bay, stamped their mark in stone with castles both large and small, like those at Abergavenny, Chepstow, Grosmont, Skenfrith and Usk. Even now there are those, the makers of our Ordnance Survey maps among them, who claim the county as part of England. Perhaps the motto on the county's coat of arms sums up the situation—*Utrique Fidelis* (Faithful to Both). However, as far as ornithology is concerned, Monmouth belongs firmly to Wales.

The county may be divided into four main areas. The most southerly of these extends between the eastern and the western boundaries, the rivers Wye and Rhymney, and is a flat alluvial plain, not exceeding 50 feet in height extending inland from the Severn for several miles. The Romans were active here; it was they who built the first coast defences. Now a modern stone embankment runs the whole length of the shore, protecting the hinterland from floods like that in 1606, commemorated as the 'Great Flood' on plaques in several local churches. Travel here, whether afoot or by vehicle and you will be immediately impressed by the extent of man's drainage activities. Everywhere there are ditches or reens running into larger channels which empty into the estuaries. Some channels were dug in the fourteenth century and now there are at least 100 miles of reens interlacing the countryside.

Moving north-east from the coastal lowlands, the terrain becomes more rolling with some hills rising to 1,000
feet, though generally the contours are much lower. To
the west the Usk sprawls through water meadows on its
way to the sea at Newport. Eastwards the Wye has
carved a narrow steep-sided valley of great beauty where
man has thought fit to plant extensive woodlands, though
from a naturalist's point of view, there are too many
conifers. There are other woodlands in this area, most
noteworthy being Wentwood, but essentially this is an
agricultural countryside with numerous hamlets and
small villages and occasional towns like Raglan and Usk.
This part of Monmouthshire seems very English in
character, and the place names are an inter-mixture,
Shirenewton rubs shoulders with Mynydd-bach and Uplands with Gaer-fawr.

The land continues to rise northwards into the third
area, that section of the Black Mountains, ridges of old
red sandstone running north to south, which lies within
Monmouthshire. North of the Usk valley, which now
runs north-west to south-east, most land is above 1,000
feet, with the highest point being on the Brecon border,
Chwarel-y-fan (2,228 feet). This whole area is included
within the Brecon Beacons National Park, declared in
1957. Although not as spectacular or dramatic as some
other upland areas in Wales, nevertheless this thinly-
populated countryside has a great charm of its own,
whether you seek birds on the high moorlands or in the
stream-chattering valleys.

South and west of the Usk valley is the fourth main
area of Monmouthshire; more high ground, this time

Lapwing   overleaf – *Common Sandpiper*

composed of coal measure rocks. Part of this, the Blorenge ridge extending southwards to the outskirts of Pontypool is also included in the Brecon Beacons National Park. Fast flowing rivers—the Ebbw, Sirhowy and Rhymney have incised deep valleys in the earth's crust as they rush, often swollen in flood, towards the Bristol Channel. These are rivers which have given their names to industrial history, for beneath the surrounding hills man has burrowed for three centuries or more in search of coal. Here it is bituminous coal, highly suitable for conversion to coke, and although the output to the layman seems prodigious (one mine alone produces half a million tons annually) vast reserves still remain. With such rich fuel supplies, it is no surprise that iron-, and more recently, steel-making has been practised here for over 200 years.

Here then is a county of contrasts. On one hand major cities and industrial centres like Ebbw Vale, Newport and Pontypool, on the other high moorland, rolling agricultural countryside and the remote Severn flats. What ornithologist could fail to be excited by the latter area, for between August and March this is the most exciting for birds in the county. Unfortunately, as with many other major estuaries, covetous eyes are cast towards it as a site for industrial development or water production through barrage schemes. If, as seems almost inevitable, such changes are wrought on Severn side one sincerely hopes that some parts can remain unspoiled. Waders breeding in the high Arctic tundra but seeking winter quarters farther south must not be completely driven away from areas such as these where bird-watchers peering through the early morning mist from the comparative safety of the sea wall, watch birds like knot and dunlin feeding in this richest of biological areas, the inter-tidal zone. On the credit side, the construction of reservoirs, in particular that at Llandegfedd, has greatly enhanced the variety and numbers of grebes and diving duck now occurring in Monmouthshire.

Reservoirs and estuaries with their high numbers of exciting birds continually attract the ornithologist. One can hardly blame them, but this means that more modest inland areas are sometimes overlooked. This is the case in Monmouthshire, where, although in general most of the county is well-watched, little is known of the status of many species in the east and north-east border areas. Here then is scope for the resident or visitor to make valuable contributions; who knows what species, not occurring or very local elsewhere in the county may breed. Among individual species about which more information is required, rather surprisingly, is the stock dove, though this may partly be due to observers failing to send information. The merlin is quite often seen in winter, even along the estuary sea wall, but does it breed? Certainly the northern uplands could well support the occasional pair, though much ground may have to be tramped by the enthusiast in search of this our smallest falcon. As in many other parts of Wales, the water rail, woodlark and hawfinch are all species about which little is known, though all are known to have nested recently.

Information

County Avifaunas
Ingram, G. C. S. and Salmon, H. Morrey, 'The Birds of Monmouthshire' *Trans Cardiff Nats. Soc.* 70 (1937).

Humphreys, P. N., *The Birds of Monmouthshire* (revised) (Newport Museum, 1963).

Bird Report
Published annually as *Monmouthshire Birds*, a journal which also includes short papers on various aspects of the counties avifauna and is available from Mrs F. Loveys, Ivybridge, Greenmeadow Drive, Parc Seymour, Penhow, Newport, or at W. H. Smith's shops in the principal towns, price 25p (by post 28p).

County Bird Recorder
W. G. Lewis, 11 Ruth Road, New Inn, Pontypool, Mon.

Ornithological Society
The Monmouthshire Ornithological Society holds a series of twelve indoor meetings during the winter months, the main venue for these being the Goytre Public Hall, Goytre, Pontypool. Field meetings are arranged throughout the year and are not restricted to the county. Members take part in several national ornithological enquiries and also operate three nest box schemes. Hon. Sec. H. W. Hamar, Andorra, Sunlea Crescent, Usk Road, Pontypool. Subscription 50p per annum (adults), 25p (Juniors).

Naturalists' Trust
The Monmouthshire Naturalists' Trust was founded in 1963 and now manages six reserves in the county. A quarterly journal—*Newsreel*—is circulated to members. This contains reports of Trust activities, reserves etc. Hon. Sec. A. T. Sawyer, 40 Melbourne Way, Newport. Subscription £1.00.

Royal Society for the Protection of Birds Representative
R. J. Hompstead, St Johns-on-the-Hill, Chepstow.

British Trust for Ornithology Representative
Dr K. Wilkinson, 9 St Tysoi Close, Llansoy, Usk. NP5 1EF

Tourist Information
An excellent handbook to the county is available from
the Public Relations Office, County Hall, Newport
(price 25p, postage extra). There is an Information
Centre of the Brecon Beacons National Park, Monk
Street, Abergavenny.

1. ABERGAVENNY SEWAGE WORKS SO2913: Sewage works,
particularly those of the older type, with their filter beds
and settling tanks prove attractive to many birds, and
this one in the mid Usk valley is no exception. The entrance is on the A465 Abergavenny to Merthyr Tydfil
road at SO293136; permission to visit must be obtained
from the Borough Engineer, Abergavenny, though much
can be seen from the road.

Water pipits occur here in most winters, as do water
rails which breed in the vicinity. An unusual record was
of a little ringed plover in April 1971, the first inland
occurrence of this species in Monmouthshire, which has
only been noted on four other occasions in the county.
Waders which occur regularly either on passage or as
winter visitors include lapwing, snipe, jack snipe, redshank, green and common sandpipers.

2. BLACKCLIFF AND WYND CLIFF ST5297: This 200-acre
National Nature Reserve on the precipitous west bank of
the River Wye two miles north of Chepstow is mainly

mixed deciduous woodland with an associated rich flora.
The Monmouthshire Naturalists' Trust and the Nature
Conservancy have, with the co-operation of the Forestry
Commission, produced a Nature Trail which enables
visitors to walk through the reserve, eventually reaching
a point on the cliffs 700 feet above the Wye. The Trail is
reached by following a minor road from the A466 at
ST521968 about half a mile north of St Arvans. Trail
leaflets are available from the Monmouthshire Naturalists' Trust or the Nature Conservancy South Wales
Regional Office.

Most common woodland birds can be seen on the
reserve, including green woodpecker, jay, coal tit, long-
tailed tit, treecreeper, blackcap, wood warbler and goldcrest. Grey herons (there is a heronry just downstream in
Piercefield Park) and cormorants are usually to be seen
on the river together with the commoner species of gull
and occasional waders like curlew and redshank.

3. BLORENGE SO2610: The red grouse which occur on the
heather moors close to Blaenavon form the most southerly
indigenous population of this bird in Britain, those on
Dartmoor and Exmoor being introduced about the beginning of the century. The Blorenge which rises to 1,833
feet north of Blaenavon and is crossed by the B4246 Abergavenny to Blaenavon road probably holds the greatest
number of birds. Others occur on Coity Mountain
SO2307 and on Mynydd Garn-clochdy to the south. Red
grouse on these moors were once keepered with a seasonal
bag averaging 205 brace, but now only haphazard shooting is carried out by people from the local towns and this
probably accounts at least partly for the present low
numbers. Other moorland species encountered include

the merlin, ring ouzel, wheatear, whinchat and meadow pipit.

4. CHEPSTOW RAILWAY BRIDGE ST538941: This is the site of a small herring gull colony, an extension of that which has existed for many years on the cliffs on the Gloucestershire side of the river at this point. It is of particular interest as there are only two other gull colonies on the Monmouthshire coast—Denny Island midway across the Bristol Channel and on rooftops in Newport Docks. Future developments concerning the gulls nesting on the bridge at Chepstow should be watched with interest, and also the incidence of roof nesting in the town where a pair occupied such a site in 1969. This is part of a general increase in this habit which has been noted in a number of coastal towns in Great Britain and probably over-looked by ornithologists in others.

5. GARNLYDAN RESERVOIR SO1713: This small reservoir in north-west Monmouthshire lies just south of the border with Breconshire and close to the head of the Monmouth-shire industrial valleys. Some 200 yards north off the A465 Abergavenny to Merthyr Tydfil road the reservoir is accessible by means of a track which leaves the main road at SO176127.

Small numbers of tufted duck winter on the reservoir, being joined not infrequently by pochard and the oc-casional goldeneye. Little grebes are also seen and there is a single record of a great crested grebe. Common sand-pipers are the most regular wader noted and in some years pairs remain long enough in the spring to establish territories. Waders noted on passage have included ringed plover, turnstone, whimbrel, black-tailed godwit and dunlin and in mid-May 1970 eight black terns were seen.

6. GOLDCLIFF ST3682 : South-east of Newport and east of the Usk Estuary is an area of saltings and mud flats centred close to the village of Goldcliff. Just east of the village an unclassified road leads to the coast near the lighthouse, while westwards a number of tracks and paths lead to the seawall.

Small numbers of all the waders regularly occurring on this section of the Severn Estuary are seen here and observations in recent years have also produced records of several rarer species including gadwall, velvet scoter, peregrine, long-tailed skua and razorbill.

7. LLANDEGFEDD RESERVOIR ST3299 : Constructed in 1964 mainly to supply water to Cardiff, this reservoir three miles east of Pontypool covers some 162 hectares (400 acres) and, unlike most in Wales, is at a sufficiently low altitude to attract large numbers of wintering wildfowl besides waders and terns on passage. Leave the A4042 Newport to Pontypool road at New Inn ST305990 and follow the signposted unclassified road to the dam at the south end of the reservoir. For access along the shore a permit is required and these may be obtained by members of the Monmouthshire Ornithological Society or the Monmouthshire Naturalists' Trust from Mrs Q. Saunders, Sandys, Glascoed, Mon. The best access route for permit-holders is from the A472 Pontypool to Usk road at ST336027 or ST342025, where unclassified roads run south to the entrance at ST331008. Although on the northern side, this is the best section for bird-watching and there is an observation hide.

In winter mallard are the most numerous duck at
Llandegfedd with up to 1,300 noted in January; wigeon
and teal also occur in large numbers with winter peaks of
about 500 and 200 respectively. Tufted duck and pochard are the most numerous diving duck, up to 200 of each
species being noted in mid-winter. Other diving duck of
regular occurrence, though only in small numbers, are
goldeneye, red-breasted merganser and goosander, while
long-tailed duck and smew have also been seen. The coot
flock has increased in size over several successive winters
and in 1970 over 1,000 were noted in January. Great
crested grebes are seen throughout the year (in 1972 the
maximum number recorded was twenty) and, although
courtship display has been noted, there are as yet no
positive records of this species breeding, though surely it
is only a matter of time before this takes place. Slavonian,
black-necked and little grebes also occur. Waders recorded on passage include oystercatcher, ringed plover,
turnstone, whimbrel, green sandpiper, wood sandpiper,
spotted redshank, greenshank and curlew sandpiper.
Terns pass through mainly in the autumn and have included black tern, thirty-six of which were seen in 1970.

8. LLANDOGO FOREST SO5204: Situated on the slopes of
Beacon Hill (1,005 feet) above the village of Llandogo is
an extensive area of mainly coniferous plantations, part
of the Tintern Forest. A Forest Walk commencing near
Llandogo Church SO526042 is described in a leaflet available from the Forestry Commission, South Wales Office,
price 5p. Although the habitat is rather limited, most
common woodland bird species will be encountered
during the three-mile walk.

9. LLANTHONY VALLEY SO2827: One of the many streams rushing south out of the Black Mountains is the Afon Honddu which flows through the Vale of Ewyas to join the river Monmow about six miles north of Abergavenny. Leave the A465 Abergavenny to Hereford road at Llanfihangel Crucorney SO326207 and follow the B4423 to Llanthony Priory more usually called Llanthony Abbey built by the Normans, though St David was said to have had a cell here four centuries before. Over the Breconshire border at Capel-y-ffin is a monastery, mostly ruined, founded towards the end of the last century. A minor road continues over the hills from here eventually to reach Hay-on-Wye.

Upland and woodland birds which may be seen in the valley include buzzard, red grouse, raven, dipper, ring ouzel, redstart, wood warbler, pied flycatcher and grey wagtail.

10. MAGOR RESERVE ST4286: A 24-hectare (60-acre) area of marshy land just south of Magor village is leased as a reserve by the Monmouthshire Naturalists' Trust. This is the largest remnant of this type of habitat in the county. Access is restricted to members of the Trust and the Monmouthshire Ornithological Society.

The reserve has an extensive list of breeding birds including mallard, moorhen, snipe, sedge warbler and reed bunting. Both garganey and shoveler have nested in recent years, the latter occurring fairly regularly as a passage migrant in spring, while reed warbler and marsh warbler have been recorded in summer—could they breed? A prominent winter feature is the large number of snipe which visit the reserve.

11. NEDERN BROOK so4888: Winding its way under a motorway, several roads and a railway before reaching the estuary near the expanding town of Caldicot is Nedern Brook, a small but interesting area of water meadows. These are easily accessible from Caldicot Castle so486885 or the coast at so488873.

Up to about 250 teal are usually here in winter when the small herd of mute swans is occasionally joined by passing whooper swans. Other wildfowl have included mallard, garganey, shoveler and pochard. Small numbers of most common waders occur on passage including snipe, curlew, green and common sandpipers.

12. PETERSTONE WENTLOOGE st2780: This is an extensive area of low-lying fields, often flooded in winter and separated from a half-mile-wide strip of mud flats, exposed at low tide, by a sea wall which runs westward to the Rhymney River and eastwards to the Usk. It is one of the most important wader sites in the county and a great deal of information concerning numbers and the species present has been collected in recent years by the Monmouthshire Ornithological Society. There are various access points from the B4239 which runs close to the shore two miles east of Rumney, Cardiff.

Lapwings and golden plover frequent the water meadows throughout the winter, while during the same season the mud flats support large flocks of knot and dunlin, both in several thousands. The ringed plover is mainly a passage migrant in both spring and autumn when up to 200 may be seen. Grey plover, on the other hand, winter in the area, the highest number noted of this, one of our most attractive waders, being about eighty. Other waders are seen on passage in small numbers, and casual visitors in recent years have included little ringed plover, turnstone, green sandpiper, greenshank, little stint, sanderling, ruff and avocet. Short-eared owls winter in this area with up to six in 1970–1.

Preece, M. V., 'Wader Populations of the Severn Estuary', *Monmouthshire Birds* 1 (1970): 177–84.

13. PEN-Y-FAN POND SO1900: Just below the 1,000-foot contour on the southern slopes of Mynydd Pen-y-fan, the ridge between Ebbw Vale and the Sirhowy Valley, is the Pen-y-fan Pond. An unclassified road leaves the A4046 Ebbw Vale road at SO208019 and, after climbing for a mile and a quarter, passes the pond before joining the B4251 at ST195987 in Oakdale. Birds are not numerous here though both stonechat and whinchat breed, the former somewhat local in Monmouthshire. The area north of the pond should be searched for woodlarks. There are few records of this species in the county, but they have been observed here in recent years; could they breed? There is usually a small passage of waders— snipe, woodcock, curlew, common sandpiper; wildfowl seen have included tufted duck, goldeneye and whooper swan.

14. RHYMNEY RIVER ST2277: A narrow estuary on the eastern outskirts of Cardiff with adjacent saltings and reed beds opening on to the mud flats of the lower Severn estuary. The river forms the boundary between Monmouthshire and Glamorgan with the best access point being in the former county. Turn south off the A48, just east of the Rhymney bridge and in just over a quarter of a mile a narrow road leading left over a rail-

way bridge terminates on the sea wall. Shelduck can be seen here for most of the year, and in winter there is normally a small flock of wigeon, joined at times by other dabbling duck including teal, shoveler and pintail. Waders include ringed plover, curlew, redshank, greenshank, knot and dunlin.

15. UNDY ST4384: This is the centre of a long section of estuarine coast backed by Caldicot Level, a huge area of water meadows interlaced with drainage ditches. What ornithological treasures would there have been before man stamped his agricultural mark here? In places the Level extends up to three miles inland, but farming and industrialisation—the Spencer steelworks sit astride the north-west sector where there were once two duck decoys—have decreased even the more recent ornithological interest. The huge expanse of mud flats known as the Welsh Grounds, remain at present intact and extend over three miles into the Severn Estuary, which at this point is five miles wide. Observations are best made from the sea wall between Magor Pill ST438848 and Collister Pill ST453857.

Turn south from the B4245 at ST425872 in the village of Magor, turn left immediately on crossing the railway bridge and continue for a mile until Magor Pill Farm at ST432855, from which a track may be followed to the sea wall at Magor Pill. A footpath runs along the sea wall both to the north-east and south-west.

Mallard are the most numerous wintering duck, up to 200 normally being present, joined by smaller numbers of teal, wigeon and the occasional pintail. Small numbers —up to about forty—Bewick's swans spend part of the winter on Caldicot Moor ST4486 just east of Undy.

Waders, with knot and dunlin predominating in winter, are the main feature of the Undy area. Up to 200 grey plover normally winter, though there were 3,500 in January 1971, while ringed plover, turnstone, curlew and redshank are numerous on spring passage when smaller numbers of whimbrel, black-tailed and bar-tailed godwits occur. More unusual visitors noted have included hen harrier, dowitcher, little stint, purple sandpiper, ruff, stone curlew and Sandwich tern. Snow buntings are regularly seen in winter and black redstarts have been reported.

Preece, M. V., 'Wader Populations of the Severn Estuary', *Monmouthshire Birds* 1 (1970): 177–84.

16. WENTWOOD RESERVOIR AND WOODS ST4293: Situated on the southern edge of what was formerly the extensive Wentwood Forest (though now all that remains is chiefly conifers) is Wentwood Reservoir, a small sheet of water from which Newport draws its supply. The reservoir is best reached by turning north off the A48 Chepstow to Newport road at Penhow ST426910, and after passing through the village of Llanvaches bear left until the reservoir dam is reached in about a mile. The road continues along the western bank, while another follows the eastern. From the reservoir head a road runs on into the woodland with a number of tracks leading off at various points, giving the visitor ample scope for exploration.

Pochard are the most numerous wintering duck on the reservoir with a maximum of just over seventy in 1970; other species recorded include mallard, teal, pintail, shoveler, tufted duck and goosander. Great crested grebes are occasionally seen and, as at Llandegfedd Reservoir, have displayed but not remained to breed.

Waders are seen from time to time, greenshank, dunlin and little stint have occurred in recent years and like any sheet of open water gulls are attracted in some numbers. Kingfishers and dippers may be seen, while the woodlands species include buzzard, tawny owl, nightjar, great spotted and lesser spotted woodpeckers. Golden orioles were seen here in 1967, 1969 and 1971.

Loveys, F. M., 'Wentwood Forest Area', *Monmouthshire Birds* 1 (1970): 188–9.

17. YNYS-Y-FRO RESERVOIR ST2889: This small reservoir just north-west of Newport is divided in two sections by a causeway complete with footpath. An unclassified road runs south from the suburb of Betwws and a track leads left from this at ST279896 and past Ynys-y-fro house to the reservoir causeway. Alternatively one can turn off the A467 Newport to Risca road at ST271888 in Rogerstown and by taking the second right will arrive at the track to the reservoir. For those wishing to approach on foot from Newport, follow the Monmouthshire and Brecon canal alongside the M4, leaving the canal where it passes under the motorway and then head north on the footpath leading to the reservoir dam.

Up to fifty coot winter on the reservoir together with small numbers of teal, tufted duck, pochard and goldeneye. Occasional visitors have included great crested and black-necked grebes, wigeon and goosander. Common sandpipers regularly occur on passage with one wintering in 1970.

Check list

RB Resident Breeder MB Migrant Breeder
wv Winter Visitor PV Passage Visitor
v Vagrant

Great Crested Grebe	RB	Bewick's Swan	wv
Black-necked Grebe	v	Buzzard	RB
Little Grebe	RB	Sparrowhawk	RB
Manx Shearwater	v	Hen Harrier	wv
Gannet	v	Hobby	v
Cormorant	PV	Peregrine	wv
Grey Heron	RB	Merlin	wv
Mallard	RB		Has bred
Teal	wv	Kestrel	RB
Garganey	MB	Red Grouse	RB
Gadwall	wv	Quail	PV
Wigeon	wv	Red-legged Partridge	RB
Pintail	wv	Partridge	RB
Shoveler	wv	Water Rail	RB
Scaup	wv	Corncrake	PV
Tufted Duck	wv	Moorhen	RB
Pochard	wv	Coot	RB
Goldeneye	wv	Oystercatcher	wv
Common Scoter	v	Lapwing	RB
Red-breasted Merganser		Ringed Plover	wv
	wv	Grey Plover	wv
Goosander	wv	Golden Plover	wv
Shelduck	RB	Turnstone	wv
White-fronted Goose	wv	Snipe	RB
Mute Swan	RB	Jack Snipe	wv
Whooper Swan	wv	Woodcock	RB

Curlew	RB	Tawny Owl	RB
Whimbrel	PV	Short-eared Owl	WV
Black-tailed Godwit	PV	Nightjar	MB
Bar-tailed Godwit	PV	Swift	MB
Green Sandpiper	PV	Kingfisher	RB
Common Sandpiper	MB	Green Woodpecker	RB
Redshank	WV	Great Spotted Wood-	
Spotted Redshank	PV	pecker	RB
Greenshank	PV	Lesser Spotted Wood-	
Knot	WV	pecker	RB
Little Stint	V	Woodlark	V
Dunlin	WV	Skylark	RB
Curlew Sandpiper	PV	Swallow	MB
Sanderling	PV	House Martin	MB
Ruff	PV	Sand Martin	MB
Great Black-backed Gull		Golden Oriole	V
	RB	Raven	RB
Lesser Black-backed Gull		Carrion Crow	RB
	MB	Rook	RB
Herring Gull	RB	Jackdaw	RB
Common Gull	WV	Magpie	RB
Black-headed Gull	WV	Jay	RB
Black Tern	PV	Great Tit	RB
Common Tern	PV	Blue Tit	RB
Arctic Tern	PV	Coal Tit	RB
Sandwich Tern	PV	Marsh Tit	RB
Stock Dove	RB	Willow Tit	RB
Woodpigeon	RB	Long-tailed Tit	RB
Turtle Dove	MB	Nuthatch	RB
Collared Dove	RB	Treecreeper	RB
Cuckoo	MB	Wren	RB
Barn Owl	RB	Dipper	RB
Little Owl	RB	Mistle Thrush	RB

Fieldfare	WV	Meadow Pipit	RB
Song Thrush	RB	Tree Pipit	MB
Redwing	WV	Rock Pipit	WV
Ring Ouzel	MB	Water Pipit	WV
Blackbird	RB	Pied Wagtail	RB
Wheatear	MB	White Wagtail	PV
Stonechat	RB	Grey Wagtail	RB
Whinchat	MB	Yellow Wagtail	MB
Redstart	MB	Waxwing	V
Black Redstart	V	Starling	RB
Nightingale	PV	Hawfinch	RB
Has bred		Greenfinch	RB
Robin	RB	Goldfinch	RB
Grasshopper Warbler	MB	Siskin	WV
Reed Warbler	MB	Linnet	RB
Marsh Warbler	PV	Redpoll	RB
Sedge Warbler	MB	Bullfinch	RB
Blackcap	MB	Crossbill	PV
Garden Warbler	MB	Has bred	
Whitethroat	MB	Chaffinch	RB
Lesser Whitethroat	MB	Brambling	WV
Willow Warbler	MB	Yellowhammer	RB
Chiffchaff	MB	Corn Bunting	PV
Wood Warbler	MB	Reed Bunting	RB
Goldcrest	RB	Snow Bunting	WV
Spotted Flycatcher	MB	House Sparrow	RB
Pied Flycatcher	MB	Tree Sparrow	RB
Dunnock	MB		

MONTGOMERYSHIRE

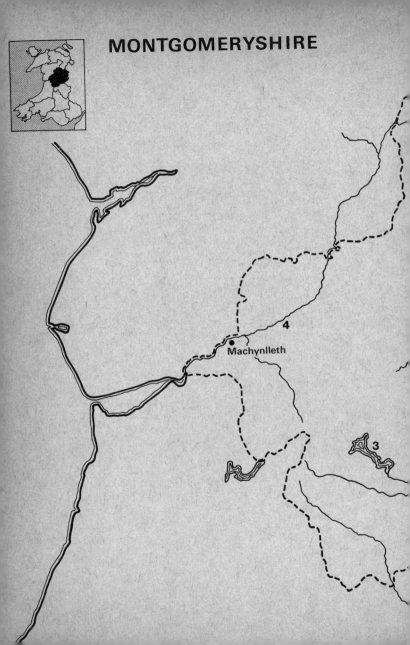

Machynlleth

4

3

5

Llanefyllin

7

Welshpool

2

8

6

1

9

11

Montgomery

Newtown

10

anidloes

0   5   10
mile

Chapter 14

Montgomeryshire

Montgomeryshire, the third largest county in Wales (797 square miles), although basically an inland area does in fact reach westwards to the estuary of the Dyfi for about three miles in its confined upper reaches. It is thus the only county to extend the full width of Wales, reaching from the Shropshire plain across the central mountains to Cardigan Bay, or rather an estuary entering Cardigan Bay. The population, like those of other mid-Wales counties, is small (46,761 in 1971) and there are few large communities. Newtown and Welshpool, fourteen miles apart in the Severn valley, are the main centres with a combined population of about 12,000, and share the local government administration of the county.

An arc of mountain and moorland sweeps across the north and west of Montgomeryshire and continues along the southern borders to reach the English marches. In the north-west the Berwyns run in heather confusion away into the upland fastnesses of Denbighshire and Merioneth. Here is the highest point in the county, Moel Sych rising to 2,700 feet. This merges with other high ground and lacks the dramatic impact of some Welsh peaks, even those of lesser heights.

The western boundary continues south, crossing the Afon Dyfi to intersect the Dyfi Forest conifer plantations before rejoining the river at Machynlleth. Leaving the river again a little lower down it ascends the lovely Llyfnant Valley to meander along moorland streams, across pools, bogs and watersheds and eventually across the eastern slopes of Plynlimon (2,470 feet). Here both the Severn and the Wye trickle into life, beginning their quite separate journeys, later to meet on the Monmouth-shire–Gloucestershire border where they enter the Bristol Channel. After crossing the upper Wye valley the bound-ary gradually turns eastwards with Radnorshire and then Shropshire as its southern neighbours, sharing with them the sheep-rearing uplands of Kerry and of Clun.

One other upland area deserves special note, the Breidden Hills rising with their three peaks to 1,324 feet at Moel-y-Golfa and dominating the Severn plain north-east of Welshpool. Of volcanic origin, the dolerite rock of which they are composed has excellent qualities for use in the surfacing of roads and is in great demand. Exten-sive quarrying has been carried out with several thousand tons of material being removed annually, resulting in one of the highest man-made cliffs in Britain. The special geological nature of the crags has resulted in rich and, in some respects, unique plant communities, with several particularly rare species occurring. Some of these have been lost and others are endangered, but naturalists and the quarry management now work in close liaison. A small area has been set aside as a nature reserve, and it is hoped that abandoned cliff faces and screes will eventually be recolonised.

The upland areas are intersected by the valleys of mainly eastward flowing rivers which gradually open out as they approach the English border. Chief among these is the Severn with its wide flood plain of rich water meadows. Smaller tributaries include the Vyrnwy, Cain and Tanat, so that fingers of the Shropshire plain seem to extend towards the very centre of Wales. It was along such natural and amenable routes that early man came. Above Montgomery one of the earliest known living sites in the central marches of Wales has been discovered—

that of a Neolithic open settlement. Later activities include the building of numerous hill forts by Iron Age
peoples and later the Romans who passed this way in
search of lead on the Plynlimon uplands. Offa, king of
Mercia, is best remembered for his embankment known
as Offa's Dyke, which in Montgomeryshire stretches from
Carreghofa south to Castlewright.

Montgomeryshire is mainly an agricultural county, but
in the nineteenth century it passed through an industrial
era with lead mining and slate quarrying in the western
hills and flannel and woollen mills in the valley towns.
Some measure of the county's prosperity at that time may
be gained from the population figures which rose to
70,000. Although rough grazing land accounts for about
40 per cent of the total land area, 85 per cent of the re-
mainder is under grass, with both dairy and beef farming
expanding.

Montgomeryshire, it is claimed, is the best wooded of
all Welsh counties, and certainly no one who has wan-
dered along one of the river valleys would dispute this. At
one time it was a recognised source of oak for the Navy,
a fact commemorated by the pillar erected on Breidden
Hill in 1782 to the victories of Admiral Rodney, which
were fought in ships made from Montgomeryshire oaks.
More recently the Forestry Commission has been active
with large areas in the upland regions now planted with
conifers. One of the major Welsh forests is the Hafren,
some 3,500 hectares (9,000 acres) close to the Cardiganshire border.

With the virtual absence of an estuarine area and no
sea coast it is hardly surprising that Montgomeryshire
has been somewhat neglected by visiting ornithologists,
who tend to seek out such sites. Resident ornithologists

are few and have a vast area, much of it difficult terrain, so that probably less is known of its avifauna than most other counties in Wales. Some areas, however, are well watched, in particular the Severn valley flats where winter wildfowl are of special note. Other parts, especially in the north and west, are greatly under recorded yet contain interesting birds and, no doubt, discoveries for those who explore there. The major reservoirs of Clywedog and Vyrnwy are probably more important than the present records indicate and every effort should be made by the visitor to reach these sites. There is certainly a great need for concentrated watching and an ornithologist with careful observation can add to our present knowledge in most parts of Montgomeryshire.

Information

County Avifaunas
Forrest, H. E., *The Vertebrate Fauna of North Wales* (London, 1907). This, together with a supplement published in 1919, is the only avifauna available, though it is long out of date.

Bird Report
Records of birds in Montgomeryshire are published annually in the reports of the Montgomeryshire Field Society, price 15p from the Hon. Sec. (see Ornithological Society).

County Bird Recorder
R. R. Lovegrove, Walkmill, Mochdre, Newtown.

Ornithological Society
The Montgomeryshire Field Society arranges a programme of lectures, some of specific ornithological interest, at monthly intervals throughout the winter; these
are generally held in Welshpool. During the summer
there are field meetings and again some of these are to
places of ornithological interest. Subscription 25p per
annum. Hon. Sec. Miss V. J. Macnair, Lower Garth,
Welshpool.

Naturalists' Trust
The North Wales Naturalists' Trust covers the counties
of Anglesey, Caernarvonshire, Denbighshire, Flintshire,
Merioneth and Montgomeryshire. Founded in 1963 the
Trust now owns or leases three reserves, together with
three roadside verge reserves, in Montgomeryshire. There
is an active branch of the Trust in the county, which holds
occasional field meetings and arranges lectures. Subscription £1.00 per annum, students 50p, juniors 25p. Hon.
Gen. Sec. Mrs. M. J. Morgan, 154 High Street, Bangor,
Caerns.

Royal Society for the Protection of Birds Representative
Not appointed.

British Trust for Ornithology Representative
R. R. Lovegrove, Walkmill, Mochdre, Newtown.

Tourist Information
County Handbook available (price 15p) from County
Offices, Welshpool.

1. CAMLAD VALLEY SJ2100: Near Church Stoke (Shropshire) several streams unite to form the River Camlad which, following a circuitous route, forms part of the county boundary before reaching the River Severn at SJ209005 near the hamlet of Forden. The water meadows on either side of the river are a favourite wintering ground for wildfowl, and may be observed from several vantage points. About two miles north of Montgomery the B4388 crosses Salt Bridge at SO227994 close to a section of Offa's Dyke. To the south-west of Forden an unclassified road crosses the river at SO214999. Originally the Hem Flash SJ2400 was the most important ornithological site in the valley. Unfortunately, from both birds' and bird-watchers' points of view, efforts have been made to improve the drainage. Although not wholly successful, these have nevertheless diminished its attractiveness.

White-fronted geese—up to 1,000 at one time, though generally fewer in recent years—winter in the valley, while wigeon are the most numerous duck. Other duck regularly occurring include mallard, teal and shoveler; scarcer visitors include garganey, pintail, shelduck, greylag goose, whooper and Bewick's swans. Waders recorded on autumn passage have included ringed plover, black-tailed godwit and ruff, with lapwings and golden plover regularly in large flocks right through the winter.

2. CHARLES ACKERS REDWOOD GROVE SJ245055: In 1958, a hundred years after the first trees, brought direct from California, were planted, the Charles Ackers Redwood Grove was presented to the Royal Forestry Society. Situated in Leighton Park about three miles south-east of Welshpool it is reached by leaving the town on the B4381 and then turning south along the B4388 for about

one mile where there is a minor road turning into Leighton Park at sj238053. Some forty-seven of the original trees still remain, the tallest being 125 feet with a girth exceeding 12 feet. Further extensive planting took place in 1935, while other species thriving in the area include wellingtonia, Douglas fir and Japanese cypress.

A census of breeding birds in the 10 hectares (25 acres) of exotic woodland showed a richness both in number and variety of species present compared to most other coniferous plantations. Goldcrests were the most numerous species with fourteen pairs, wood pigeon, wren, blackbird, robin and chaffinch also being common. Hole-nesting species are for the most part absent, the timber, in first class condition, providing few suitable nesting sites. Other birds breeding in the redwood grove include tawny owl, crow, jay, coal tit, long-tailed tit, song thrush and chiffchaff.

Williamson, K., 'Birds in a Redwood Grove', *Countryman* 77 (1972): 145–9.

3. CLYWEDOG RESERVOIR SN8988: Completed in 1968 this 250-hectare (615 acre) reservoir north-west of Llanidloes acts primarily as a regulating reservoir for water abstraction by the Montgomeryshire Water Board farther downstream. During the construction eighteen farms were flooded or partially flooded. When full, the reservoir is six miles long with a maximum width of about 500 yards, and contains 11,000 million gallons of water. A Nature Trail has been laid out around part of the reservoir by the North Wales Naturalists' Trust, with access from the road at SN904872.

The main ornithological interest is during the winter, but common and Arctic terns have been observed on passage and, no doubt, further observation will provide an indication that waders also occur even though their stay may be brief. Mallard, teal, tufted duck and pochard are regular throughout the winter; other visitors have included cormorant, goldeneye and red-breasted merganser.

4. DYFI VALLEY SN6997 TO SH8614: The Afon Dyfi extends from the border with Cardiganshire at Dovey Junction, on its upper estuarine reaches, inland for some sixteen miles to Dinas Mawddy (Merioneth) a southern gateway to the Snowdonia National Park. Three miles downstream from this point the river passes out of the Park and into Montgomeryshire. For the most part the valley floor is barely half a mile wide, edged by steep slopes, in some places wooded. Numerous streams and two main tributaries, the Afon Dulas and Afon Twymyn dash from the uplands to join the main watercourse of the Dyfi. Below Machynlleth the A487 runs parallel to the river, while upstream the A489 and 4084 follow the south bank with the B4404 on part of the north.

Red-breasted mergansers have nested in the Dyfi valley for some years, they first nested in Wales as recently as 1954, and should be looked for on the lower reaches of the river. Other water birds include common sandpiper, kingfisher, dipper and grey wagtail. Buzzards, redstarts, wood warblers and pied flycatchers occur in the woodlands along the valley sides, while the higher ground supports birds like ring ouzel, wheatear and whinchat.

5. LAKE VYRNWY SH9921: On the western borders of Montgomeryshire and surrounded by hills rising to

nearly 2,000 feet is Lake Vyrnwy, a reservoir constructed in 1888 by throwing a dam across the Afon Vyrnwy, just upstream from Llanwyddyn, in order to supply water to Liverpool. The B4393 runs west from Llanfyllin SJ1419 and follows the whole perimeter of the reservoir, which is lined with extensive conifer plantations.

Common sandpipers and grey wagtails breed around the shore, but the main ornithological interest is concerned with visiting birds, though unfortunately records are few due to an absence of observers in this remote area. Cormorants are frequent visitors throughout the year, while in winter up to about four great crested grebes are usually present. Mallard and teal are regular winter visitors as are small parties of tufted duck and pochard, and rarer species have included goosander and common scoter. Redstarts, pied flycatchers and redpolls can be seen among the plantations and one should always look carefully for siskins, a few pairs of which have nested here since about 1964.

6. LEIGHTON FLATS SJ2305: An extensive area of water meadows on the south bank of the river Severn just upstream from Welshpool. Leave Welshpool on the B4381 which crosses Leighton Bridge and then turn south on the B4388; minor roads run down towards the Severn from this road at SJ239058 and SJ237050. Normally any wildfowl present can be adequately observed from the gate at the end of each road; there is no need to proceed on to the water meadows, which are private land, and cause undue disturbance.

Canada geese were introduced into Montgomeryshire, near Leighton, about 1860, and have thrived ever since. They spend much of their time outside the breeding

season in large flocks, one of their favourite haunts being
the river and water meadows of Leighton Flats. Peak
numbers are normally reached in December and January,
when up to 250 have been noted, local stock being aug-
mented by birds moving in from outside the county. In
view of the large numbers of this bird in Montgomeryshire, it seems surprising that it is so scarce in some other
Welsh counties including neighbouring Cardiganshire.
White-fronted geese are regular winter visitors with peak
numbers of about 400 occurring in January and February. Other winter wildfowl on the flats include mallard,
teal and wigeon, while the river itself sometimes attracts
diving duck. Waders, which occur on passage though
only in very small numbers, include oystercatcher, ringed
plover, green sandpiper, common sandpiper, greenshank
and dunlin.

7. LLYN DU SJ1712: This small pool on Broniarth Hill
above the Dyffryn Meifod is adjacent to the unclassified
road which crosses the hill. Leave Meifod in an easterly
direction from SJ153131 or travel westwards from the
A490 Llanfyllin to Welshpool road at SJ209115.

   Great crested grebes and coot regularly breed. Cormorants visit the pool, and common and Arctic terns
have been observed on passage, while waders have included green sandpiper and greenshank. Wintering duck
include, though in no great numbers, mallard, teal,
wigeon, tufted duck, pochard and goldeneye.

8. LLYN HIR SJ0205: This moorland pool on Mynydd
Waun Fawr is reached by way of the unclassified road
running south through Nant Menial from the village of
Llanerfyl SJ033097 on the A458. After about a mile a

track leads south-east up the hill at sj025088.

At too high an altitude it only attracts a few mallard and teal in winter, but in summer it holds one of the largest inland gull colonies in Wales, usually about 700 pairs of black-headed gulls. This whole upland area is well worth exploring.

9. LLYN MAWR SO0097: This rather fine upland lake of about eight hectares (20 acres) is situated at 1,250 feet on the moorland north-west of Caersws. The lake, together with a narrow strip of surrounding land, is a reserve of the North Wales Naturalists' Trust who purchased it in 1970 with the aid of grants from the World Wildlife Fund and other bodies. Access is unrestricted to members of the Trust; enquiries concerning the reserve should be made to the Secretary, Llyn Mawr Management Committee, Binian, The Fron, Newtown. The lake is reached by taking the unclassified road near Pontdolgoch SO005944 on the A489 Caersws to Machynlleth road.

The lake is less acid than most upland waters in Wales and the consequent rich and varied flora has no doubt encouraged its interesting avifauna. Breeding birds include great crested grebe, heron, mallard, teal, tufted duck, snipe, curlew, black-headed gull and whinchat. Wigeon, pochard and goldeneye are winter visitors and a small flock of white-fronted geese is usually present during January and February.

10. NEWTOWN SEWAGE FARM SO1292: Due to alterations the attractiveness to birds of this small sewage farm, situated between the A483 Newtown to Welshpool road just to the east of Newtown, has now diminished.

A few waders still call, mainly during the autumn

passage when green sandpiper, spotted redshank, greenshank and dunlin have been noted. Yellow wagtails
breed, while an unusual species to do so has been the
greylag goose, undoubtedly feral birds, possibly from
Anglesey where up to 130 have been seen.

11. SHROPSHIRE UNION CANAL SO1493 TO SJ2620: This
long-disused canal originally carried traffic from the
Llangollen Canal at Welsh Frankton (Shropshire) to
Newtown. Parts are now filled in or drained, but much of
the Montgomeryshire section still contains water, though
is much overgrown in places. It is easily accessible at
many points from the A483 which it follows for much of
its length. This provides an interesting linear habitat for
many birds including mallard, mute swan, coot, moorhen, sedge warbler and reed bunting.

Check list

RB Resident Breeder   MB Migrant Breeder
WV Winter Visitor   PV Passage Visitor
              V   Vagrant

Great Crested Grebe	RB	Gadwall		V
Little Grebe	RB	Wigeon		WV
Cormorant	PV	Pintail		V
Grey Heron	RB	Shoveler		WV
Mallard	RB	Tufted Duck		RB
Teal	RB	Pochard		WV
Garganey	V	Goldeneye		WV

Common Scoter	V	Woodcock	RB
Red-breasted Merganser		Curlew	RB
	RB	Whimbrel	PV
Goosander	WV	Green Sandpiper	PV
Shelduck	RB	Common Sandpiper	MB
Greylag Goose	V	Redshank	RB
Feral birds breed		Dunlin	PV
White-fronted Goose	WV	Great Black-backed Gull	
Pink-footed Goose	V		PV
Canada Goose	RB	Lesser Black-backed Gull	
Mute Swan	RB		PV
Whooper Swan	WV	Herring Gull	PV
Bewick's Swan	WV	Common Gull	WV
Buzzard	RB	Black-headed Gull	RB
Sparrowhawk	RB	Common Tern	PV
Hen Harrier	PV	Arctic Tern	PV
Peregrine	V	Stock Dove	RB
Merlin	RB	Woodpigeon	RB
Kestrel	RB	Turtle Dove	MB
Red Grouse	RB	Collared Dove	RB
Black Grouse	RB	Cuckoo	MB
Partridge	RB	Barn Owl	RB
Pheasant	RB	Little Owl	RB
Water Rail	RB	Tawny Owl	RB
Corncrake	MB	Long-eared Owl	RB
Moorhen	RB	Short-eared Owl	RB
Coot	RB	Swift	MB
Oystercatcher	PV	Kingfisher	RB
Lapwing	RB	Green Woodpecker	RB
Ringed Plover	PV	Great Spotted Wood-	
Golden Plover	RB	pecker	RB
Snipe	RB	Lesser Spotted Wood-	
Jack Snipe	WV	pecker	RB

Skylark	RB	Sedge Warbler	MB
Swallow	MB	Blackcap	MB
House Martin	MB	Garden Warbler	MB
Sand Martin	MB	Whitethroat	MB
Raven	RB	Lesser Whitethroat	MB
Carrion Crow	RB	Willow Warbler	MB
Rook	RB	Chiffchaff	MB
Jackdaw	RB	Wood Warbler	MB
Magpie	RB	Goldcrest	RB
Jay	RB	Spotted Flycatcher	MB
Great Tit	RB	Pied Flycatcher	MB
Blue Tit	RB	Dunnock	RB
Coal Tit	RB	Meadow Pipit	RB
Marsh Tit	RB	Tree Pipit	MB
Willow Tit	RB	Pied Wagtail	RB
Long-tailed Tit	RB	White Wagtail	PV
Nuthatch	RB	Grey Wagtail	RB
Treecreeper	RB	Yellow Wagtail	MB
Wren	RB	Starling	RB
Dipper	RB	Hawfinch	RB
Mistle Thrush	RB	Greenfinch	RB
Fieldfare	WV	Goldfinch	RB
Song Thrush	RB	Siskin	RB
Redwing	WV	Linnet	RB
Ring Ouzel	MB	Redpoll	RB
Blackbird	RB	Bullfinch	RB
Wheatear	MB	Chaffinch	RB
Stonechat	RB	Brambling	WV
Whinchat	MB	Yellowhammer	RB
Redstart	MB	Reed Bunting	RB
Robin	RB	House Sparrow	RB
Grasshopper Warbler	MB	Tree Sparrow	RB
Reed Warbler	MB		

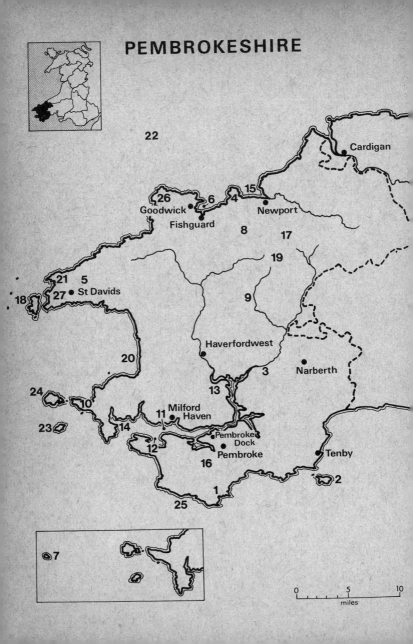

PEMBROKESHIRE

22

● Cardigan

26
Goodwick
Fishguard
6
4
15
Newport

8
17

19

21
5
27
● St Davids
18

9

20

Haverfordwest

24
10
23
14
12

11
Milford
Haven

13
3

● Narberth

Pembroke
Dock
Pembroke
16

● Tenby
2

1
25

7

0   5   10
miles

Chapter 15

Pembrokeshire

Pembrokeshire, the most south-westerly county in Wales, protrudes into the Bristol and St George's Channels, where it receives both the full Atlantic swell and the benefits of the Gulf Stream. It is one of the windiest parts of Britain, second only to north-west Ireland and can expect to have at least thirty-two gales annually, mostly in winter. Small wonder that trees in coastal areas, save for those in sheltered hollows, are stunted and wind twisted. Not until the more central and easterly parts of the county are reached do large areas of woodland occur. The maritime plant communities, which thrive in the salt-laden air on exposed cliffs sidings, make up for the virtual absence of trees; the profusion of species and colour, particularly during May and June, is quite remarkable and should not be missed by the visitor.

The county is very rich geologically; there is much of interest to be explored both by the complete beginner and the advanced student. The most ancient of rocks are found here, cooled two thousand million years ago, from which run an unbroken series of volcanic lavas and sedimentary rocks until the coal measures of two hundred and fifty million years ago. More recent deposits are not found in Pembrokeshire. Perhaps they have been eroded away, or were never laid down due to the land already being above sea level. Much of south Pembrokeshire is now a 200-foot-high marine platform deeply incised by glacial and river action. It is not possible to stand anywhere in the county more than eight miles from salt

overleaf – *Oystercatcher*

water at high tide and nearly one-third of the county is
within two miles of the sea. In the north the Presely
ridge commences at the St David's peninsula and climbs
eastwards to a summit of 1,760 feet forming the western
bastion for higher ground in Cardiganshire and Carmarthenshire.

Essentially an agricultural county, dairy and beef
farming is dominant in the south with early potatoes
being locally important in coastal areas. The poorer and
higher ground to the north supports large flocks of sheep.
Milford Haven was once an important fishing port and
during the early years of this century the sixth largest in
Britain. A decline has taken place since the Second World
War and landings of fish have dropped from 60,000 tons
in 1946 to less than 10,000 tons per annum during the
late 1960s. More recently the deep water harbour has
become one of Europe's largest ports in terms of tonnage
handled, this being due entirely to the growth of the oil
industry around its shores. The first refinery opened in
1960. Now there are three with a fourth under construction, while oil is pumped from another terminal via a
storage tank farm to Llandarcy, Swansea, sixty miles
east. Another development on the shore of Milford Haven
has been the establishment of an oil-fired power station;
its 600 foot main chimney is now a landmark throughout
southern Pembrokeshire.

The three most important regions of the county are included in the Pembrokeshire National Park established
in 1952. A coastal strip of varying depth runs the whole
way from the border with Carmarthenshire to that with
Cardiganshire traversed by the 170-mile coastal footpath

Baird's Sandpiper

completed in 1970. The upper reaches of the Cleddau estuaries and their adjoining creeks are also included in the Park as are the higher parts of the Presely ridge. A Chief Warden with three assistants has his headquarters at the County Offices, Haverfordwest. There are staffed information centres at Tenby, Pembroke, Haverfordwest and Fishguard, and others are planned. In 1969 the Pembrokeshire Countryside Unit was established by the Countryside Commission and Field Studies Council at Broad Haven. With its information officer, exhibition space and full programme of field excursions between Whitsun and September, the Unit has played an important part in creating a greater awareness about the Pembrokeshire countryside and the heightening pressures it faces.

The coastline, although with many superb sandy beaches, is essentially a rocky shore with cliffs and steep slopes in most places. Offshore the islands with their Norse names—Grassholm, Skokholm, Middleholm—have long been famous for their seabird colonies and migrant passerines. They have dominated the attention of both resident and visiting ornithologists to Pembrokeshire. Even so, other aspects of the county's bird life should not be neglected and there are many mainland opportunities for the beginner, casual observer or for more advanced workers. The north coast headlands have been shown to have many opportunities for observation on visible migration about which virtually nothing is known at present in this area. Estuarine habitats are virtually restricted to Milford Haven and its tributaries which although full of interest do not compare, for variety of species and numbers, with those elsewhere in Wales. Could they become more important as some of our larger estuaries are developed and altered by barrages and greater industrialisation? Upland areas are generally at too low an altitude to attract any number of moorland birds and because of this they tend to be neglected. More detailed watching might show that they are more important than is realised. With so few areas of open fresh water in the county, the newly-constructed Llys-y-fran reservoir could well prove most attractive to wintering flocks of diving duck, but this remains to be seen.

Information

County Avifaunas
Mathew, M. A., *The Birds of Pembrokeshire and its Islands* (London, 1894). Long out of date, but still of interest.
Lockley R. M. *et al.*, *Birds of Pembrokeshire* (Haverfordwest, 1949).
   Now in urgent need of revision due to the vast amount of new information collected during the years since its publication.

Bird Report
No county bird report is available, but a joint report with Cardiganshire and Carmarthenshire known as the *Dyfed Bird Report* is published by the West Wales Naturalists' Trust, price 20p.

County Bird Recorder
J. W. Donovan Esq., The Burren, Dingle Lane, Crundale, Haverfordwest.

Ornithological Society

No Society as such; this role has been taken over by the West Wales Naturalists' Trust (see Naturalists' Trust). The quarterly bulletin produced by the Trust usually contains a brief section concerned with the more unusual species seen within the county.

Naturalists' Trust

The West Wales Naturalists' Trust (see also Ornithological Society) covers the counties of Cardiganshire, Carmarthenshire and Pembrokeshire. Formerly the West Wales Field Society it changed to a Trust in 1961, and now owns or leases some eight reserves in Pembrokeshire, including Skokholm and Skomer Islands. Members receive the journal *Nature in Wales* and a quarterly Bulletin, while there is an extensive range of winter lectures in Haverfordwest, Newport and Tenby, together with numerous field meetings. Subscription £2.00 per annum (adults), 50p (children and students). Hon. Gen. Sec. Dillwyn Miles, 4 Victoria Place, Haverfordwest.

Royal Society for the Protection of Birds Representative

J. W. Donovan Esq. (see County Bird Recorder).

British Trust for Ornithology Representative

J. W. Barrett, MA, FIBiol, Anchor Cottage, Dale, Haverfordwest.

Tourist Information

West Wales Tourist Association, 4 Victoria Place, Haverfordwest, or when in the county from this office or any of the information offices in Tenby, Pembroke, Haverfordwest and St David's, also the Countryside Unit, Broad

Haven. Official Guide to Pembrokeshire (price 15p).

1. BOSHERSTON LILY PONDS: SR9795: During the winter
months when there is little disturbance, small numbers
of duck, both dabbling and diving, congregate here, including gadwall which now winter regularly in the
county. More unusual visitors have included goosander
and a ring-necked duck—the first record for Wales of this
wanderer from North America.

2. CALDEY AND ST MARGARET'S SS1396 AND 1297: Unlike
the western islands of the county, Caldey and its satellite
St Margaret's, to which it is joined at low tide, has comparatively few seabirds. Caldey is extensively farmed by
its community of Cistercian monks and there is also an
extensive area of woodland. The most recent account of
its bird life is given by Sage (1956). It has the largest
herring gull colony in south-west Wales with 3,250 pairs
in 1970, but few other seabirds nest. The landbird population does not include any unexpected species, though
the variety is richer than the other islands and includes
sparrowhawk, collared dove, blackcap, goldcrest and
yellowhammer. No studies have yet been made on Caldey
of bird migration.

St Margaret's Island is a reserve of the West Wales
Naturalists' Trust from whom permission is required to
land. It is, however, far better to sail around on one of
the many boat trips arranged from Tenby; all the seabird
colonies may then be seen with ease. Kittiwakes, razorbills and guillemots nest in small numbers and there are
still several pairs of puffins. The cormorant colony with
260 pairs in 1969 and 328 in 1973 is the largest in Wales
and one of the largest in Britain and Ireland.

Sage, B. L., 'Notes on the Birds of Caldey and St Margaret's Islands, Pembrokeshire', *Nature in Wales* 2 (1956): 332–40.

3. CANASTON AND MINWEAR WOODS SN0513 AND 0713: An area of deciduous and conifer woodland to the south of Canaston Bridge on the A40 road at SN067152. A National Park view point at SN055137 gives fine views of the river and is adjacent to an interesting Forest Trail through the conifer plantations. (Leaflet price 5p from Forestry Commission, South Wales Office.) Farther on in the deciduous woods about SN0413 a path leads down to the river and a good chance of seeing herons; there is a heronry in Slebech Park on the opposite bank. Shelduck nest on this section and can usually be seen, while small numbers of curlew and redshank are frequently present. In the woods birds like nightjars, redstarts and wood warblers should be looked for.

4. DINAS ISLAND SN0140: Although the name is misleading, this is in fact another of the fine Pembrokeshire headlands; this one dividing the Fishguard and Newport Bays. It is best reached from Cwm-yr-eglwys SN015400 from where a path runs right round the head. A booklet describing the geological and natural history features of the headland, (price 8p) is available from West Wales Naturalists' Trust.

The most important point for ornithologists is Needle Rock SN016409 where both razorbills and guillemots nest; the latter, unfortunately, only on the seaward side, though they can be observed flying to and fro. Fulmar petrels and shags also nest on the cliffs, while buzzards, ravens, even the occasional peregrine falcon may be seen.

Cwm Dewi, the valley which runs west from Cwm-yr-eglwys and divides the headland from the mainland proper, has some sheltered woodland where summer visitors like whitethroats, blackcaps and garden warblers nest. A small marshy area has sedge warblers, grass-hopper warblers and reed buntings.

5. DOWROG COMMON SM7727: An unfenced single track road crosses the common from SM782268 to SM769278. Montagu's harriers usually occur on passage, particularly during April and May, while during the winter hen harriers, merlin and short-eared owls are normally resi-dent. A large pool near Maen Dewi Farm at SM768268 once contained a black-headed gull colony, but is now too choked, while excessive shooting keeps winter duck numbers low. Both water rails and spotted crake are heard most years in spring; do they ever breed? The whole area is particularly rich entomologically and botanically and has much of interest to the general naturalist.

6. FISHGUARD HARBOUR SM9538: The sheltered water here is most attractive in winter to divers and grebes; the central breakwater at SM955383 being the best observation point. Red-throated divers are the most frequently en-countered, though the other two species occur and, in particular, the great northern. Several great crested grebes winter here and all the other British grebes are seen from time to time. Other visitors to the harbour include shelter-ing razorbills and guillemots and duck like red-breasted mergansers and common scoter. Purple sandpipers can regularly be seen on the outer side of the main break-water SM962391. In the old quarry area at SM952395

wintering black redstarts may be encountered. The gulls which frequent the harbour area should be scrutinised; there is always a chance of wintering Iceland or glaucous gulls becoming mixed up in the flocks, while a great skua once wintered here.

7. GRASSHOLM SM5909: This 22-acre island, a reserve of the Royal Society for the Protection of Birds, is situated six miles due west of Skomer. Its small size and isolated position makes landing difficult, so that few visits are made each year. A settled period of weather with little or no swell is required and intending visitors should make enquiries with boatmen at Dale.

Grassholm, despite its small size, has the fourth largest gannet colony in the North Atlantic with 16,000 pairs in 1969, barely 100 years since they first nested there. The colony is easily visible from the mainland in good visibility. Small numbers of shags, herring gulls, kitti-wakes and guillemots also nest. The list of visiting land birds is full of interest considering its isolated position and includes wood pigeon, kingfisher, rook, blackbird, robin, chiffchaff, red-breasted flycatcher and goldcrest.

8. GWAUN VALLEY SM9636 TO SN0736: One of the best known Pembrokeshire beauty spots the steep-sided valley of the Afon Gwaun extends inland for some six miles from Lower Fishguard. A road runs for much of its length and there are numerous access points, the best being from Newport SN0539. Buzzards and ravens may be seen soaring over the wooded escarpments, while dippers and grey wagtails nest along the river. Willow tits, redstarts and wood warblers, all of somewhat restricted range in Pembrokeshire, may be seen in the Gwaun Valley.

9. LLYS-Y-FRAN RESERVOIR SN0324: This newly completed reservoir was officially opened by H.R.H. Princess Margaret in 1972 and is intended to ensure that a regular supply of water is available for extraction plants on the River Cleddau farther downstream. When approaching from the south leave the B4329 at SM966177 and follow the signs through Clarbeston Road to Llys-y-fran village and the reservoir dam; from the north leave the B4329 at Tufton SN040282. There is a viewing point at the dam, and from this a footpath has been constructed right around the reservoir, the most attractive area for birds being the upper reaches of the eastern arm.

Being newly completed it is too early to assess the reservoir's value to winter wildfowl, but the comparative shortage of open fresh water in south-west Wales suggests that this large area will in time become the most important. In the winter of 1971–2, as the reservoir filled, over 100 pochard were present, and other duck in smaller numbers included mallard, teal, tufted duck and golden-eye. A longtailed duck spent the 1973–74 winter at the reservoir, while cormorants are now regular there. Clearly this is a site worth watching, not only in winter but also at passage times when waders and terns should also occur.

10. MARLOES PENINSULA SM7808–7509: The peninsula, with the village of Marloes at its base, is an ideal place for a visitor to view the islands of Ramsey, Skomer and Skokholm. From the highest point SM758093 on the Deer Park headland at the westerly extremity of the peninsula the whole expanse of St Brides Bay north to Ramsey and the Bishop and Clerks nine miles away can be seen. Directly in front across Jack Sound is Middleholm, beyond which is the massive bulk of Skomer. To the south-

K *

west across two miles Broad Sound is Skokholm.

Although it has no breeding seabirds of its own, the Deer Park enables visitors to see some of those from the islands and this is particularly valuable when boats are not running. Jack Sound, with its swift currents, overfalls and up-wellings, provides a rich feeding ground for gannets—which can be seen plunge diving—as well as kittiwakes and the larger gulls, together with smaller numbers of shags, razorbills, guillemots and puffins. Observations are best made from Wooltack Point SM755095 when the tide flows north, which it does for about three hours either side of high water. When flowing south the feeding birds tend to congregate in Broad Sound, so that only more distant views are obtained. During evenings throughout the summer months large numbers of Manx shearwaters gather in St Brides Bay and Broad Sound, the Deer Park headland being the best mainland site in the county to watch the flocks. Numbers vary greatly depending on weather conditions as does the proximity to the shore that the birds come.

Ravens and choughs are usually to be seen about the Deer Park; stonechats and grasshopper warblers breed there. The coastal footpath runs towards Marloes village on both sides of the peninsula. The north cliffs are rather overgrown, though they are a good place to see buzzards, while near Musselwick Sands SM786091 a small colony of fulmars has existed for some years. On the southern side the maritime plant communities provide a good feeding area for choughs, while the shelving rocks always attract oystercatchers. Turning inland just north of Gateholm Island a path runs beside Marloes Mere SM776083, a reserve of the West Wales Naturalists' Trust. This when flooded in winter regularly attracts mallard, teal, shoveler and wigeon.

11. MILFORD HAVEN AND CLEDDAU ESTUARIES: This estuary and river system stretches eastwards from St Ann's Head SM8002 to Haverfordwest SM9515 on the Western Cleddau and Canaston Bridge SN0616 on the Eastern Cleddau. There are many tributaries and bays off the main stream and these are worth examining for waders and wildfowl between August and April. The main areas are:

12. ANGLE BAY SM8802: A fine area of mudflats on the south side of Angle Bay with access points at Kilpaison SM897022 and Angle SM867028. Not watched as regularly as other more easily-reached areas it is, nevertheless, one of the most important in Pembrokeshire as a wintering ground for waders and wildfowl. Among the more un-usual species both grey plover and bar-tailed godwits winter here in small numbers; divers and grebes are regular offshore.

13. CLEDDAU WILDFOWL REFUGE: Mainly on the Western Cleddau from Little Milford SM9612 downstream to a line across the Daucleddau from SM998102 to SN004102 and including the mouth of the Eastern Cleddau. Access is best achieved at Little Milford SM970116, Hook SM990121 and near Picton Point SM010122. The resident Canada geese at Boulston SM978123 attract wintering parties of wild geese—usually white-fronted—from time to time, while a barnacle goose has also been recorded. Wigeon and teal are the predominant species of duck, but smaller numbers of most dabbling species can be seen in-cluding shelduck which breed on the river. Goldeneye and red-breasted mergansers are regular here, the latter could well remain to breed as further extensions of its range in Wales take place. The main waders are lapwing,

golden plover, curlew, redshank and dunlin. The autumn passage months are particularly good with groups of both black-tailed and bar-tailed godwits, knot and greenshank occurring. Unusual visitors have included flamingo, spotted redshank and black guillemot.

14. THE GANN SM8106: This small estuary backed by several lagoons near Dale attracts many waders and, because of its small size, there are ample opportunities for close-range observation. Because of this it is one of the best watched estuaries in south-west Wales. The lagoons are generally too disturbed during the summer months, save for the occasional migrant terns, but little grebe and goldeneye are always present in the winter being joined on occasions by red-throated divers, Slavonian grebes and red-breasted mergansers. Offshore there is generally a wintering flock of up to 300 wigeon and most autumns small parties of brent geese call briefly while on passage. The saltings upstream attract, among other waders, greenshank, small numbers of which have wintered here since at least the 1950s. The silt trap below the sand pit at SM813078 is well worth checking for birds like green sandpiper and little stint. More unusual species seen on the estuary have included little egret, Mediterranean gull, Baird's sandpiper and white-winged black tern.

15. NEVERN ESTUARY SN0539: A small estuary, but the only one in the county outside the Milford Haven–Cleddau rivers complex. Good views of the upper reaches may be obtained from the road bridge at SN063395, from which footpaths on either side of the Afon Nyfer lead towards the sea. Mute swans and mallard breed, but the main interest centres around the passage and winter

visitors. Up to ten little grebes winter on the estuary and
are occasionally joined by coot, particularly in hard
weather when inland waters are frozen. Grey herons find
the estuary attractive and up to ten have been noted
fishing at one time. Small numbers of waders winter, including oystercatcher, ringed plover, curlew, redshank,
greenshank and dunlin, while in 1970–1 a flock of thirty-
five bar-tailed godwits could regularly be seen. Unusual
visitors have included scaup, red-breasted merganser,
white-fronted goose and jack snipe.

16. ORIELTON SR9599: At the Orielton Field Centre a
Nature Trail has been laid out through the woodland and
past the now disused duck decoy. All the more common
woodland birds can be seen in this area while lesser
spotted woodpeckers have been recorded here, one of
their few sites in Pembrokeshire. In the past, woodlarks
nested here until the early 1960s. Among the duck on the
pool is usually a small flock of up to ten of wintering gadwall, while diving duck like tufted duck and pochard are
also present. The Nature Trail leaflet is available free at
the Field Centre.

17. PRESELY MOUNTAINS SN03 AND 13: The mountains,
though perhaps more truly hills, cover much of the above
two 10-kilometre squares, and rise to 1,760 feet at Foel-
cwmcerwyn SN094312. The whole upper slopes of the
Presely's are sheep- and pony-grazed turf and heather
with several extensive conifer plantations. Virtually the
only rock faces and scree slopes are the man-made ones
at the now disused Rosebush slate quarries SN078302.
Bird life in these upland regions is somewhat limited and
does not include species like the red grouse found farther

inland in Wales, but even so they should not be neglected by ornithologists. Redpolls are now numerous in the plantations around Rosebush and a great grey shrike has wintered there for several years. On the higher ground ring ouzels should be looked for at likely points; buzzards and ravens are always in view and merlins may sometimes be seen. There are two mid-winter records of snow buntings, one a flock of thirty birds; with so few visits by ornithologists at that time of year this bird may indeed winter regularly on the tops.

18. RAMSEY ISLAND SM7023: This, the most northerly of the Pembrokeshire islands, is reached by boat from the lifeboat slip at St Justinian's SM723252. Crossings are made daily, weather permitting, during the summer months. There is a landing fee of 25p, children half price. The island is privately owned, but managed as a Nature Reserve by the Royal Society for the Protection of Birds, whose warden is resident at the old farmhouse. The western cliffs are some of the most spectacular in Wales, while the whole coast is riddled with caves and inlets, and offshore there are many stacks and islands. It is well worth going round the island by boat, the passage at the southern end through the 50-foot channel of Twll y Dillyn, with the cliffs and Ynys Cantwr and Midland towering above the tide race, is something never to be forgotten.

The seabird colonies on Ramsey do not include puffins which are said not to nest because of the brown rats. However, manx shearwaters, another burrow-nesting species were found breeding in 1971; the full extent of the colony has yet to be determined. Fulmars, shags, kittiwakes, guillemots and razorbills all nest, mainly on the western side. Black guillemots have been observed

off the island for several years now and may breed in
the near future, if they are not already doing so. Ramsey,
like Skokholm and Skomer, undoubtedly attracts migrants, though to what extent is not yet known, it is certainly the least known ornithologically of the western
Pembrokeshire islands. More unusual species have included American bittern, corncrake, green sandpiper and
Alpine swift.

19. ROSEBUSH RESERVOIR SN0629: Situated high on the
Presely Mountains the reservoir at Rosebush, until the
Llys-y-fran reservoir was completed, was one of the
largest freshwater areas in the county. Unfortunately, its
exposed position and acidic waters restricts the winter
wildfowl population. A path leaves the B4329 at SN060297
and runs to the shore; the narrow upper reaches are best
observed from the long disused railway track, as this prevents unnecessary disturbance.

Mallard and teal, up to about fifty, are here throughout the winter, being joined by small parties of wigeon,
tufted duck, pochard and the occasional goldeneye.
Cormorants regularly fish on the reservoir, although it is
eight miles from Fishguard Bay. In August and September, as the water level drops, passing waders such as lapwing, snipe, curlew, green and common sandpipers find
the exposed mud attractive.

20. ST BRIDES BAY SM7918: Even in August the popular
holiday beaches of Broad Haven SM8513, Little Haven
SM8512 and Newgale SM8422 attract migrant terns. All
except the roseate have been seen fishing offshore, while
waders will rest at the tide edge during the early morning
before many people are about. During September young

Manx shearwaters, mainly from Skomer, are often 'wrecked' on these beaches after a period of south-westerly gales. Some are dead on arrival or are speedily picked off by predatory gulls. However, many others are healthy and can be collected to be released at some point in the north of the county where the wind will carry them into St George's Channel and not back to land. The winter months are particularly interesting. A flock of several hundred common scoter can usually be observed off Newgale and this is joined at times by such other duck as velvet scoter, eider and long-tailed duck. Red-throated divers appear off Broad Haven, while in the more shel-tered water off Little Haven Slavonian grebes occur each year.

21. ST DAVID'S HEAD SM721278: Best approached by means of the coastal footpath from Whitesand Bay SM734272. The whole area is good for birds like stone-chats, rock pipits and linnets while there is a good chance of seeing buzzards, kestrels, ravens, choughs and possibly peregrine falcon. The Head is superbly placed for watching passing seabirds; all those breeding in Pem-brokeshire save for British storm petrels may, in the right season, be seen at close quarters. Waters (1968) provides an account of visible migration; during 39 hours of watching at the Head in the autumns of 1963 and 1964 he observed, besides the resident species, divers, Balearic shearwater, long-tailed duck, common scoter, whooper swan, great and Arctic skuas. Land bird movement at the Head seems to be extensive during the autumn and early winter months and this, together with the seabird pass-age, warrants further investigation.
Waters, W. E., 'Visible Migration at St David's Head', *Nature in Wales* 11 (1968): 20–7.

22. ST GEORGE'S CHANNEL: The British Rail ferries which operate on the Fishguard to Rosslare, Co. Wexford run, include excursion trips between July and September and normally one or two cruises along the Pembrokeshire and Cardiganshire coasts and islands. The excursions to Ireland normally leave Fishguard at 07.15 hrs, the crossing taking about two and a half hours, and return by 22.15 hrs. Enquiries should be made at the Fishguard booking office. The excursions and coastal cruises provide opportunities for observing seabirds on passage, which are normally only seen at a distance from the Pembrokeshire headlands. Species noted have included Cory's, great and sooty shearwaters, great, Arctic and pomarine skua, besides more regular birds such as the auks and terns.

23. SKOKHOLM SM7304: The site of the oldest bird observatory—established in 1933—in Great Britain and Ireland the island is now managed by the West Wales Naturalists' Trust who have a warden ashore from March to October. Hostel accommodation is provided by the Trust; there is only a boat once a week and no facilities for day visitors. Although there are excellent seabird colonies, particularly of Manx shearwater, British storm petrel and puffin, Skokholm is particularly noted for the bird migration which may be observed there. Annual reports are published by the West Wales Naturalists' Trust; that for 1972 being available (price 25p) from the Trust Office. Besides a systematic bird list, the reports include short papers on various aspects of the island's wildlife which has been extensively studied over the years. Research on seabirds there is now under the direction of the Edward Grey Institute, Department of Zoology, Oxford. Like all bird observatories, Skokholm has been visited by many exciting bird migrants. Unusual

visitors in recent years have included sooty shearwater,
osprey, quail, dotterel, Sabine's gull, Sardinian warbler,
pied wheatear, Bonelli's warbler, yellow-browed warbler
and Lapland bunting.

24. SKOMER SM7209: Without question one of the finest
seabird islands in Europe; although the numbers of some
species are not high compared with more northern
colonies, they are easily visible, some at particularly close
range. Boats run daily from Martinshaven SM760092,
weather permitting, between May and September, the
crossing taking about fifteen minutes. There is a landing
fee of 30p for adults, 10p for children. Skomer is a
National Nature Reserve managed by the West Wales
Naturalists' Trust, whose warden is normally resident
from March to October. There is some simple accommodation and enquiries regarding this and early-season
visits should be made to the Trust Office.

A Self-Guiding Nature Trail is on sale at 15p at the
landing place or from the Trust Office. Day visitors must
follow this in order to make the most advantageous use of
their time ashore and to minimise disturbance. Skomer
is a large island and the seabird colonies, mainly kittiwakes, razorbills and guillemots, at High Cliff, Kittiwake
Cove and The Wick should not be missed. The largest
puffin colony is in the vicinity of the warden's house
above North Haven; they even sit along the house roof.
There is a huge Manx shearwater colony though day
visitors will not see this bird. The interior plateau has
large lesser black-backed gull colonies and numerous
breeding oystercatchers, also curlews, lapwings, short-
eared owls and wheatears. Despite its large size, proximity to the mainland and areas of thick cover, Skomer does

have an impressive list of rare migrants. Species noted in recent years include lesser yellowlegs, pectoral sandpiper, little gull, alpine swift, subalpine warbler, barred warbler and woodchat shrike. The best general account of the island and its wildlife is provided by Buxton and Lockley (1950), while annual bird reports were published in *Nature and Wales* for the years 1960 to 1966.

Buxton and Lockley, *Island of Skomer* (Staples, London, 1950).

25. STACK ROCKS SR9294: Also known as Elegug Stacks, *Elegug* being the south Pembrokeshire dialect name for guillemot, this is the most easily observed cliff seabird colony in the county and possibly in the whole of Britain and Ireland. Situated on the south side of the Castle-martin peninsula a single track road leaves the B4319 at SR932970 and terminates at the cliff overlooking the Stacks. As the surrounding area is a tank range, access on weekdays may be restricted. Red flags fly when firing is in progress and the times are published in the two Pembrokeshire papers, or enquiries may be made at Bosherston Post Office. From the cliff top visitors can easily see the colonies on the one large and three small stacks which are very close inshore. The colony seen to best advantage is that on the most westerly stack, just off the Green Bridge of Wales rock arch; here in 1971 nearly 400 guillemots were nesting. Other seabirds which can be seen are fulmar, shag, herring gull, great black-backed gull, kittiwake and razorbill. A cliff path runs east from the Stacks to St Govan's Head, a distance of four miles. Although seabirds on this section are few, there is a good chance of seeing oystercatcher, raven, chough, wheatear and stonechat.

26. STRUMBLE HEAD SM8941 : This most prominent of the north Pembrokeshire headlands is reached by way of the unclassified road which climbs away from the A40 at SM945383 in Goodwick, and continues to a small car park directly opposite the lighthouse rock. A footbridge across a narrow channel provides access to the rock.

From the vantage point on the north side below the lighthouse wall from March until early September, large numbers of Manx shearwaters may be seen most evenings moving south from their Irish Sea feeding grounds to the colonies on Skomer and Skokholm. Return movements take place an hour or so after dawn. An extensive passage of other seabirds has been noted during the autumn; gannets, kittiwakes, razorbills and guillemots being the main species involved, with smaller numbers of fulmars, common scoter and terns. More unusual species recorded include Balearic shearwater, eider duck, little gull, great and Arctic skuas. The tide race close in to the head proves an attractive feeding area for many seabirds, among them red-throated divers, seventeen having been seen together on one occasion.

27. TREFEIDDAN POOL SM734252 : A boggy area beside the St David's to St Justinian's SM723252 road, from which it may be easily viewed. The pool is best in winter when there is a large area of shallow water. Like Dowrog Common there was once a black-headed gull colony and winter disturbance keeps duck numbers low. Garganey are regular here in March and early April, and small numbers of other dabbling duck are usually present. Herons are often to be seen feeding; and of the waders, snipe and ruff seem almost resident throughout the winter.

Check list

RB Resident Breeder   MB Migrant Breeder
wv Winter Visitor   PV Passage Visitor
      v Vagrant

Black-throated Diver	v	Scaup	wv
Great Northern Diver	wv	Tufted Duck	wv
Red-throated Diver	wv	Pochard	wv
Great Crested Grebe	wv	Goldeneye	wv
Red-necked Grebe	v	Long-tailed Duck	wv
Slavonian Grebe	wv	Velvet Scoter	v
Black-necked Grebe	v	Common Scoter	wv
Little Grebe	wv	Eider	v
Fulmar	RB	Red-breasted Merganser	
Manx Shearwater	MB		wv
Great Shearwater	PV	Goosander	v
Sooty Shearwater	PV	Smew	v
British Storm Petrel	MB	Shelduck	RB
Leach's Petrel	v	Greylag Goose	v
Gannet	RB	White-fronted Goose	v
Cormorant	RB	Brent Goose	v
Shag	RB	Barnacle Goose	v
Grey Heron	RB	Canada Goose	RB
Mallard	RB	Mute Swan	RB
Teal	wv	Whooper Swan	wv
Garganey	PV	Bewick's Swan	wv
Gadwall	wv	Buzzard	RB
Wigeon	wv	Rough-legged Buzzard	v
Pintail	wv	Sparrowhawk	RB
Shoveler	wv	Marsh Harrier	v

Hen Harrier	WV	Wood Sandpiper	PV
Montagu's Harrier	PV	Common Sandpiper	PV
Has bred		Redshank	WV
Hobby	V	Spotted Redshank	WV
Peregrine	RB	Greenshank	WV
Merlin	WV	Knot	WV
Has bred		Purple Sandpiper	WV
Kestrel	RB	Little Stint	PV
Red-legged Partridge	RB	Dunlin	WV
Partridge	RB	Curlew Sandpiper	PV
Quail	PV	Sanderling	PV
Pheasant	RB	Ruff	PV
Water Rail	WV	Grey Phalarope	V
Spotted Crake	PV	Great Skua	PV
Corncrake	PV	Arctic Skua	PV
Has bred		Pomarine Skua	V
Moorhen	RB	Great Black-backed Gull	
Coot	RB		RB
Oystercatcher	RB	Lesser Black-backed Gull	
Lapwing	RB		MB
Ringed Plover	WV	Herring Gull	RB
Has bred		Common Gull	WV
Grey Plover	WV	Little Gull	V
Golden Plover	WV	Black-headed Gull	RB
Turnstone	WV	Kittiwake	RB
Snipe	WV	Black Tern	PV
Jack Snipe	WV	Common Tern	PV
Woodcock	WV	Arctic Tern	PV
Curlew	RB	Little Tern	PV
Whimbrel	PV	Sandwich Tern	PV
Black-tailed Godwit	WV	Razorbill	RB
Bar-tailed Godwit	WV	Guillemot	RB
Green Sandpiper	PV	Black Guillemot	V

Puffin	MB	Magpie	RB
Stock Dove	RB	Jay	RB
Woodpigeon	RB	Chough	RB
Turtle Dove	PV	Great Tit	RB
Collared Dove	RB	Blue Tit	RB
Cuckoo	MB	Coal Tit	RB
Barn Owl	RB	Marsh Tit	RB
Little Owl	RB	Willow Tit	RB
Tawny Owl	RB	Long-tailed Tit	RB
Long-eared Owl	V	Nuthatch	RB
Short-eared Owl	RB	Treecreeper	RB
Nightjar	MB	Wren	RB
Swift	MB	Dipper	RB
Kingfisher	RB	Mistle Thrush	RB
Hoopoe	V	Fieldfare	WV
Green Woodpecker	RB	Song Thrush	RB
Great Spotted Wood-		Redwing	WV
pecker	RB	Ring Ouzel	PV
Lesser Spotted Wood-			Has bred
pecker	RB	Blackbird	RB
Wryneck	V	Wheatear	MB
Woodlark	V	Stonechat	RB
	Has bred	Whinchat	MB
Skylark	RB	Redstart	MB
Swallow	MB	Black Redstart	PV
House Martin	MB	Robin	RB
Sand Martin	MB	Grasshopper Warbler	MB
Golden Oriole	V	Reed Warbler	V
Raven	RB	Sedge Warbler	MB
Carrion Crow	RB	Blackcap	MB
Hooded Crow	V	Garden Warbler	MB
Rook	RB	Whitethroat	MB
Jackdaw	RB	Lesser Whitethroat	PV

Willow Warbler	MB	Starling	RB
Chiffchaff	MB	Hawfinch	V
Wood Warbler	MB		May breed
Goldcrest	RB	Greenfinch	RB
Firecrest	V	Goldfinch	RB
Spotted Flycatcher	MB	Siskin	WV
Pied Flycatcher	PV	Linnet	RB
Dunnock	RB	Twite	V
Meadow Pipit	RB	Redpoll	RB
Tree Pipit	MB	Bullfinch	RB
Rock Pipit	RB	Crossbill	V
Water Pipit	V	Chaffinch	RB
Pied Wagtail	RB	Brambling	WV
White Wagtail	PV	Yellowhammer	RB
Grey Wagtail	RB	Reed Bunting	RB
Yellow Wagtail	PV	Snow Bunting	WV
Waxwing	V	House Sparrow	RB
Great Grey Shrike	V	Tree Sparrow	RB

RADNORSHIRE

Knighton

2 ● Rhayader

1

6

Presteigne

Llandrindod
Wells
4

5

3   7

0   5   10
      miles

Chapter 16

Radnorshire

One of the smaller (471 square miles) Welsh counties, Radnorshire with a population of only 18,262 (1971 census) is the most sparsely occupied in Wales and indeed the whole of southern Britain. Rural depopulation here has in most cases meant complete migration from the county, for there are few urban centres and virtually no industries to provide alternative employment. There are but four towns, all small—Knighton, Llandrindod Wells (administrative centre), Presteigne (county town) and Rhayader. Llandrindod Wells and Rhayader are considered potential growth points for developments in central Wales, and the implementation of such plans should reverse the population movement to some extent.

The River Wye, flowing from the Cardiganshire uplands, forms a convenient western boundary to Radnorshire from near Rhayader to Hay-on-Wye. To the north of Rhayader a salient, part of which is bounded by two of the Elan reservoirs, extends into Cardiganshire with Breconshire on the southern flank. Montgomeryshire is the northern neighbour to Radnorshire, the border here crossing much high ground towards its meeting with Shropshire in the Forest of Clun. This is not a wooded area, but rather a section of open country used in medieval times for hunting. The border now runs south-east along the course of the River Teme, a tributary of the Severn which it joins to the south of Worcester. About four miles east of Knighton the border turns south out of the valley to wander over high ground like Llanwen Hill, Hergest Ridge and Clyro Hill and valleys like those of the Rivers Arrow and Lugg, before reaching Hay-on-Wye.

The lowest point in the county is about 250 feet in the lower Wye valley and the highest point is 2,166 feet in the Radnor Forest. Radnorshire can boast of one hundred peaks between 1,500 feet and 2,000 feet and has only 3 per cent of its total area below the 500-foot contour. Despite this high ground, the fact that all the rivers eventually run east or south-east towards England has meant that man from earliest times has found easy access to these parts. Because of this, Radnorshire is more inclined towards England than most other parts of Wales. Many place names are English, having long replaced their Welsh counterparts and very little Welsh is spoken even in the remoter upland areas. This is mirrored in the naturalist's organisations, for both the Ornithological Society and the Naturalists' Trust are linked with Herefordshire rather than the adjacent Welsh counties.

The Roman withdrawal from these parts in the fourth century saw the commencement of intermittent warfare between the princes of Powys (approximately present-day Montgomeryshire), and Brycheiniog (approximately present-day Breconshire), which was to smoulder here for six centuries. Radnorshire, lying between these two areas, was the scene of many a bloody skirmish. Following the Norman invasion of England it was not long before powerful barons were thrusting their private armies along the river valleys into Wales. Radnorshire was one of the first areas they prised from Welsh rule and by 1100 they had built a castle at New Radnor. Families like the Mortimers and de Brasnoses established Marcher lordships, but this did not deter the Welsh and there followed nearly three centuries of pillage and counter-pillage, am-

overleaf – *Buzzard*   *Dipper*

bushes and larger affrays. This only ceased after the Acts of Union in 1536 and 1542 when Henry VIII joined the Mortimer and Warwick lordships to form what is now present-day Radnorshire.

The county may be divided on the basis of its geology into three main areas. The smallest is in the extreme south-east, where an extension of Old Red Sandstone from the Black Mountains intrudes across the Wye as far as the tumbling Bach Howey with its waterfalls and rapids. The lowland in this part of Radnorshire is a particularly rich agricultural area. Northwards and westwards towards the Ithon and beyond are older Silurian rocks. Amongst these and exposed by the erosion of centuries are igneous rocks which stand above the surrounding countryside. For the botanist several limestone hills provide an even greater variety in the flora, and no doubt discoveries await the enthusiast.

Since the early 1960s some fourteen factories have been established in Radnorshire in an effort to alleviate its depopulation. These concerns now employ some 750 workers and manufacture items diverse as gearboxes for satellite-tracking antennae to percussion instruments. Although other light industries may find the county attractive the main employment will remain in agriculture. Farms in Radnorshire tend to be larger than the average for Wales and many have grazing rights on the numerous commons. The higher ground supports large sheep flocks while the lower parts store cattle and breeding stock. About one-fifth of the land is arable. Forestry Commission activities are centred on Radnor Forest southwest of Knighton and Coed Sarnau north-east of Rhayader, the two combining to cover about 4,800 hectares (12,000 acres).

Radnorshire has few resident ornithologists and is perhaps the least visited of all Welsh counties. It is perhaps safe to say that more needs to be known concerning the status of all birds occurring in the county, with the emphasis on breeding species. At the same time there are no areas which can claim to be well known, so that observations from any part of the county will add greatly to our knowledge of this part of mid-Wales.

Information

County Avifaunas
Ingram, G. C. S. and Salmon, H. Morrey, *A Handlist of the Birds of Radnorshire* (Hereford, 1955).

Bird Report
The Herefordshire Ornithological Club publishes an Annual Report which contains classified notes concerning birds in Radnorshire. Price $22\frac{1}{2}$p plus postage from the Hon. Secretary.

County Bird Recorder
A. J. Smith, 4 The Orchard, Moreton-on-Lugg, Hereford.

Ornithological Society
The Herefordshire Ornithological Club also covers Radnorshire. Field meetings are held at sites throughout the two counties, but indoor meetings are confined at present to a venue in Hereford. Subscription 75p per annum (adults), $37\frac{1}{2}$p (juniors). Hon. Sec. R. H. Baillie, Wyche House, Kington, Hereford.

Naturalists' Trust
The Herefordshire and Radnorshire Nature Trust was founded in 1962 and now has seven reserves, of which two are in Radnorshire though others are planned. The Trust operates probably the largest nestbox scheme in Britain with over 1,000 boxes distributed between forty-five sites. Members receive a regular newsletter and Radnorshire members the journal *Nature in Wales* which appears twice yearly. Subscription £1.00 (£1.50 family membership). Hon. Sec. (Radnorshire) W. I. Hughes, County Hall Annex, Ithon Road, Llandrindod Wells LD1 6AS.

Royal Society for the Protection of Birds Representative
H. McSweeney, Tyneydd, Aberedw, Radnor.

British Trust for Ornithology Representative
Mrs J. Bromley, The Garth, Kington, HR5 3BA, Hereford.

Tourist Information
County Handbook available from the County Offices, County Hall, Llandrindod Wells.

1. ELAN VALLEY RESERVOIRS SN9163: Lying partly in Breconshire and flooding a section of the lower Claerwen valley is Caban Coch, ornithologically the most important of the Elan Valley reservoirs. These supply water —80,000,000 gallons daily—to Birmingham, and have become a major tourist attraction in mid-Wales. The reservoirs are reached from Rhayader by means of the B4518 to Elan village, then an unclassified road which runs along or close to the shore line, ultimately joining the mountain road to Cwmystwyth in Cardiganshire.

Caban Coch and adjoining Carreg ddu are the most interesting reservoirs, the main species being the diving duck which winter here. Tufted duck and pochard are numerous, but other regular visitors include red-breasted merganser, goldeneye and goosander; rarities have included scoter, smew and Bewick's swan.

2. GLAN LLYN SN9469: A small lake north-west of Rhayader, which is reached by turning north off the B4518 on the outskirts of the town. Great crested grebe have bred recently, but wintering duck, mallard, tufted duck and pochard predominating, are the main attraction.

3. LLAN BWCH-LLYN LAKE SO1146: One of the most important of the natural lakes in Radnorshire lies at about 1,000 feet on the southern slopes of Llandeilo Hill and covers some 10 hectares (25 acres). Leave the A479 at SO089437 just north of Erwood and head for Llandeilo Graban, pass through the village and continue for about two miles, the lake is then visible just south of the road.

Both great crested and little grebe breed here as does tufted duck. A whiskered tern seen in 1956 was the first record of this species for Wales, confirming that no water, however small or far inland, should be neglected by the ornithologist.

4. LLANDRINDOD WELLS PARK LAKE SO0660: This 14-acre lake, partially surrounded by woodland is situated in the park and gardens on the southern outskirts of the town.

Although numbers of winter wildfowl are not high, several interesting species for such a small inland site in Wales have been noted in recent years, including wigeon, goosander and common and Arctic tern.

5. LLYN HEILYN SO1658: This pool is easily viewed from the A481 about a mile west of Llanfihangel-nant-Melen SO185584.

Coot are the most numerous water bird both as a resident and winter visitor, but little grebes also breed, and mallard, teal, tufted duck, pochard and goldeneye are regular winter visitors in small numbers.

6. RADNOR FOREST SO1964: A large tract of hill land almost in the centre of the county and rising to 2,166 feet at Great Rhos. Extensive conifer plantations have been planted in some parts, most particularly on the northeast slopes towards Bleddfa. Although main roads run right around the perimeter, access to the interior of this area is not so easy for there are hardly any roads or tracks. A good route is that leading from SO203605 just west of New Radnor up Harley Dingle, a steep-sided valley terminating amongst the high ground of the central region. This valley has been used by I.C.I. for experiments with explosives so access may at times be restricted, however a footpath does exist. Another approach is the Water-break-its-neck valley from SO1959, though there is no access to vehicular traffic. The Warren Wood, although small, can prove attractive and should not be missed.

Red grouse occur on the high ground while other species likely to be encountered include ring ouzel, wheatear, whinchat, redstart, wood warbler and goldcrest. Casual visitors to be looked for are merlin and golden plover.

7. RHOSGOCH COMMON SO1948: On the southern slopes of Llanbedr Hill and close to Painscastle is the marshy area

of Rhosgoch Common. Leave the A4153 at Clyro
so213436, or the A479 at so089437 near Erwood and
head for Painscastle, then north for a further two miles to
Rhosgoch, beyond which lies the marsh.

Rhosgoch Common once held the largest black-headed
gull colony in Radnorshire, though for some unknown
reason none have nested here since 1967. This is a very
good area for snipe, curlew, sedge warbler and reed
bunting, with mallard and teal also normally present.
There are a number of old (pre-1940) records of spotted
crakes breeding at Rhosgoch where at one time they were
regular summer visitors. Regular observations during
spring and early summer might prove of interest in con-
nection with this species.

Check list

RB	Resident Breeder	MB	Migrant Breeder
WV	Winter Visitor	PV	Passage Visitor
	V	Vagrant	

Great Crested Grebe	RB	Pochard	WV
Little Grebe	RB	Goldeneye	WV
Cormorant	PV	Red-breasted Merganser	
Grey Heron	RB		WV
Mallard	RB	Goosander	WV
Teal	RB	White-fronted Goose	V
Wigeon	WV	Canada Goose	PV
Pintail	V		Has bred
Shoveler	V	Mute Swan	RB
Tufted Duck	RB	Buzzard	RB

Sparrowhawk	RB	Black Tern	V
Red Kite	PV	Common/Arctic Tern	V
Peregrine	PV	Stock Dove	RB
	Has bred	Woodpigeon	RB
Merlin	RB	Turtle Dove	PV
Kestrel	RB	Collared Dove	RB
Red Grouse	RB	Cuckoo	MB
Black Grouse	RB	Barn Owl	RB
Partridge	RB	Little Owl	RB
Pheasant	RB	Tawny Owl	RB
Water Rail	RB	Long-eared Owl	RB
Corncrake	V	Short-eared Owl	PV
Moorhen	RB	Nightjar	PV
Coot	RB	Swift	MB
Oystercatcher	V	Kingfisher	RB
Lapwing	RB	Green Woodpecker	RB
Golden Plover	PV	Great Spotted Wood-	
	Has bred	pecker	RB
Snipe	RB	Lesser Spotted Wood-	
Jack Snipe	WV	pecker	RB
Woodcock	RB	Skylark	RB
Curlew	RB	Swallow	MB
Green Sandpiper	PV	House Martin	MB
Common Sandpiper	MB	Sand Martin	MB
Redshank	RB	Raven	RB
Dunlin	V	Carrion Crow	RB
Great Black-backed Gull		Rook	RB
	WV	Jackdaw	RB
Lesser Black-backed Gull		Magpie	RB
	PV	Jay	RB
Herring Gull	WV	Great Tit	RB
Common Gull	WV	Blue Tit	RB
Black-headed Gull	RB	Coal Tit	RB

Marsh Tit	RB	Chiffchaff	MB
Willow Tit	RB	Wood Warbler	MB
Long-tailed Tit	RB	Goldcrest	RB
Nuthatch	RB	Spotted Flycatcher	MB
Treecreeper	RB	Pied Flycatcher	MB
Wren	RB	Dunnock	RB
Dipper	RB	Meadow Pipit	RB
Mistle Thrush	RB	Tree Pipit	MB
Fieldfare	WV	Pied Wagtail	RB
Song Thrush	RB	Grey Wagtail	RB
Redwing	WV	Yellow Wagtail	RB
Ring Ouzel	MB	Great Grey Shrike	V
Blackbird	RB	Starling	RB
Wheatear	MB	Greenfinch	RB
Stonechat	PV	Goldfinch	RB
	Has bred	Siskin	RB
Whinchat	MB	Linnet	RB
Redstart	MB	Redpoll	RB
Robin	RB	Bullfinch	RB
Grasshopper Warbler	MB	Crossbill	V
Sedge Warbler	MB	Chaffinch	RB
Blackcap	MB	Brambling	WV
Garden Warbler	MB	Yellowhammer	RB
Whitethroat	MB	Reed Bunting	RB
Lesser Whitethroat	MB	House Sparrow	RB
Willow Warbler	MB	Tree Sparrow	RB

Appendix

A list of Welsh bird names

The following list of birds includes all species which have been recorded in Wales, even those which have occurred only once. The ornithologist wishing to look up and use the Welsh name for many species has in the past encountered problems. Due possibly to the isolating effect of the mountainous terrain, different districts have adopted their own bird names so that for well-known and widely-distributed species there may be up to about a dozen names to choose from. The question of which one should be used is not easily answered. This confusion and uncertainty has at last been remedied by P. Hope Jones and E. Breeze Jones in their List of Welsh Birds published in 1973 by the National Museum of Wales. They have, after much discussion with ornithologists and language experts, selected the most appropriate Welsh name for each species of bird to have occurred within the Principality. The authors, together with the National Museum of Wales, have kindly consented to my reproducing this authoritative list of Welsh bird names and to them I am deeply grateful.

Black-throated Diver *Gavia arctica*	Trochydd Gyddfddu
Great Northern Diver *Gavia immer*	Trochydd Mawr
Red-throated Diver *Gavia stellata*	Trochydd Gyddfgoch
Great Crested Grebe *Podiceps cristatus*	Gwyach Fawr Gopog
Red-necked Grebe *Podiceps grisegena*	Gwyach Yddfgoch

Slavonian Grebe *Podiceps auritus*	Gwyach Gorniog
Black-necked Grebe *Podiceps nigricollis*	Gwyach Yddfddu
Little Grebe *Tachybaptus ruficollis*	Gwyach Fach
Fulmar *Fulmarus glacialis*	Aderyn-Drycin y Graig
Manx Shearwater *Puffinus puffinus*	Aderyn-Drycin Manaw
Little Shearwater *Puffinus assimilis*	Aderyn-Drycin Bach
Great Shearwater *Puffinus gravis*	Aderyn-Drycin Mawr
Sooty Shearwater *Puffinus griseus*	Aderyn-Drycin Du
British Storm Petrel *Hydrobates pelagicus*	Pedryn Drycin Prydeinig
Leach's Petrel *Oceanodroma leucorhoa*	Pedryn Gynffon-fforchog
Gannet *Sula bassana*	Hugan
Cormorant *Phalacrocorax carbo*	Mulfran
Shag *Phalacrocorax aristotelis*	Mulfran Werdd
Grey Heron *Ardea cinerea*	Crëyr Glas
Purple Heron *Ardea purpurea*	Crëyr Porffor
Little Egret *Egretta garzetta*	Crëyr Bach
Squacco Heron *Ardeola ralloides*	Crëyr Melyn
Night Heron *Nycticorax nycticorax*	Crëyr y Nos
Little Bittern *Ixobrychus minutus*	Aderyn-bwn Lleiaf
Bittern *Botaurus stellaris*	Aderyn y Bwn

American Bittern *Botaurus lentiginosus*	Aderyn-bwn America
White Stork *Ciconia ciconia*	Ciconia Gwyn
Spoonbill *Platalea leucorodia*	Llwybig
Glossy Ibis *Plegadis falcinellus*	Crymanbig Ddu
Mallard *Anas platyrhynchos*	Hwyaden Wyllt
Teal *Anas crecca*	Corhwyaden
Garganey *Anas querquedula*	Hwyaden Addfain
Blue-winged Teal *Anas discors*	Corhwyaden Asgell-las
Gadwall *Anas strepera*	Hwyaden Lwyd
Wigeon *Anas penelope*	Chwiwell
American Wigeon *Anas americana*	Chwiwell America
Pintail *Anas acuta*	Hwyaden Lostfain
Shoveler *Anas clypeata*	Hwyaden Lydanbig
Red-crested Pochard *Netta rufina*	Hwyaden Gribgoch
Scaup *Aythya marila*	Hwyaden Benddu
Tufted Duck *Aythya fuligula*	Hwyaden Gopog
Ring-necked Duck *Aythya collaris*	Hwyaden Dorchog
Pochard *Aythya ferina*	Hwyaden Bengoch
Ferruginous Duck *Aythya nyroca*	Hwyaden Lygadwen
Goldeneye *Bucephala clangula*	Hwyaden Lygad-aur

Long-tailed Duck *Clangula hyemalis*	Hwyaden Gynffon-hir
Velvet Scoter *Melanitta fusca*	Môr-hwyaden y Gogledd
Surf Scoter *Melanitta perspicillata*	Môr-hwyaden yr Ewyn
Common Scoter *Melanitta nigra*	Môr-hwyaden Ddu
Eider *Somateria mollissima*	Hwyaden Fwythblu
Ruddy Duck *Oxyura jamaicensis*	Hwyaden Goch
Red-breasted Merganser *Mergus serrator*	Hwyaden Frongoch
Goosander *Mergus merganser*	Hwyaden Ddanheddog
Smew *Mergus albellus*	Lleian Wen
Hooded Merganser *Mergus cucullatus*	Hwyaden Benwen
Shelduck *Tadorna tadorna*	Hwyaden yr Eithin
Ruddy Shelduck *Tadorna ferruginea*	Hwyaden Goch yr Eithin
Greylag Goose *Anser anser*	Gŵydd Wyllt
White-fronted Goose *Anser albifrons*	Gŵydd Dalcen-wen
Lesser White-fronted Goose *Anser erythropus*	Gŵydd Dalcen-wen Leiaf
Bean Goose *Anser fabalis*	Gwydd y Llafur
Pink-footed Goose *Anser brachyrhynchus*	Gŵydd Droedbinc
Brent Goose *Branta bernicla*	Gŵydd Ddu
Barnacle Goose *Branta leucopsis*	Gŵydd Wyran
Canada Goose *Branta canadensis*	Gŵydd Canada

Red-breasted Goose	Gŵydd Frongoch
Branta ruficollis	
Mute Swan	Alarch Dof
Cygnus olor	
Whooper Swan	Alarch y Gogledd
Cygnus cygnus	
Bewick's Swan	Alarch Bewick
Cygnus bewickii	
Golden Eagle	Eryr Euraid
Aquila chrysaetos	
Buzzard	Bwncath
Buteo buteo	
Rough-legged Buzzard	Bod Bacsiog
Buteo lagopus	
Sparrowhawk	Gwalch Glas
Accipiter nisus	
Goshawk	Gwalch Marth
Accipiter gentilis	
Red Kite	Barcud
Milvus milvus	
White-tailed Eagle	Eryr y Môr
Haliaeetus albicilla	
Honey Buzzard	Bod y Mêl
Pernis apivorus	
Marsh Harrier	Bod y Gwerni
Circus aeruginosus	
Hen Harrier	Bod Tinwen
Circus cyaneus	
Montagu's Harrier	Bod Montagu
Circus pygargus	
Osprey	Gwalch y Pysgod
Pandion haliaetus	
Hobby	Hebog yr Ehedydd
Falco subbuteo	
Peregrine	Hebog Tramor
Falco peregrinus	
Gyrfalcon	Hebog y Gogledd
Falco rusticolus	
Merlin	Cudyll Bach
Falco columbarius	

Red-footed Falcon	Cudyll Troedgoch
Falco vespertinus	
Kestrel	Cudyll Coch
Falco tinnunculus	
Red Grouse	Grugiar
Lagopus lagopus	
Black Grouse	Grugiar Ddu
Lyrurus tetrix	
Red-legged Partridge	Petrisen Goesgoch
Alectoris rufa	
Partridge	Petrisen
Perdix perdix	
Quail	Sofliar
Coturnix coturnix	
Pheasant	Ffesant
Phasianus colchicus	
Crane	Garan
Grus grus	
Water Rail	Rhegen y Dŵr
Rallus aquaticus	
Spotted Crake	Rhegen Fraith
Porzana porzana	
Sora Rail	Rhegen Sora
Porzana carolina	
Baillon's Crake	Rhegen Baillon
Porzana pusilla	
Little Crake	Rhegen Fach
Porzana parva	
Corncrake	Rhegen yr Ŷd
Crex crex	
Moorhen	Iâr Ddŵr
Gallinula chloropus	
Coot	Cwtiar
Fulica atra	
Great Bustard	Ceiliog y Waun
Otis tarda	
Little Bustard	Ceiliog y Waun Lleiaf
Otis tetrax	
Oystercatcher	Pioden y Môr
Haematopus ostralegus	

Lapwing	Cornchwiglen
Vanellus vanellus	
Ringed Plover	Cwtiad Torchog
Charadrius hiaticula	
Little Ringed Plover	Cwtiad Torchog Bach
Charadrius dubius	
Kentish Plover	Cwtiad Caint
Charadrius alexandrinus	
Grey Plover	Cwtiad Llwyd
Pluvialis squatarola	
Golden Plover	Cwtiad Aur
Pluvialis apricaria	
Dotterel	Hutan y Mynydd
Eudromias morinellus	
Turnstone	Cwtiad y Traeth
Arenaria interpres	
Long-billed Dowitcher	Gïach Gylfin-hir
Limnodromus scolopacous	
Snipe	Gïach Gyffredin
Gallinago gallinago	
Great Snipe	Gïach Fawr
Gallinago media	
Jack Snipe	Gïach Fach
Lymnocryptes minimus	
Woodcock	Cyffylog
Scolopax rusticola	
Upland Sandpiper	Pibydd Cynffonir
Bartramia longicauda	
Curlew	Gylfinir
Numenius arquata	
Whimbrel	Coegylfinir
Numenius phaeopus	
Black-tailed Godwit	Rhostog Gynffonddu
Limosa limosa	
Bar-tailed Godwit	Rhostog Gynffonfrith
Limosa lapponica	
Green Sandpiper	Pibydd Gwyrdd
Tringa ochropus	
Wood Sandpiper	Pibydd-y Graean
Tringa glareola	

Common Sandpiper	Pibydd y Dorlan
Tringa hypoleucos	
Spotted Sandpiper	Pibydd Brych
Tringa macularia	
Redshank	Pibydd Coesgoch
Tringa totanus	
Spotted Redshank	Pibydd Coesgoch Mannog
Tringa erthropus	
Greater Yellowlegs	Melyngoes Mawr
Tringa melanoleuca	
Lesser Yellowlegs	Melyngoes Bach
Tringa flavipes	
Greenshank	Pibydd Coeswerdd
Tringa nebularia	
Knot	Pibydd yr Aber
Calidris canutus	
Purple Sandpiper	Pibydd Du
Calidris maritima	
Little Stint	Pibydd Bach
Calidris minuta	
Temminck's Stint	Pibydd Temminck
Calidris temminckii	
Baird's Sandpiper	Pibydd Baird
Calidris bairdii	
White-rumped Sandpiper	Pibydd Tinwen
Calidris fuscicollis	
Pectoral Sandpiper	Pibydd Cain
Calidris melanotos	
Dunlin	Pibydd y Mawn
Calidris alpina	
Curlew Sandpiper	Pibydd Cambig
Calidris ferruginea	
Semipalmated Sandpiper	Pibydd Llwyd
Calidris pusilla	
Sanderling	Pibydd y Tywod
Calidris alba	
Buff-breasted Sandpiper	Pibydd Bronllwyd
Tryngites subruficollis	
Broad-billed Sandpiper	Pibydd Llydanbig
Limicola falcinellus	

Ruff   Pibydd Torchog
Philomachus pugnax
Avocet   Cambig
Recurvirostra avosetta
Black-winged Stilt   Hirgoes
Himantopus himantopus
Grey Phalarope   Llydandroed Llwyd
Phalaropus fulicarius
Red-necked Phalarope   Llydandroed Gyddfgoch
Phalaropus lobatus
Wilson's Phalarope   Llydandroed Wilson
Phalaropus tricolor
Stone Curlew   Rhedwr y Moelydd
Burhinus oedicnemus
Cream-coloured Courser   Rhedwr y Twyni
Cursorius cursor
Great Skua   Sgiwen Fawr
Stercorarius skua
Pomarine Skua   Sgiwen Frech
Stercorarius pomarinus
Arctic Skua   Sgiwen y Gogledd
Stercorarius parasiticus
Long-tailed Skua   Sgiwen Lostfain
Stercorarius longicaudus
Ivory Gull   Gwylan Ifori
Pagophila eburnea
Great Black-backed Gull   Gwylan Gefnddu Fwyaf
Larus marinus
Lesser Black-backed Gull   Gwylan Gefnddu Leiaf
Larus fuscus
Herring Gull   Gwylan y Penwaig
Larus argentatus
Common Gull   Gwylan y Gweunydd
Larus canus
Glaucous Gull   Gwylan y Gogledd
Larus hyperboreus
Iceland Gull   Gwylan yr Arctig
Larus glaucoides
Mediterranean Gull   Gwylan Môr y Canoldir
Larus melanocephalus

Little Gull	Gwylan Fechan
Larus minutus	
Black-headed Gull	Gwylan Benddu
Larus ridibundus	
Sabine's Gull	Gwylan Sabine
Larus sabini	
Kittiwake	Gwylan Goesddu
Rissa tridactyla	
Black Tern	Corswennol Ddu
Chlidonias niger	
White-winged Black Tern	Corswennol Adeinwen
Chlidonias leucopterus	
Whiskered Tern	Corswennol Farfog
Chlidonias hybrida	
Gull-billed Tern	Morwennol Ylfinbraff
Gelochelidon nilotica	
Caspian Tern	Morwennol Fwyaf
Hydroprogne caspia	
Common Tern	Morwennol Gyffredin
Sterna hirundo	
Arctic Tern	Morwennol y Gogledd
Sterna paradisaea	
Roseate Tern	Morwennol Wridog
Sterna dougallii	
Sooty Tern	Morwennol Fraith
Sterna fuscata	
Bridled Tern	Morwennol Ffrwynog
Sterna anaethetus	
Little Tern	Morwennol Fechan
Sterna albifrons	
Sandwich Tern	Morwennol Bigddu
Sterna sandvicensis	
Razorbill	Llurs
Alca torda	
Little Auk	Carfil Bach
Plautus alle	
Guillemot	Gwylog
Uria aalge	
Black Guillemot	Gwylog Ddu
Cepphus gyrlle	

Puffin	Pâl
Fratercula arctiva	
Pallas's Sandgrouse	Iâr y Diffeithwch
Syrrhaptes paradoxus	
Stock Dove	Colomen Wyllt
Columba oenas	
Rock Dove	Colomen y Graig
Columba livia	
Woodpigeon	Ysguthan
Columba palumbus	
Turtle Dove	Turtur
Streptopelia turtur	
Collared Dove	Turtur Dorchog
Streptopelia decaocto	
Cuckoo	Cog
Cuculus canorus	
Great Spotted Cuckoo	Cog Frech
Clamator glandarius	
Yellow-billed Cuckoo	Cog Bigfelen
Coccyzus americanus	
Barn Owl	Tylluan Wen
Tyto alba	
Scops Owl	Tylluan Scops
Otus scops	
Snowy Owl	Tylluan yr Eira
Nyctea scandiaca	
Little Owl	Tylluan Fach
Athene noctua	
Tawny Owl	Tylluan Frech
Strix aluco	
Long-eared Owl	Tylluan Gorniog
Asio otus	
Short-eared Owl	Tylluan Glustiog
Asio flammeus	
Nightjar	Troellwr Mawr
Caprimulgus europaeus	
Swift	Gwennol Ddu
Apus apus	
Alpine Swift	Gwennol Ddu'r Alpau
Apus melba	

Kingfisher *Alcedo atthis*	Glas y Dorlan
Bee-eater *Merops apiaster*	Gwybedog y Gwenyn
Roller *Coracias garrulus*	Rholydd
Hoopoe *Upupa epops*	Copog
Green Woodpecker *Picus viridis*	Cnocell Werdd
Great Spotted Woodpecker *Dendrocopus major*	Cnocell Fraith Fwyaf
Lesser Spotted Woodpecker *Dendrocopus minor*	Cnocell Fraith Leiaf
Wryneck *Jynx torquilla*	Pengam
Short-toed Lark *Calandrella cinerea*	Ehedydd Llwyd
Woodlark *Lullula arborea*	Ehedydd y Coed
Skylark *Alauda arvensis*	Ehedydd
Shore Lark *Eremophila alpestris*	Ehedydd y Traeth
Swallow *Hirundo rustica*	Gwennol
House Martin *Delichon urbica*	Gwennol y Bondo
Sand Martin *Riparia riparia*	Gwennol y Glennydd
Golden Oriole *Oriolus oriolus*	Euryn
Raven *Corvus corax*	Cigfran
Carrion Crow *Corvus corone*	Brân Dyddyn
Rook *Corvus frugilegus*	Ydfran
Jackdaw *Corvus monedula*	Jac-y-do

Magpie *Pica pica*	Pioden
Nutcracker *Nucifraga caryocatactes*	Malwr Cnau
Jay *Garrulus glandarius*	Ysgrech y Coed
Chough *Pyrrhocorax pyrrhocorax*	Brân Goesgoch
Great Tit *Parus major*	Titw Mawr
Blue Tit *Parus caeruleus*	Titw Tomos Las
Coal Tit *Parus ater*	Titw Penddu
Marsh Tit *Parus palustris*	Titw'r Wern
Willow Tit *Parus montanus*	Titw'r Helyg
Long-tailed Tit *Pegithalos caudatus*	Titw Gynffon-hir
Nuthatch *Sitta europaea*	Delor y Cnau
Treecreeper *Certhia familiaris*	Dringwr Bach
Wren *Troglodytes troglodytes*	Dryw
Dipper *Cinclus cinclus*	Bronwen y Dwr
Bearded Tit *Panurus biarmicus*	Titw Barfog
Mistle Thrush *Turdus viscivorus*	Brych y Coed
Fieldfare *Turdus pilaris*	Socan Eira
Song Thrush *Turdus philomelos*	Bronfraith
Redwing *Turdus iliacus*	Coch dan-aden
Ring Ouzel *Turdus torquatus*	Mwyalchen y Mynydd

Blackbird *Turdus merula*	Mwyalchen
Olive-backed Thrush *Hylocichla ustulata*	Corfronfraith
Grey-cheeked Thrush *Hylocichla minima*	Bronfraith Fochlwyd
Wheatear *Oenanthe oenanthe*	Tinwen y Garn
Black-eared Wheatear *Oenanthe hispanica*	Tinwen Clustiog Du
Pied Wheatear *Oenanthe pleschanka*	Tinwen Fraith
Stonechat *Saxicola torquata*	Clochdar y Cerrig
Whinchat *Saxicola rubetra*	Crec yr Eithin
Redstart *Phoenicurus phoenicurus*	Tingoch
Black Redstart *Phoenicurus ochruros*	Tingoch Du
Nightingale *Luscinia megarhynchos*	Eos
Bluethroat *Luscinia svecica*	Bronlas
Robin *Erithacus rubecula*	Robin Goch
Grasshopper Warbler *Locustella naevia*	Troellwr Bach
River Warbler *Locustella fluviatilis*	Telor yr Afon
Savi's Warbler *Locustella luscinioides*	Telor Savi
Great Reed Warbler *Acrocephalus arundinaceus*	Telor Mawr y Cyrs
Reed Warbler *Acrocephalus scirpaceus*	Telor y Cyrs
Marsh Warbler *Acrocephalus palustris*	Telor y Gwerni
Sedge Warbler *Acrocephalus schoenobaenus*	Telor yr Hesg

Aquatic Warbler *Acrocephalus paludicola*	Telor y Dŵr
Melodious Warbler *Hippolais polyglotta*	Telor Pêr
Icterine Warbler *Hippolais icterina*	Telor Aur
Olivaceous Warbler *Hippolais pallida*	Telor Llwyd
Blackcap *Sylvia atricapilla*	Telor Penddu
Barred Warbler *Sylvia nisoria*	Telor Rhesog
Garden Warbler *Sylvia borin*	Telor yr Ardd
Whitethroat *Sylvia communis*	Llwydfron
Lesser Whitethroat *Sylvia curruca*	Llwydfron Fach
Sardinian Warbler *Sylvia melanocephala*	Telor Sardinia
Subalpine Warbler *Sylvia cantillans*	Telor Brongoch
Dartford Warbler *Sylvia undata*	Telor Dartford
Willow Warbler *Phylloscopus trochilus*	Telor yr Helyg
Greenish Warbler *Phylloscopus trochiloides*	Telor Gwyrdd
Chiffchaff *Phylloscopus collybita*	Siff-saff
Wood Warbler *Phylloscopus sibilatrix*	Telor y Coed
Bonelli's Warbler *Phylloscopus bonelli*	Telor Bonelli
Arctic Warbler *Phylloscopus borealis*	Telor yr Arctig
Yellow-browed Warbler *Phylloscopus inornatus*	Telor Aelfelen
Radde's Warbler *Phylloscopus schwarzi*	Telor Radde

Goldcrest *Regulus regulus*	Dryw Eurben
Firecrest *Regulus ignicapillus*	Dryw Penfflamgoch
Spotted Flycatcher *Muscicapa striata*	Gwybedog Mannog
Pied Flycatcher *Ficedula hypoleuca*	Gwybedog Brith
Collared Flycatcher *Ficedula albicollis*	Gwybedog Torchog
Red-breasted Flycatcher *Ficedula parva*	Gwybedog Brongoch
Dunnock *Prunella modularis*	Llwyd y Gwrych
Alpine Accentor *Prunella collaris*	Llwyd y Mynydd
Richard's Pipit *Authus novaeseelandiae*	Corhedydd Richard
Tawny Pipit *Anthus campestris*	Corhedydd Melyn
Meadow Pipit *Anthus pratensis*	Corhedydd y Waun
Tree Pipit *Anthus trivialis*	Corhedydd y Coed
Red-throated Pipit *Anthus cervinus*	Corhedydd Gyddfgoch
Rock Pipit *Anthus spinoletta*	Corhedydd y Graig
Pied Wagtail *Motacilla alba*	Siglen Fraith
Grey Wagtail *Motacilla cinerea*	Siglen Lwyd
Yellow Wagtail *Motacilla flava*	Siglen Felen
Waxwing *Bombycilla garrulus*	Cynffon Sidan
Great Grey Shrike *Lanius excubitor*	Cigydd Mawr
Lesser Grey Shrike *Lanius minor*	Cigydd Glas

Woodchat Shrike	Cigydd Pengoch
Lanius senator	
Red-backed Shrike	Cigydd Cefngoch
Lanius collurio	
Starling	Drudwen
Sturnus vulgaris	
Rose-coloured Starling	Drudwen Wridog
Sturnus roseus	
Red-eyed Vireo	Telor Llygatgoch
Vireo olivaceous	
Yellow Warbler	Telor Melyn
Dendroica petechia	
Blackpoll Warbler	Telor Tinwen
Dendroica striata	
Baltimore Oriole	Euryn Baltimore
Icterus galbula	
Hawfinch	Gylfinbraff
Coccothraustes coccothraustes	
Greenfinch	Llinos Werdd
Carduelis chloris	
Goldfinch	Nico
Carduelis carduelis	
Siskin	Pila Gwyrdd
Carduelis spinus	
Linnet	Llinos
Acanthis cannabina	
Twite	Llinos y Mynydd
Acanthis flavirostris	
Redpoll	Llinos Bengoch
Acanthis flammea	
Serin	Llinos Frech
Serinus serinus	
Bullfinch	Coch y Berllan
Pyrrhula pyrrhula	
Scarlet Rosefinch	Llinos Goch
Carpodacus erythrinus	
Crossbill	Gylfin Groes
Loxia curvirostra	
Two-barred Crossbill	Croesbig Wenaden
Loxia leucoptera	

Chaffinch *Fringilla coelebs*	Ji-binc
Brambling *Fringilla montifringilla*	Pinc y Myndd
Summer Tanager *Piranga rubra*	Euryn yr Haf
Corn Bunting *Emberiza calandra*	Bras yr Ŷd
Yellowhammer *Emberiza citrinella*	Bras Melyn
Black-headed Bunting *Emberiza melanocephala*	Bras Penddu
Cirl Bunting *Emberiza cirlus*	Bras Ffrainc
Ortolan Bunting *Emberiza hortulana*	Bras y Gerddi
Rock Bunting *Emberiza cia*	Bras y Graig
Rustic Bunting *Emberiza rustica*	Bras Gwledig
Little Bunting *Emberiza pusilla*	Bras Lleiaf
Reed Bunting *Emberiza schoeniclus*	Bras y Cyrs
Lapland Bunting *Calcarius lapponicus*	Bras y Gogledd
Snow Bunting *Plectrophenax nivalis*	Bras yr Eira
Song Sparrow *Melospiza melodia*	Llwyd Persain
White-throated Sparrow *Zonotrichia albicollis*	Llwyd Gyddfwyn
Rose-breasted Grosbeak *Pheucticus ludovicianus*	Gylfindew Brongoch
House Sparrow *Passer domesticus*	Aderyn y To
Tree Sparrow *Passer montanus*	Golfan y Mynydd